Transforming
Local Government

Transforming Local Government

*A Practical Management Guide
to Local Government Restructuring
and Renewal*

GUY HOLLIS

Published by Longman Information and Reference,
Longman Group Ltd, 6th Floor,
Westgate House, The High, Harlow, Essex CM20 1YR
Telephone: Harlow (0279) 442601; Fax: Harlow (0279) 444501
Telex: 81491 Padlog

A catalogue record for this book is available from the British Library

ISBN 0-582-24664-4

Printed by Page Bros, Norwich

Contents

Preface

Local government's world has been turbulent for as long as most of us can remember. There has been continuing debate about local government's purpose, roles, responsibilities, functions, activities, structure and internal management since the term local government was first coined well over a hundred years ago.

The present decade will be no exception - major change continues unabated. This book's immediate background is the Government's current review of the structure of local government, and in particular, the process currently under way to introduce mainly single tier unitary local authorities to replace the current two tiers of counties and districts in England and Wales, and regions and districts in Scotland. The timescales for change are short - decisions are being taken now, and implementation of the new structure of local government is expected to be completed by 1996 in Scotland and Wales and by 1997 in England. There is an urgent need for practical advice for members and officers in local government about how they should approach the process of setting up new authorities and making them work. This book is designed in part to meet that need.

But the mechanics of structural change are only part of the story. Local authorities, at the end of the twentieth century, face a much sterner challenge - how to re-establish the relevance and excitement of local government in a political system where local democracy is, more often than not, taken entirely for granted. Many voters appear to know little about local government and care little for local issues. This raises fundamental issues concerning the functions of local government, local democracy and local accountability.

It is not fanciful to suggest that fundamental and comprehensive transformation is called for, of which structural change is only a part. The book's principal aim is therefore to help senior policy makers and decision takers in local government, both elected members and officers, in existing and new authorities alike, to define the nature of this transformation and to implement it successfully.

The book is in two parts. Part I, 'Local government restructured and renewed', considers the agenda of issues local authorities will have to deal with as they seek to achieve structural and/or transformational change. It is divided into five chapters, as follows:

- **1:** the background to the current reorganisation debate, and local government's changing place in the wider political and institutional framework; this history puts the rest of the text in context and begins to demonstrate the need for change

- **2**: key policy issues and trends impacting upon local government in the future, and the implications for local government's vision of itself; this chapter describes the opportunities that transformational change can present even where structural change is not involved

- **3**: how local authorities can draw on corporate experience to plan for and manage change successfully and respond to the challenges and opportunities they face

- **4**: the main tasks involved in implementing structural change - specifically, the transfer of responsibilities between old and new authorities, winding down old authorities and setting up new ones

- **5**: priorities for senior decision-takers, both members and officers, in unifying and integrating new authorities, and, generally, in bringing about longer-term change

Part II, 'Doing it well and getting it right', introduces the individual management tools and techniques that are likely to be most useful in helping local authorities to respond to their agenda of change, which may be considerable. The main focus is on the need to develop the ability of authorities to plan, manage and respond positively to change, both as whole organisations and as groups of individuals. Tools and techniques relevant to the particular circumstances and nature of the changes facing local government are also included.

Two points of qualification are necessary at the outset. First, because there is a rolling programme across the country of decision making and implementation of reorganisation area by area, this book has of necessity been written before all decisions have been made for the UK as a whole, and before all official regulations and guidance have been published. Where definitive guidance has been available at time of going to print, it has been taken fully into account. But the reader is encouraged to pursue the primary sources given in the book for current chapter and verse on detailed matters. Second, there are some significant differences between the processes of review and implementation under way in England, Scotland and Wales, reflecting the variety of practice in matters of local government in these countries and, to an extent, their different political circumstances. Where appropriate these differences are noted. But they do not materially affect the book's principal theme of how best to respond to the twin challenge of structural and transformational change.

In addition, the style of the book is not 'task specific'. Many detailed professional and technical information issues are outside the scope of such a book. Readers seeking such guidance should refer to many of the excellent checklists and follow events on structural change already available from the professional bodies, the Audit Commission and the Local Government Management Board.

Finally, I would like to thank my colleagues in Coopers & Lybrand, in particular Gail Ham and Dr Mark Pegg, who helped enormously to shape the book and contributed much valuable material. Also Paula Gilder and Lucy Dennett who shouldered much of the editorial burden, Howard Davies, Roger Jefferies, Peter Hanney, Julia Speller, Dr Chris Emin, Chris Gibbons, Janet Baker and Helen Cottam for individual sections and our experienced Expert Panel, consisting of John Harman, Heather Rabbats, Denis Cleggett, Sylvie Pierce and Pat Crowson, who made useful comments and suggestions on the book's content and style. Many thanks also to senior colleagues in the Coopers & Lybrand Local Government Practice, Ken Crossland, Philip Halsall, Andrew Heley and Simon Humberstone whose support and cooperation in this venture I much appreciate. Thanks are also due to Shelley Couper at Longman for her help and forbearance.

Guy Hollis

July 1994

PART I

Local Government Restructured and Renewed

1

GIVING LOCAL GOVERNMENT BACK TO LOCAL PEOPLE

Background: local government review

The current review of local government has been presented by the Government as 'the most radical this century' - part of a wide-ranging reassessment of form, function, finance and accountability, designed to 'give local government back to local people' (Hansard 27 March 1991 col. 973) Yet the review has been carried out largely without any fundamental debate at a policy level about local government's role, its powers, or its responsibilities. Instead, issues have been dealt with in a fragmented manner without specific focus on the dual strategic and operation roles of local government. The finance system has been reformed through the Council Tax, further improvements in efficiency are to be encouraged through the extension of compulsory competitive tendering, quality of service delivery is to be promoted through a further range of mechanisms and incentives under the Citizen's Charter and a review of internal management may lead to legislation allowing authorities to adopt different methods of operating.

The question of structure remains now the outstanding issue. The Government is proceeding on the basis that the introduction of unitary (single tier) authorities may further improve the accountability of, and increase empathy with, local government. In England, a Local Government Commission has been established to review structure, electoral arrangements and boundaries, area by area. Notwithstanding the recent challenge in the High Court by Lancashire and Derbyshire County Councils to the terms of its policy guidance to the Commission, the Government continues to indicate a strong preference for a pattern of unitary authorities to replace the current county and district structure (Hansard 3 February 1994 col. 880). In Wales and Scotland, the Secretaries of State have proceeded (without benefit of a commission) to redraw the map on the basis of 21 and 32 unitary authorities respectively, replacing eight counties and 37 districts in Wales, nine regions, three islands (already unitary authorities) and 53 districts in Scotland. New unitary authorities are expected to be larger than most districts but smaller than most counties/regions.

Though many commentators have attempted to broaden the terms of the debate to include more wide-ranging consultation about local government's purpose and role, current public discussion at an official level has been limited to the different ways of reconfiguring current authorities in each area to achieve a unitary pattern able to command local support. There is to be no change elsewhere in the institutional structure (for example, at the parish council level, or indeed at the regional level in England) and other ways of looking at local government, for example, changing relationships between tiers, or transferring functions and responsibilities, have been excluded from the review (except insofar as the possibility of joint boards for certain activities, such as police and fire services, has been raised by the Government as a means of dealing with particular needs).

But this book is not directly concerned with the familiar issues of the merits and demerits of alternative forms of local government structure. The 'transformation' of the title is not one driven by the Government's review, though this provides the context. Instead the book's central proposition is that there is now a vital need for local government to complete a thorough and fundamental transformation of itself from within. Such a transformation requires a new vision for local government, and new approaches to all aspects of management, organisation and behaviour, whether within a unitary structure or not. In this sense, structure is almost beside the point. But for those authorities which will come into being as substantively new entities, the change in structure creates a real opportunity.

The book's principal theme is therefore to explore the opportunity presented by parallel structural and transformational change, and to provide practical guidance on how to manage it. But before considering these issues, it is appropriate to take a step back to look at the wider context of local government's changing place in the country's political and institutional framework. This introductory chapter therefore looks at the background to the review and at what this means for local government's current purpose and role.

Conspiracy or confusion?

The constitutional position of local government is a matter of custom and practice rather than principle or theory. Whether one likes it or not, there is currently no inalienable right for local government to exist: 'The position of local government in our political system is ... governed by constitutional convention as well as by the fact that it derives its existence and powers from Parliament. It would, however, be wrong to assume that such constitutional convention amounts to or derives from any natural right for local government to exist. It is a convention based on, and subject to, the contribution which local government can bring to good government.' (The Widdicombe Report).

The ambiguity created by 'constitutional convention' has allowed very different attitudes to local government to exist within the present constitutional and political framework. In the 1970s, for example, the view of the relationship between central and local government was described as 'partnership'. In the 1980s this was replaced by a more overtly hostile rhetoric. Yet both these very different attitudes are based on a view of local government not as an independent and coherent whole, with integrated powers and responsibilities, but as a kind of portmanteau institution, acquiring and losing functions as central government needed and circumstances demanded. In the absence of clarity about local government's real democratic role (and without any express commitment to local self-government as a fundamental principle of democracy) it is not surprising if local authorities have come to be seen as being little more than central government's agents, with no permanent locus or separate identities of their own. Such a view has tended to suit central governments, of varying complexions, and it is only in recent years that local government has itself woken up to the disadvantages of constitutional convention.

This view of local government runs counter to trends elsewhere in Europe. In France, for example, there is a long history of highly centralised administration. In the past, central government has tightly controlled all local decision making, not least through the powers of the prefect. But in the radical reforms of the early 1980s, the prefect's powers were reduced, regions and their councils were established to devolve functions from central government and all levels of local government were enabled to take decisions without state intervention. These changes represented a policy of substantial decentralisation and, to an extent, reflected a growing tendency on the part of some political activists to sidestep national government and build an independent, regional powerbase.

In Germany's federal structure, the nation state is decentralised and fragmented to a greater degree than perhaps any other in Western Europe. This reflects a long history of particularism and regional pride, combined with post-war fears of a resurgence of a centralised German state which encouraged both the occupying powers and German politicians themselves to adopt a highly federal constitution. In consequence, the German Länder run most of their own affairs, with funds to match. They also participate in the making of national legislation through their delegations in the Bundesrat (Federal Assembly). Lower levels of local government (the Landkreise and Gemeinden), through long German tradition, also have considerable autonomy and responsibility. They act both as independent local authorities competent to take any necessary action in their community's interest and as agents of federal and state laws.

With unification, this highly decentralised approach has had to respond to new pressures to provide a consistent approach in matters of national policy, and the autonomy of the Länder has been in consequence gradually reduced. But responsibility has also been pushed from the Länder to the local level, where authorities are encouraged to see their role as that of contributing to a comprehensive national network of public administration and service provision within the newly unified state.

There is bound to be tension, especially in a democracy, between the 'top-down' requirements to implement national policies in a consistent way, and the 'bottom-up' need to allow for diverse expression of community identity. In some places, these tensions are considerably more than issues in the abstract. Expressions of community identity can operate at quite large, even regional levels of aggregation and can have an impact within even a well established nation state. The development of the regional level in France, for example, was in part a response to the demands for greater autonomy from Brittany and Corsica.

In addition, a decentralised structure has been seen as providing some sort of check upon, or correction to, totalitarianism, whether of the right or left. Both Italy and Portugal, for example, have adopted programmes of decentralisation to assist the move away from the authoritarian regimes of their modern histories and reflect growing pressure for recognition of regional and local identity. Each country continually seeks to achieve an institutional structure appropriate to its immediate needs, its history and its political culture. But, notwithstanding countries' different histories, it appears that in western Europe both federal and unitary systems have a tendency to seek out a middle ground, somewhere between centralisation and decentralisation.

This middle ground is reinforced by general acceptance within the European Union of the right to local self-government, a principle given official recognition in the European Charter of Local Self-government (1985). Self-government is defined there as local authorities' right to 'regulate and manage a substantial share of public affairs under their own responsibility in the interests of the local population'. Most EU countries have both signed and ratified the Charter - the UK has done neither. Reflecting this, the power of general competence is the norm for local government in most parts of the EU. Such a power enables authorities to take any action in the interests of the local community unless specifically prohibited by statute from doing so. In the UK, the opposite is true. Authorities are empowered only to carry out those activities specifically assigned to them by Parliament.

Partly this is due to the UK's different history, and to its different constitutional and legal traditions. But it is probably fair also to see the UK's position on these issues as symptomatic of markedly different attitudes to the relative importance of local government as part of the country's political and institutional framework. The UK does not seek to achieve a pragmatic balance between top-down and bottom-up, but instead to assert the permanent superiority of the national mandate over any other, an interpretation of 'subsidiarity' unique in Europe.

In the past, local government's formal position of 'subservience to the Crown in Parliament' tended to be seen as a matter of constitutional nicety, rather than a question of political significance. But recent changes in functions and finance have made the matter of local government's constitutional position and powers an issue in itself. Also, the sheer volume of legislative change has put pressure on local authorities' ability to maintain and develop good standards of service delivery. These have combined to lead some commentators to speculate that an intentional process of steady emasculation is under way, whereby once independent and powerful local authorities have been gradually stripped of their more important functions, and have lost more and more autonomy and decision making powers. By this interpretation, the review of local government is one more step along this road, with the objective to create authorities without significant powers or resources, unable to present any challenge to central government, with limited capacity to identify and exploit strategic opportunities and incapable of taking on any substantially new constitutional role.

If it were indeed the objective so to rearrange the balance of power in the state, this would scarcely amount to 'giving local government back to local people'. A less pessimistic view, however, sees the review not as part of a great centralising conspiracy, but more as a reflection of long standing failure to think clearly about local government's purpose in the UK's system of government. While central-local relations have obviously changed considerably in practice, it can equally well be argued that this has happened almost by default rather than by design. This has been reinforced by an undoubted trend within local government itself towards what has been called the 'nationalisation of local politics', which has tended to obscure the local nature of local government.

Pride, prejudice and politics: he who pays the piper ...

A driving force behind changing UK central to local relations over the past 20 years has undoubtedly been the policy of the two major parties in government to reduce public expenditure. The post-war institutional framework combined central control and initiative over policy with considerable local discretion in implementation. A key feature of the system was the rate support grant, introduced in 1958 in place of specific service grants, which allowed local authorities to allocate funds between services as they thought fit. This was reinforced with the power to set rate levels without restriction. A variety of mechanisms combined to create pressures for uniformity - legal, administrative, political and professional - but local authorities were broadly free to make decisions about the desired level of funding for each service at the local level and about the way in which services should be delivered. Overt conflict between central and local government was unusual.

Central government control over the level of central grant to local authorities began in the mid 1970s, with the introduction of cash limits for rate support grant in 1976. The need to control expenditure in cash terms conflicted with local government's view that finance should be increased to maintain spending in real terms. When the Layfield Report on Local Government Finance suggested in 1976 that local accountability required the removal of local government expenditure from the public expenditure planning process, together with the introduction of a new local income tax to replace the rates, the Labour Government rejected it, essentially because of the impact on tighter central government economic and financial management.

When a Conservative Government was elected in 1979, it initially was intended to lessen central controls as such, but in combination with an overriding commitment to reducing public expenditure. Failure initially to control spending to the Government's satisfaction led to a series of radical changes in local government finance, particularly in England, in the first half of the 1980s, which substantially reduced the extent of authorities' previous discretion. These created a highly confrontational situation but still failed, as the Government accepted, in their main aim of reducing expenditure. This failure was attributed to weaknesses in the local government finance system as a whole, whereby those who paid for local government services were not necessarily the primary beneficiaries of local government spending.

Specific controls on spending, therefore, were replaced by wholesale change in the system of local government finance. Under the Abolition of Domestic Rates (Scotland) Act 1987, and the Local Government Finance Act 1988, domestic rates were abolished for Scotland in 1989, and for England and Wales in 1990, and business rates were fundamentally altered. The domestic rate was replaced by the Community Charge, or poll tax, which was essentially a flat-rate levy on all individual adults. Business rates were retained but, instead of being set locally, were set centrally and differently for Scotland, Wales and England, hence the term Uniform Business Rate (though the business rate is not yet uniform in Scotland).

Though the rating system had long been widely recognised as in need of change, the Government's approach to its replacement, the Community Charge, was generally seen as substantially increasing central control over local spending levels, especially when combined with technical changes in central assessments of spending need, and continuing ratecapping powers. But widespread criticism of the Community Charge focused less on questions of the balance between central and local government powers than on problems with the charge itself as a robust system of local taxation. In particular:

- it was widely seen as regressive and, hence, unfair
- it was administratively difficult and costly to collect
- there were substantial problems of non-payment

No tax is popular, but the poll tax was spectacularly unpopular. Following unparalleled public hostility to the Community Charge as it was implemented, it was replaced by the present Council Tax following the necessary legislation in 1992. The Council Tax has been described as a modern property tax - each household is taxed according to the value of the property which is assessed in eight bands. The bands, and the ratios between them, are set by the Government. A minor personal element remains, in that each household is assumed to consist of two adults, but a discount of 25% on the total bill is available where there is only one adult (and larger households do not pay more). No change has been made to the Uniform Business Rate.

Most other countries base their system of local finance upon a local property tax. Though there has been criticism of the continuing personal element of the tax, of the detail of the approach to property valuation, and of the continuation of capping as the final control on local revenue raising, to an extent this change has successfully defused the issue of local government finance as a particular source of confrontation. But there is no doubt that the changes of the past 20 years in the systems and methods of local government finance have made a major contribution to changing relationships between central and local government, and to shifting power and influence away from the local level.

The challenge to consensus

To an extent, changes in financing might have been expected whatever the political complexion of central government. Objections to the rates in particular were long-standing across all political parties, and tighter controls on public expenditure were already a feature of government before the Conservatives came to power. But relations between local and central government also took on in the 1980s an ideological and overtly political dimension, reflecting conservative free-market thinking and a challenge to 'consensus' and corporatism.

Local government's functions of course have from the outset been subject to reform and restructuring. In the early part of this century local authorities were the primary agents through which public services and utilities were developed and delivered. But as these services grew in national importance, so did the arguments against small-scale, variable local provision. Thus, local government lost functions in the 1930s and 1940s - for example, trunk roads (1936), main highways (1946), hospitals (1946), electricity (1947) and gas (1948) - and some commentators even then interpreted this as the death of local government. But the welfare state at the same time increased local government's role in providing redistributive and welfare services, especially education, housing and social services.

Both major parties supported local 'freedom' when it suited them - the Conservatives in opposing comprehensive education in the 1960s, and the Labour Party in opposing market rents for council housing in the early 1970s. In general, however, 'consensus politics' acted primarily to reinforce the perception of local government as the primary local agent of the state, increasingly funded by central government grants, guided and managed by central government circulars, inspectors, and administrators, but nonetheless secure in 'a well-understood and accepted constitutional relationship', in which confrontation remained unusual. It was also based in practice on 'big' government, both centrally and locally, so that the public sector grew substantially as a provider of services and hence as an employer.

This cosy consensus disappeared when the Conservative Government came to power in 1979. Their commitment to reduce the role of the welfare state, increase individual choice, and promote private enterprise presented an obvious challenge to local government. In the early 1980s legislation reforming housing, transport, education and planning gave more powers to central government either to compel compliance from local authorities or to work through other, new, local agencies set up for the purpose. Auditing powers were increased and auditing authorities given an extended remit to investigate and report on local authorities' financial management and their achievement of value for money.

But even these changes were not primarily motivated by the desire to reduce the local mandate as such. Professional administrative bureaucracies in central and local government, nationalised industries and public utilities alike were increasingly regarded as inefficient and unresponsive, and market mechanisms were becoming seen as a more effective way of providing services to meet consumers' real needs. The process of introducing market mechanisms was itself seen to require more central controls, and the need for such controls was seen to intensify when some local authorities opposed the changes.

This central-local conflict was given a further twist by the fact that much of this opposition came from the radical left-wing local groups which gained control of some urban councils. The early 1980s saw a number of Labour authorities elected on more explicitly politicised and radical manifestos than in the past, which antagonised the Government and led to further constraints. In the case of the Greater London Council and other metropolitan authorities, where resistance was seen to be concentrated, it led as far as outright abolition.

The pace of change intensified still further in the late 1980s. Though still presented and managed as separate policy initiatives in key areas, radical change occurred on several fronts simultaneously, amounting to significant cumulative impact on local government's role. Probably the most important of these were:

- substantial changes in the role, remit and powers of local education authorities in England through the Education Reform Act 1988

- fundamental changes in the role of local authorities as housing providers in the 1988 and 1989 Housing Acts

- further requirements to contract out direct works services in the Local Government Act 1988 and subsequent legislation

Added to the contemporary changes in local government finance, and to other changes in the local economic development field such as the creation of Training and Enterprise Councils and Local Enterprise Councils in Scotland, these reforms were seen as reducing still further local authorities' autonomy and restricting their influence in local affairs. And yet, in the midst of changes apparently designed to achieve a permanent worsening in local government's position, the Government implemented the Griffiths Report on community care, which designated local authorities as the responsible body for co-ordinating and planning care in the community across the full range of provision from NHS facilities, voluntary bodies, private sector providers and local government itself. Though central government approves overall community care plans, it is left to local government to decide what care is provided and how.

Though this decision may reflect the particular problems of community care, rather than a change in more fundamental philosophy about central-local relations, it provides yet another instance of the way in which local government historically has tended both to acquire and lose significant functions simultaneously. Furthermore, even those changes which have reduced local government's powers are not necessarily completely synonymous with greater centralisation. For example, the introduction of Local Management of Schools (England) and the facility to 'opt out' as a Grant Maintained School were presented as a way of shifting decision making powers to schools and parents, albeit constrained by the national curriculum and national standards testing. In housing, 'right to buy' and 'Tenants' Charter' changes were similarly intended to shift ownership and decision making powers to council house occupants.

Such developments are linked with the vexed and much disputed concept of the 'enabling' authority, which is discussed further in the next chapter. The enabling concept is supposed to represent a new philosophy of public service provision, 'the key to good local government' as the Prime Minister John Major put it, is where a council 'acts on behalf of the public, not the providers ... to buy in the best quality at the best price, whether from its own workforce or outside, and then to put it to the benefit of its local community' (speech, Conservative Local Government Conference, 2 March 1991).

On the face of it, therefore, enabling need imply no diminution of local government's essential purpose; it is about means, not ends. But taken in the context of specific policies (such as education and housing in particular) it begins to look much more like a rationale for reducing local authorities' powers and functions by handing them to other bodies, and seems to be based on a very narrow view of local government as service manager rather than strategist, or policy maker. In reaction to this, other views of enabling have attempted to popularise a wider interpretation, sustaining a new definition of the role of local government, acting in a wide variety of ways in the community's interests. This wider view is usually necessarily linked, however, with new powers and new freedoms for local government, within a new constitutional settlement for the country as a whole, something clearly not on the present Government's policy agenda.

Whatever one's politics and whatever one's view of what enabling should, or does, mean there is no doubt that the changes introduced by the Government simultaneously to so many areas of local government's activity have produced a fundamental, and probably lasting, change in local government's traditional character. Perhaps it is not surprising if this change has been interpreted by many people, both inside and outside local government, as a threat to local government's very existence, even if it were not so intended in the first place.

'Nationalisation' of local politics

As local government has increasingly become the agent of national government, so local politics has increasingly been swamped by national politics. The changes of the past fifteen years have turned local government itself into something of a political issue and have undoubtedly contributed to its politicisation as an institution. This is sometimes seen as evidence of decline in truly 'local' government. It is argued that the politicisation of local authorities somehow usurps their true role as representatives of community identity, since the influence of party politics tends to lead to greater uniformity in policy and practice, and may obscure local needs and inhibit local independence.

It is true that the growth of party politics in local government has been marked over the last 20 years or so. Prior to the last reorganisation, the majority of small authorities were entirely or mostly non-partisan, few or no seats were held by party nominees. Politicisation was in the main limited to older urban centres, where it was well-established. The reorganisation itself did much to transform this situation. Incorporation of major towns into county areas, and the creation of larger district councils, together with the uncertainties of control in these newly created authorities, encouraged the political parties to extend their operations into rural areas, competing both with one another and with independent candidates. Such candidates were inevitably at a disadvantage compared to those backed by the party machines. By 1985, when the Widdicombe Committee looked at party influence in local government, only 3% of authorities reported no political party representation.

However, not all councils on which parties are represented are controlled by a party as such. A recent study on the politics of local government since Widdicombe showed that, though most councillors wear a party label, non-party control is still usual in well over half of rural authorities, and that in such areas, independent patterns of behaviour persist among elected members, notwithstanding their party affiliation (Young and Davies 1990). Instead, the pattern indicated by the study is one of increasing divergence in the character of local politics between largely urban and largely rural areas. On the other hand, the experience of the previous reorganisation suggests that, if the present review leads to the amalgamation of many smaller districts, this will tend once again to increase politicisation, as the smaller authorities absorb the practices of the larger.

Politicisation is not necessarily a bad thing, if it improves decision making and generally enlivens local democracy. Indeed, it can be argued that the absence of strong political and strategic control by members tends to hand over too much influence to (unelected) officers. But there is some indication that the changing character of local government in recent years may have contributed to increased distrust by the public of their local representatives. In a survey in 1990 of attitudes to local government (Block and John 1991), people were asked about their views on the value of voting in local elections, and their responses compared with the answers to the same questions put by the Maud Committee in 1965.

Then, 77% of respondents agreed with the statement that 'the way people vote at council elections is the main thing that decides how things are run in this locality'; and 56% of respondents agreed that 'the people you vote for say they'll do things for you, but once they're in they forget what they've said'. In 1990, the percentages agreeing were 68% and 67% respectively, suggesting perhaps increased scepticism about the value of elections and about the motives of local councillors.

Some commentators have interpreted trends like this as an indication of a deep malaise in 'civic culture', suggesting distrust and cynicism of political institutions and democratic processes. And yet attitude surveys continue also to show reasonable levels of satisfaction with local government's performance, and that the majority of people think that local government should continue to be responsible for running local services, even though there continues to be some considerable public confusion about what services actually fall within its jurisdiction.

The final nail in the coffin?

In this context, it is a legitimate prior question in any discussion of the shape and structure of local government to ask what 'giving local government back to local people' really means. Does it mean more local government, or less? What place is local government expected to have within the future national, and international, political and institutional framework?

Local government, it is clear, faces radical reorganisation against a background of significant change in both the mechanisms and the climate of central-local relations. Yet the outcome has been to increase the ambiguity of local government's 'conventional position' (to use the language of the Widdicombe Report) rather than any clear perception of some lesser purpose for local government. That local government has lost much of its previous discretion is undoubtedly true, and that its traditional character has already profoundly changed is obvious.

But there is still no single coherent pattern across functions, and no consistent statement of principle beyond the generalities of political rhetoric, from which to sustain a view of these changes as intentional centralisation. And though some commentators continue to discern a sense of hostility to local government as an institution, even this has abated recently as the pace of legislative change has once more slowed. It thus remains very unclear whether the reorganisation is designed to weaken local government as an institution, or to strengthen it, or indeed to achieve any specific shift in either direction for central-local relations.

It is this book's contention that this very ambiguity amounts to a significant opportunity for local government to exploit reorganisation to determine its own vision and purpose. In the abstract, there is a strong constitutional and political case for effective local government as a key dimension of any country's system of government. But, in the absence of any written constitution for the UK, and until constitutional change itself becomes a political issue at a national level, such arguments have little real political relevance or practical clout. In these circumstances, local government is thrown back on its own resourcefulness and performance to demonstrate its credibility as a source of power in the state.

The challenge for all local authorities therefore, especially new authorities as they emerge from the reorganisation process, is to turn the political rhetoric of 'giving local government back to local people' into a reality which strengthens local government's position, bringing truly participative, accountable 'local' government, rather than something which is seen to undermine it. The immediate task is to implement structural change successfully - the longer-term task is to achieve a more fundamental transformation which renews local government's importance in the system of government in practice, as well as in theory. The next chapter therefore looks at the key policy issues and trends which will impact upon local government in the future, and at the implications for local government's vision of itself.

2

BRAVE NEW WORLD
New approaches to community leadership

Taking the longer view

Though the current proposed reorganisation and its objectives are the immediate background, to look only at these specific issues would be to take too restricted a view of the context for change. Local government institutions have, in general terms, a long history - before the nineteenth century, government was always 'local' in character. But when government at the 'centre' began steadily to expand in scope, this required a new rationale to be invented to justify the government of local communities. Such a rationale was found in the systematic democratisation of local government, matching the development of the national franchise, and sustained as the century progressed by improvements in management, control, and overall effectiveness.

Since then, government as a whole, both centrally and locally, has continued steadily to increase its functions. But it has also become more standardised and uniform in character, and, at least in the UK, both more centralised and more diversified in organisation and approach. Government is no longer predominantly local, and is unlikely ever to be so again, as the policy and institutional environment increases in complexity.

Recent changes in particular have tended to depress local government's confidence in itself, and are seen generally to have weakened local democracy. Its rationale is no longer clear, as it once was. But even though the specific changes promoted by the current reorganisation debate may be an unavoidable preoccupation, local government must take the long view in considering its future direction, if this trend is to be reversed.

For authorities subject to reorganisation, substantial change is unevitable. For others it is perhaps more difficult to see the need for voluntary, transformational change. Certainly, in a situation where so much new legislation requires implementation and where customer demands and expectations are changing it is understandable if authorities are reluctant to add to the change agenda. Change for the sake of change is not being advocated but, for the reasons outlined in this chapter, all authorities should be exploring the possibility that radical, transformational change is in their interests, both long- and short-term, as well as in the interests of local government as a whole.

A vision for local government into the twenty-first century must begin with some attempt to define the external factors likely to impact upon local government in the future. This chapter therefore seeks to point out possible future challenges and opportunities likely to be most relevant in determining the nature and style of future local government. It goes on to look at some key aspects of the way in which local authorities will need to be managed, in order to respond effectively to their changing environment.

The international dimension

Perhaps one of the most fundamental developments of recent years is that the sovereign state is no longer the predominant unit of economic life and hence no longer the only effective unit for economic policy. Sovereign states react to, rather than control, events in global capital markets - there is an almost autonomous world economy of money, credit, and investment. Production facilities can be located anywhere in a global market - goods are produced abroad and imported 'home', where they were once made at home and exported.

Increasingly in this environment, governments seek to mediate national economic relations through regional trading blocks, such as the European Union, rather than through traditional patterns of bilateral relationships between individual countries. Through such trading blocks, and through reciprocal international agreements, ready access is gained to a very large market, and a measure of protection derived for key industries. But countries' membership also requires them to conform to certain explicit and implicit community-wide economic policies, which constrain internal economic flexibility and, to an extent, the development of social policy also. In particular, constraints on public sector borrowing, and on levels of inflation and interest rates, form a clear framework within which national macro-economic policy is conducted. This has required Sweden, for example, as an applicant for enlarged membership of the EU, to introduce a major reduction in public expenditure to achieve the necessary measure of economic alignment.

In the UK, the drive to reduce public spending has had a significant impact on central-local relations and on the practical extent of local government's autonomy (*see* Chapter 1). Continuing constraints on public sector borrowing of course depend on the extent and pace of future economic growth, relative to other members of the EU. Latterly, after a brief period of debt repayment, the UK has once again returned to deficit funding, and the effects of this situation continue to be felt by local government through tight controls on both revenue expenditure and credit approvals.

The public sector resource environment thus currently remains very tight and, while the financing regime continues to restrict local government's ability to raise money independently, the scope for spending increases is likely to remain small, whatever the colour of the future ruling party nationally. The pressures for continuous improvement in performance and efficiency will remain very strong, and choices about resource allocation will remain difficult.

That said, EU membership is likely also to continue to offer local authorities specific funding opportunities through structural funds, the Regional Development Fund and the Social Fund, and other economic development initiatives. And the completion of the Single European Market already requires an increasing role for local and regional government in monitoring, implementing and enforcing EU legislation in trading standards and environmental health. The extension of EU competence further into economic development and environmental protection will have an impact on policy making and funding both at national and local levels, and this will create an international dimension to local government's activities.

With the development of 'Europe of the Regions', there is an opportunity for local authorities to play a role on a wider stage; to create new partnerships; and learn about different ways of doing business. It is quite striking that almost any feature about which there is hot debate in the UK may be found somewhere in Europe, and found to work; and it is also striking that most Western European countries' systems of local government are characterised by a substantial degree of stability. Wider debate within the European Union about government structures may yet prompt a reassessment of central/local relationships in a more fundamental way, and challenge the narrowness and parochialism of much debate in the UK about local government's form and function.

Pressures to standardise services?

If economic growth remains slow, and the requirements of economic convergence tight, this will continue to force to the top of the political agenda the question of levels of public service provision, and the standards of service to be achieved. It is possible to see that, increasingly, achieving economic convergence across

Europe may also mean convergence on a level playing field for public service provision.

It is already possible to see a trend emerging of increasing dissemination of levels of service provision across countries through comparative studies, business comparisons and exchange visits. National standards definition is already being emphasised in the UK in attainment testing in schools, charter standards in health, standardised performance indicators and moves towards sub-national bodies for some services such as police and fire. Such standards may mean levelling up, but are more likely, as social welfare costs increase, to mean levelling down. There may therefore be increasing emphasis on promoting and achieving uniformity on acceptable minimum standards for 'core' services in key areas of social welfare such as education, social services, and health.

Such standardisation need not imply the absence of all or any opportunity for local initiative. But it may mean a reassessment of the scope for local variation in service management and delivery. It may also argue for a more overtly contractual relationship between local and central levels of government, where national (or even European) government specifies explicit standards and levels of service, eligibility, indicative unit costs, and expected outcomes, and funds local authorities accordingly. It is possible to envisage further changes in the grant regime to reflect such an approach. But more importantly, this would require an explicit recognition of local government's role as preferred agent for certain core services. Greater clarity could therefore replace current ambiguities, though at the price of less room for local manoeuvre in core services. By contrast, discretionary areas of provision could be explicitly recognised as areas where local authorities were expected and encouraged to innovate and to reflect diverse needs.

Democratic decline?

One corollary of increasing emphasis on service standards, however, seems to be an increasing manifestation of 'consumerism' in government. Service users want certainty of supply, guarantees of quality, impartiality in provision and scrupulousness in the management of resources. The 'charter movement', with its emphasis on performance standards and rights of redress, focuses on individuals exercising their specific rights as 'customers', rather than their collective rights as voters, to whom elected representatives are ultimately accountable. This is gradually shifting the balance of power in traditional relationships between individuals and their local authorities and it is also altering its nature emphasising the distinction between responsiveness to the consumer and accountability to the citizen.

Some commentators have seen this as contributing to the emergence of a phenomenon termed 'designer politics', whereby political parties base their policies and programmes increasingly on market surveys of public opinion and expectations. It is argued that this leads to convergence on a crowded centre ground, and to confusion about what different parties actually stand for, at the more fundamental level of ideas and ideology. There are some signs that membership of political parties is in decline as old certainties recede, and that the dominance of the two-party system may be ending. If so, the politicisation of local government of the last twenty years may be replaced by a more fragmented politics, in which 'hung' councils are increasingly the norm and there is less long-term stability in political direction and control than members, officers and indeed voters have typically experienced.

On the one hand, this may help to defuse the confrontational atmosphere of central-local relations that the UK has experienced in the recent past. But it may also contribute to the sense of decline in the importance of local democracy, unless local authorities take positive steps to assert and develop their democratic and representative functions, as well as respond to the aspirations and expectations of their 'customers'. It seems that, in a developed democracy, people need to be actively encouraged to act in the collective civic interest as citizens, as well as in their own interests as individual consumers.

A complex policy agenda

Realistically the portfolio of local government's functions is likely to continue to change, but it is by no means clear that this need involve any less breadth in local government's preoccupations. Certainly, substantial policy issues continue to face local and central government alike across the current portfolio. Most of the major issues of the late twentieth century are having an impact on local government's functions and services in one way or another, for example:

- how to care effectively and at affordable cost for the needs of vulnerable individuals
- how to improve educational standards and equip young people to respond to the needs of a rapidly changing economy
- how to reconcile the demand for economic growth with the need to minimise environmental damage
- how to reduce crime and recreate a sense of public security
- how to improve the quality of life and equality of opportunity for increasingly economically and socially diverse communities

Comprehensive responses to complex issues like these require an expert and integrated approach across traditional functional and service boundaries. The challenge is to develop more generic approaches to the delivery of services without losing the benefits of professional specialisms. This will require effective inter-agency working, with other authorities, local businesses, voluntary groups and many different national and sometimes international bodies. It will also require an investment in a long-term approach, and the flexibility to innovate and, where necessary, to adapt plans and methods to circumstances as they change.

This can be seen as the true practical meaning of 'enabling', rather than sterile debate about the political orthodoxies of collective provision versus 'rolling back the state'. Enabling increasingly is seen to involve in practice:

- a strategic orientation defining a vision for the future of a local community, within the given remit of role, function and territory

- a readiness to deploy new, different, and many modes of action, as circumstances require and allow

- a focus on process and performance

- multi-agency working - sometimes leading, sometimes following

- promoting effective communication with, and participation from, users and interest groups

This all implies a highly diversified, flexible and participative style of government, potentially very different from the traditional, hierarchical and standardised organisations of the past. It also implies no one particular configuration as the general pattern of internal organisation and management - there need be no Bains and Paterson reports for this restructuring. Indeed the Government's response to the working party set up in England to review internal management (HMSO, July 1993) specifically endorses its encouragement of experimental approaches and radical proposals.

It is notable that the continuing debate in the UK about whether services should be provided by direct labour or bought in is a particularly British preoccupation. In most other countries it is not a major issue. Many European countries, for example, have a long history of buying in services and, indeed, of collaborating very effectively with the private sector in the operation of a mixed economy. Widely varying arrangements for service provision may be found involving central government, local government, the private sector, mixed organisations, non-statutory and voluntary organisations. Experimentation with such flexible arrangements in the UK may demonstrate their practical advantages, although there may be political hurdles, both central and local, to overcome first.

Changing patterns of community

Population change and settlement trends have in the past had a major impact on administrative structures. Rapid growth of towns and cities contributed to pressures for electoral and administrative reform in the nineteenth century, and suburban growth was one of the factors prompting further change in the twentieth century. Settlement trends now are diverse. Population migration has continued away from traditional industrial and inner-city areas, to smaller urban centres, new towns and retirement areas. Previously remote and rural areas have experienced a switch into growth after many decades of depopulation.

Cities in particular face significant issues. There have been shifts of employment and resources away from city centres to the periphery. An outer ring of wealth often surrounds an inner centre of poverty. Yet (and partly in response to this) there has been a re-emergence in Europe of the city in terms of a focus of economic development and community identity. Barcelona, Milan, Lyon, Frankfurt, Brussels, Amsterdam and Birmingham have all made great strides in promoting a 'brand image' emphasising their distinctive positions both as locations for inward investment, and as democratic entities. A major challenge faces large cities in terms of:

- providing diverse service requirements to meet the needs of their many communities

- developing transportation systems which reconcile economic development and social needs with environmental protection

- renewing other aspects of infrastructure first developed in the previous century

- competing internationally for investment and employment creation

Large cities will need to demonstrate considerable capacity for imagination and effective action to respond to this challenge, within the context of an enlarged European Union and the single market. Smaller cities and towns are also likely to need to accommodate and respond to rapid change in settlement, working and leisure patterns, as local economies develop and interact in new ways with the growth of part-time working, increasing numbers of small firms, teleworking, and the growth of knowledge and service industries.

These trends will in turn have an impact upon notions of 'local identity' and concepts of 'community', which have been much in evidence in the present debate. In current society, many factors work against cohesive, stable local communities. People have greater choice about where to live, where to work, and with whom to mix. Better transport and communications, increased leisure time and rising disposable income may all cut across the locality as a primary source of sense of identity. Towns and cities accommodate many different interest groups and creating a sense of shared identity across these differences represents a major

21

challenge. Yet many people continue to feel a strong sense of attachment to where they live, even if community identity is no longer as strong a social force as it once was. Promoting a sense of 'community', across different interests, must continue to be a key theme of local government, notwithstanding or perhaps even because of, rapidly changing settlement trends.

A new focus for community leadership

Pulling these threads together, what are the implications for local government's vision of itself and of its role? In what direction do these trends point? Three key issues emerge. First, resources are likely to remain severely constrained, and will be coupled with continuing emphasis on achieving explicit performance standards across a changing portfolio of functions. But whatever the differences of political opinion and interpretation about enabling, new relationships, ways of working, and patterns of internal management have to be on local government's own agenda as it responds to complex policy issues requiring a strategic view and more, rather than less, flexibility and innovation.

Second, and notwithstanding the Government's view of the superiority of the national mandate, the European dimension cannot be ignored. European policy making creates its own imperative for effective local government, and the continuing debate about the structure of the European Union itself creates a new context for debate about local government's place within it. International developments and institutions are therefore likely to play an increasing part in local government's development. While this does not mean any less importance for specifically local concerns, it will mean a reduction in parochialism and a new awareness of policy and economic issues in an international, as well as national and local, context.

Third, though local government continues to command support as part of the country's institutional framework, like all institutions, it can no longer take anything for granted. Hard work will be needed to refresh and renew local government's democratic and representative functions, to ensure that they remain relevant within the political system, and effective as expressions of community identity.

The previous chapter of this book has argued that there is no clear perception of local government's role, no definitive statement of purpose commanding universal acceptance, which local authorities may take off the shelf. They must reach their own view of the implications of these trends, and determine their own response to these challenges. Uncertainty is high and there is no shared vision or blueprint. In such an environment, there may be a sense that to confront these issues head-on is high-risk. But new authorities in particular have an opportunity to consider central questions of purpose and vision in a way which authorities unaffected by the reorganisation may find more difficult.

Furthermore, in the case of new authorities, decisions taken at the outset about how the authority sees itself as a unit of local government will become an important part of its strategy and culture and will be difficult to reverse later. They need to be robust and establish clearly what type of authority the new organisation needs to be, and what its response will be to the challenges identified above. New unitary authorities will predominantly inherit members and officers from previous constituent authorities. They will come with preconceived ideas about purpose, role, and modes of operation, and with powerful memories of previous practice. It would be all too easy simply to replicate the old in the new, unless there is a conscious effort to consider these issues at the earliest possible opportunity.

The challenges outlined here amount to a new vision for local authorities as democratic leaders of local communities. This means a new stress on strategic and policy issues, rather than the minutiae of service provision. It means new emphasis on ensuring accountability for performance, and on encouraging representation, participation and partnership by moving away from paternalism and consultation mechanisms which present a one-way communication and decision making process. Local government has to be, and has to be seen to be:

- making a real contribution to policy development through its local experience and track record

- putting the user's interest first (and not the producer's)

- responsive - delivering what communities need, to those who need it, in the way they want

- open - promoting devolution and encouraging participation by local communities in decision making

- efficient, publicly accountable, and scandal-free in its management and use of resources and in the conduct of its business

This means in turn a new focus for elected members, as community leaders and advocates. Yet this reorganisation comes at a time when the role of the local councillor is seen by many to be arduous and unattractive. Recent studies have shown that there tends to be high turnover amongst local authority members, and that councillors by and large are not very representative of the population (Game and Leach, 1993). There are significant time pressures on councillors, and therefore on their families. The commitment to serve may also mean sacrifice in terms of career opportunities. Increasing politics in local government can make the job less appealing for those without strong political convictions, and the impact of party politics on decision making may restrict the individual member's scope for influence. And even when they do have power within the council, they are seen to be less relevant outside it. They nonetheless operate within strict legal guidelines, which can put individuals at risk.

Local government must therefore not only define a new role for its elected members appropriate to the issues identified in this chapter, but must do so in a way which increases their effectiveness and personal satisfaction. This goes to the heart of the way authorities are managed. Any vision for local government must include clear thinking about internal management, as well as specific strategies in response to external circumstances and key policy issues. It involves important decisions about:

- the style of the authority and its relations with other local bodies
- the extent to which it is prepared to decentralise decision-making and increase participation
- decision-making and scrutiny processes
- the nature of political management within the authority
- member-officer relations
- key officer responsibilities and structures

The next section of this chapter looks at each of these key areas.

The authority's style of community leadership

A prerequisite of community leadership is a clear picture of the needs and resources, strengths and weaknesses of the area. Vision and strategy must relate to the present reality of the area as experienced by those who live and work there. Internally, leadership requires political direction, effective decision making processes for matters of policy, strategy and resource allocation, and mechanisms to ensure proper monitoring of performance in implementing decisions and delivering services. Externally, processes are needed which ensure that there is adequate dialogue with service users, with other service providers, both private, public and voluntary sector, and with organisations representing local associations and interest groups.

Essentially, the authority can be one voice amongst many or endeavour to assert a wider role in speaking for the area as a whole, although it has to be recognised that the community will contain a diverse range of often conflicting interests. The complexity and difficulties associated with true representation cannot be underestimated, but the council cannot speak for the community without making sure that the community is equally able to speak to the council.

This will raise issues about relationships with other organisations exercising local functions in its area. As experience with community care has illustrated, such organisations do not work in isolation - decisions taken in one have an effect elsewhere. The authority will want to co-operate and to build a sense of partnership with other players - will it also want to monitor their activities and performance, and question them on behalf of local people? What processes will be put in place to ensure that councillors representing their authority on other bodies, such as Joint Boards, will be able to exercise a leadership role? How will the authority communicate and win support for its decisions and views?

Joint arrangements

Joint bodies formed by two or more councils, usually to administer a single service, are a well known phenomenon. Less well known are some of the practical problems to which they give rise, perhaps because, with some notable exceptions created after the abolition of the metropolitan counties and the GLC, many joint bodies administer quite small services. Commonly they are found administering cemeteries and crematoria, parks and open spaces which straddle boundaries and occasionally libraries. They may also operate as consortia to provide supplies or other services to the councils themselves.

There is an important distinction to be made between a joint committee and a joint board. A joint committee is not a body corporate, while a joint board is. A joint committee is therefore a subordinate body of the constituent councils which create it, each of which delegates to that joint committee all or part of its powers to deliver the particular service in question. A joint board by contrast is a body in its own right to which the constituent councils appoint representatives but it is capable of holding land in its own right and its powers derive from its own constitution. It is subordinate to the councils only in the sense, normally, of deriving revenue funding from them and being politically influenced by them.

This constitutional distinction has some important practical consequences as does the size of the undertaking in question. If, as seems possible, the current reorganisation generates further examples of these bodies it is important to establish the basis of their operation at the outset. It is frequently the case that later generations of officers and councillors have had to handle disputes in joint bodies where inadequate attention was paid to detail in the original arrangements.

Councillor representatives on joint bodies have to fulfil difficult roles. They may be in a political minority on the joint body although representing the majority view in their own council. The joint body may administer a single service and the tasks of the councillors and their participation in the joint body may seem different to their role in the multifunctional committee setting of their local authority. For example, unless the body covers a large number of councils, it is likely that there will be few councillors on the board, which will lead to a different style of participation more akin to that of an executive board. And indeed councillors may be able to take a more direct and influential role in the deliberations of a board simply because there are fewer of them. This may be in contrast to the culture within their own authorities where wide consultation and decentralised decision making may be the norm.

Although they are directly elected to the joint body councillors have nevertheless a representative role to perform. The geographical coverage of the joint body may mean it is difficult to act independently in the interests of the joint body instead of acting as the representative of a particular physical part. Also the interests and activities of the joint body may be at variance with those of the councillor's own authority.

This could particularly be the case in respect of joint boards which some councils could feel are outside their control unless political pressure can be brought to bear. These joint boards may be made up of members elected to council but only appointed to the joint board. The problem of who members are accountable to is one shared with other appointed bodies.

In summary, therefore, it is essential that each authority represented on a joint board or committee has a clear view of what it is seeking to achieve in terms of service delivery, to focus the role of representatives involved in joint arrangements. Equally important is the need to establish clear arrangements for accountability and consultation.

Officers employed by the constituent councils but asked to service a joint body may need to swap loyalties in working for it and not simply assert the values and interest of their employing council. Officers will need to be aware and sensitive to the mixed and sometimes vexed roles of councillors on such bodies.

Decentralisation, participation and representation

Turnout in local elections is relatively low (though increasing in recent years) and is in any case a somewhat infrequent and even imprecise method of participation by people in their local government. Furthermore, new local authorities may cover quite large areas, and there will be fewer councillors per head of population than under the previous structure of counties, regions and districts. New approaches to encouraging more direct participation will be needed if local people are not to feel distanced from the new authority. Individual members will need to have adequate time to ensure that they are able to hear the views of their constituents, and represent those views in debates about strategy and performance.

New councils must decide how they are to ensure the representation of citizens' views before decisions are taken, and how to be sensitive in policy development and service management to the differing needs and views of their various communities. A requirement for decentralisation plans to be presented to the Secretary of State for approval is built into the legislation for Scotland where some new authorities will cover very large geographical areas.

Successful models of service devolution through area offices already exist. To this could be added area or community committees, either on a consultative basis or with some delegated operational or budgetary powers, for which models also exist, though more controversially. Alternatively the new authority could work with parish, town and community councils to offer delegation agreements and consultation arrangements. This would raise questions about the extent to which those elected to parish, town and community councils could have powers to take decisions and vary budgets, alongside elected members of the unitary authority in some appropriate structure.

Other models of decentralisation may be based around groups of people with particular interests or needs, not necessarily on a geographical basis and which may cross committee or departmental boundaries. Issues such as provision for children under five or access for people with disabilities might be addressed in this way. The key issues are first to establish the extent to which the authority wants to decentralise and then to explore the applicability of a wide range of means of achieving this.

Decision making and scrutiny processes

Both tradition and past legislation tend to push councils towards a committee system of decision making based on departments. Yet traditional processes are bureaucratic and time-consuming - how much of a councillor's time is to be spent in meetings? How will they be involved in setting strategy and performance standards? How will they provide an effective scrutiny function, and spend enough time talking to, and representing, the views of their constituents? What will be the role of the full council - will it be a forum for general debate, and involve the public as well as councillors? What powers will be delegated to committees? How far will the council use ad hoc panels, working groups, and small sub-committees to develop policy options and assess alternatives?

Delegation, and more focused decision making, could remove much of the rationale for traditional committee approaches. Instead, the focus needs to be on ensuring effective mechanisms of accountability. In the past, councillors have often been criticised for being too involved in the detail of administration, and of failing to concentrate on issues of importance to constituents. Now there is an opportunity for them to concentrate on policy and on the quality, efficiency, and performance of service providers, especially where services have been specified under contract. This role requires them to become less involved in the detailed running of services and more involved in scrutiny processes such as complaints-handling and in customer satisfaction reviews, which are traditionally the preserve of officers, but which, combined with their local knowledge, provide valuable information to feed back into the policy making and implementation processes.

Political management

The political and party dimension is an important aspect of internal management. New authorities will have new political groupings; some may be newly party political, requiring adjustment from members and officers alike. Essentially, the key question involves the willingness of the body of councillors in a majority party to pass over to a smaller group the de facto power to make the major decisions of the authority, in the style of 'cabinet'. This requires consideration of the relationship of such a group to their colleagues, within a party group structure, and of the relationship between these arrangements and decision taking in the council as a whole. On the one hand, a highly participative style involves all members in taking important decisions, on the other, it is time-consuming and may delay or confuse matters. If a strongly party-oriented approach is taken, what is the role of opposition group members in policy development and review? How independent should these processes be of party decision making? Whatever approach is adopted, the conventions by which the system will operate should be clearly defined in advance, and open to scrutiny.

Interesting reading on this topic includes a recent publication by the Local Government Management Board (LGMB) called *Fitness for Purpose* which describes political management in some detail with possible models of political leadership; the Audit Commission's *We can't go on meeting like this*, which pinpoints opportunities for improving the political process, and recent reports by the Joseph Rowntree Foundation.

Member-officer relations

It is members who have the political, legal and representative responsibility for the authority. But they are not the managers of the services. The member-officer relationship should be a partnership, but it is frequently sensitive and a source of tension. Getting it right is an important aspect of the new authority's management and is an important way of ensuring that councillors have time to devote to their proper roles, while enhancing officers' management role.

In the past, relations have evolved gradually, and have rarely been made explicit. The circumstances of a new authority provides the opportunity to define a more formal framework for addressing the delegations that members will make to officers and the conventions of working relations. Members need to consider what services they need from officers, how they will obtain the advice they require, and how officers and members will work together without blurring accountability for setting policy and delivering performance. This will require an implicit consensus to be reached, which may vary significantly between authorities according to both style and personalities.

The most important aspect of the relationship is to ensure that both sides are clear about who does what. Officers need to be given the space and authority to manage - members need to be clearly seen to have the responsibility for policy and for the authority's strategic direction. A culture needs to be established in which members set the objectives which they expect the officer administration to achieve, and by which the officers will be held to account. This will in turn set the framework within which those actually delivering services, whether inside or outside the authority, will be managed.

Key officer responsibilities and structures

The chief executive is a key figure in leading the officer organisation and in translating member priorities into workable policy, understood within the authority. There is inevitably some tension between the characteristically powerful position of the chief executive, and the power which members wish to exercise. Some overseas jurisdictions make the chief executive, or equivalent, solely responsible for the conduct of the administration, with the corollary that the person is placed on a fixed term contract subject to satisfactory administrative performance. Such an approach could be used to clarify the authority vested in the chief executive, and the limits on members' powers to intervene in day to day administration and management.

The role of the chief executive's senior management team also needs careful consideration. Councillors will continue to need skilled professional advice across the authority's portfolio of responsibilities, roles and functions. They will continue to expect to have senior officers who will be held accountable for the performance of the managers under their control, functioning within a management structure which assigns clear responsibilities, and which in operational terms reflects policy objectives. Such officers are likely to be far less concerned with the day-to-day management of operations which will increasingly be devolved and sometimes contracted out. Their role essentially will be to support members through setting strategic policy and the direction of services, monitoring performance, undertaking research, communicating information and sustaining the dialogue between the public and their elected representatives.

The advantage for a new authority is that it need not assume that a departmental structure is required, or that there must be chief officers for every main statutory function, or that it need carry out every function with its own staff. Choices exist on all these issues, and there is an opportunity in setting up the authority to take a fresh approach. Where a service has been contracted out, what will remain is the commissioning and performance monitoring function. Where it remains in-house, but has been devolved through an area structure, there is the opportunity to establish a similarly lean headquarters structure by allowing local managers to hold budgets and personnel responsibility and to decide how much central support they need. The role of central support services will need redefinition in the light of the approach chosen so that opportunities for flexibility are maximised whilst ensuring that essential controls and key policy objectives are sustained. Similarly, customer care and consultation processes are increasingly widespread, and can be institutionalised in the new authority from the outset.

Towards a brave new world?

Local authorities, whether well or newly established, whether or not affected by the reorganisation, face a demanding, if not alarming, future. There is a very real need to strengthen local democracy, to develop a strategic perspective, and build anew a reputation for consistently high standards of performance. A comprehensive and innovative vision of dynamic community leadership is required, which will mean a new focus for elected members, and new approaches to every aspect of internal management.

New authorities especially have the chance to start with a clean sheet. Newly elected members will be able to take a fresh view of the needs, aspirations and resources of their locality. They can build new relationships with other local organisations. And they can from the outset put into place internal structures and processes focusing on active community leadership, representation, and accountability for performance.

The fourth chapter of Part I explores the practical options available to respond to these challenges and the steps necessary to develop new authorities and new structures. However, to transform local government successfully in this way, and gain lasting benefits, those involved must come to terms with extensive institutional and procedural changes, but they must also deal with substantial behavioural changes - major changes to the way people work and perform. Changes in structures, processes and working practices will also involve thoroughgoing changes in culture.

The next chapter therefore explores the issues involved in managing cultural and behavioural change on a major scale, to identify what local authorities will need to do successfully to meet the challenges they face in the future.

3

BUILDING THE NEW WORLD
Managing change successfully

By most commonly accepted criteria, local government is facing a period of great challenge. Not only are there to be wide-ranging changes in institutions and structures, involving significant change in management processes and systems, but, as previous chapters have indicated, radically new approaches are required to the way in which local government conceives of, and carries out, its role. Each of these would, in their own right, have a major impact on the people working within local government; together they involve major changes in every function and activity, and at every level. No one will remain untouched.

This presents an immense challenge to senior decision takers in local government. Implementing and sustaining a programme of major change of this kind will require change management skills of the highest calibre. Change management is the means of aligning the people and culture in an organisation with changes in strategy, structure, systems and processes. The aim is to achieve three objectives: first, shared ownership of and commitment to change from all those people directly affected; second, sustained and measurable improvement in performance (or why do it?); and third, creating the capability to continue managing change in the future.

Keys to success

Clearly the first stage in the process is to identify whether there is a need for change and, if so, what it is aiming to achieve. There are many techniques useful in doing this and then in managing the change process. Some of these are described in Part II, Chapter 12 of this book. The present chapter aims to illustrate how an awareness of change management theory and test experience can help local authorities to manage the process of change successfully.

Local government is not, of course, unique in facing major change. There is much useful experience to draw upon from managers working elsewhere in the economy, from the traditional heartlands of manufacturing to the leading edge of the financial services industry. The pace of change in business life is constantly accelerating, and new management techniques are needed to deal with it. Active management of change is now familiar territory but success is not inevitable. It has to be worked at and examples of failure abound. Whatever the change involves, introducing new information systems, raising standards of customer care, or improving quality management, all too often the original objectives have had to be scaled down and there have been cost and time overruns, but, most importantly, planned performance improvements have not been achieved. In the worst cases, the programmes have had to be abandoned completely.

The common factor in many of these failures has been that insufficient attention has been paid to the human aspects of change programmes. Invariably, managers have been left confused and dispirited because the hoped for gains from new systems, organisations or quality programmes have not been realised even though, on paper, they appeared to be robust in design and technical specification and, although challenging, did not appear to present insuperable problems for the workforce to overcome. Yet failure rates are high - and the causes of failure are largely due to employee reluctance to embrace change. A recent Management Consultancies Association survey (January 1993) of major projects in businesses, such as new systems and total quality programmes, showed that 40% of the projects surveyed were deemed to have failed, of which roughly half of these had failed because of insufficient attention to change management aspects.

When things start to go badly, defeatism abounds and builds on itself - employees become more and more cynical and do not believe that change is achievable. Or, worse, staff actively resist, either overtly or covertly, wilfully obstructing the programme. And, having failed to cross the Alps of change on one occasion, there is a mountain of Himalayan proportions to climb the next time because the bad experience lingers in the minds of employees long after the programme has come to an end.

But success stories also exist. By learning from the past successes and failures of others and gaining a better understanding of change management issues, tools and techniques, many organisations have managed to implement change successfully. Local government need be no exception. Learning from change management experience elsewhere can have significant benefits, in terms of saving time and avoiding obvious mistakes. Many of the principles of effective change management hold good whatever the business or working environment, and skills and experience are readily transferable. Key success factors are:

- understanding and managing people's response to change

- recognising and managing change as a project in its own right and/or a support for other projects within the overall change programme

- deploying new tools and techniques to facilitate the effective implementation of change and building up the capability to manage change more successfully in the future

In particular, timing the use and application of change management tools and techniques is all important. It is vital to start using them as early as possible, building them into the overall project programme, and in being proactive in using the tools and techniques, anticipating the problems associated with major change rather than reacting to them when the problems emerge and the going gets tough.

An appreciation and understanding of these issues from the outset will be essential to ensuring that a complex process of change is successfully managed. Local government in general faces a significant challenge in maintaining and renewing the relevance of local democracy. And for those authorities directly affected by the reorganisation, transformation is intimately connected with the process of structural change. There is a real risk for such authorities that, in dealing with the technicalities and complexities of structural change, they may lose sight of the wider vision, and lose the opportunity for lasting transformation. Yet these technical problems will themselves require thorough and systematic management. There will be little tolerance of failure.

Twin-track approach

New authorities will therefore need to follow a twin-track route: on the one hand, developing a vision for unitary local government for their new areas, across the full range of local government's functions; and on the other, successfully building confidence and maintaining services until the time is right to implement fully their new vision. The process of twin-tracking structural and transformational change is illustrated in Figure 3.1. It is both complex and demanding, because major, long-term changes in strategy, structure, systems and behaviour must be managed in tandem with the achievement of a tight timetable for setting up new authorities and transferring responsibilities to them from outgoing authorities.

This book focuses primarily on the former; it attempts to provide a context for change and suggests how change might be managed. It is therefore strategic and behavioural in its focus, and its theme is TRANSFORMATION in the longer term. The second theme of STRUCTURAL CHANGE is largely task specific and short-term and most chief executives, leaders of councils and chief officers will look to checklists produced by the LGMB, the Audit Commission, the local authority associations and the professional bodies for more specific guidance.

It is a central theme of this book that each and every stage of this twin-track process will need to be supported by active change management, if it is to succeed. This chapter therefore introduces the most important issues in managing change, and provides guidance on how to deal with them. The main areas are:

- understanding change - showing how building an understanding among the workforce about the key features of change is an important part of winning the battle to effect major change

- building commitment to change - describing ways of avoiding the most common pitfalls, and how the emotions aroused can be turned to management's advantage

- taking charge of change - outlining the essential requirements for managers in managing major change successfully.

The next chapter then goes on to consider at a practical level the main tasks that will be faced by authorities involved in the reorganisation; the process of transferring responsibilities; the issues involved in setting up new authorities and in making them work; and the challenge of winding down old authorities.

Understanding change

A large part of the battle to persuade people working in an organisation that change is necessary, is in helping them to understand the reason for and the nature of that change and particularly to come to terms with their own reaction to it. Even where some difficult or possibly unpleasant things are involved in undertaking the change a better understanding of what is happening will generally support conditions that facilitate that change.

In developing a better understanding of change, the main objective is to analyse why people often fear change and why they try to stop it, either by benign neglect or active resistance. By undertaking this analysis, managers are then in a much better position to deal with emotional responses to change and, therefore, to help their people come to terms with that change.

Resistance to change can take many forms - some may have a perfectly rational basis, others may be founded on emotional factors. But whether rational or not, change can be seen all too readily as a threat that must be resisted. The most obvious influence in resisting changes is a reluctance to break a routine; a change in lifestyle may be involved and the comfortable nature of present existence may be threatened. There is the simple fear of the unknown and the state of uncertainty that goes with it. Staff may quite quickly make what seems to them the rational judgement that, at best, career development will be more limited or, worse still, that their own job will be under threat and the dole queue will beckon.

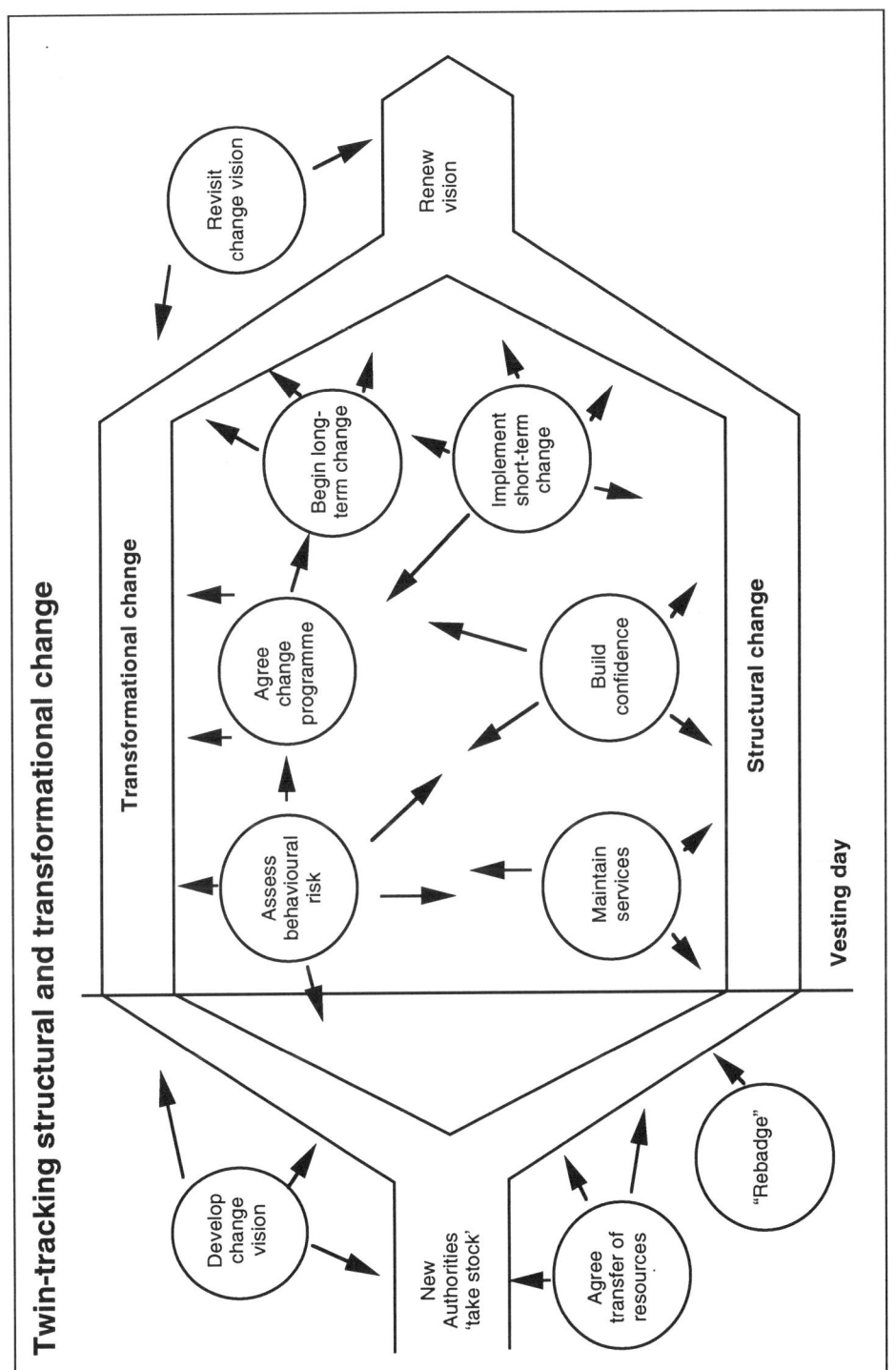

Twin-tracking structural and transformational change

Transformational change

Structural change

Vesting day

Revisit change vision

Renew vision

Begin long-term change

Implement short-term change

Agree change programme

Build confidence

Assess behavioural risk

Maintain services

Develop change vision

New Authorities 'take stock'

Agree transfer of resources

"Rebadge"

Figure 3.1

It may also be that change is seen as a threat to a particular skill base, much in the way that the Luddites smashed looms fearing the impact of new machinery on their cottage industry. Another factor may be change overload: the cry that 'all we need is a period of stability' is often heard, and is a sure sign that staff are experiencing some degree of stress in coping with the rate of change.

But perhaps the most important factor of all in building resistance to change is the lack of perceived motive for change. People ask themselves: 'why should I change when the way things are done now is perfectly satisfactory and the alternative does not seem to be appreciably better?' If people do not feel that they have a compelling need to change, they are unlikely to sustain the motivation required to implement that change. If, however, the alternative can be promoted effectively to show that it is a markedly better way of working, so that the status quo is seen as more painful and less desirable than change, then a compelling need has been established, even if the change is perceived to be no more than the lesser of two evils. To convince staff that there is a compelling need is an important responsibility for those who want to manage change successfully.

Perhaps the best example of a compelling need for change is described by Daryl Connor in his book *Managing at the Speed of Change* (1993). In it he describes the decision by the survivor of the Piper Alpha disaster to jump to probable death from the burning oil rig platform. Figure 3.2 summarises how the parallels with the 'burning platform' can help to shape the approach to change management.

Piper Alpha - The burning platform

In July 1988, Piper Alpha, an oil drilling platform in the North Sea exploded and burned, 168 people lost their lives, just 63 survived. One survivor, a superintendent on the rig - told his story. On hearing the explosion, he ran from his quarters and jumped some 150 feet from the burning platform into a freezing sea covered in flaming oil and debris. When asked why he made the potentially fatal jump, he said 'it was either jump or fry'. He chose possible death over certain death because he had no choice - the price of staying on the platform was higher.

Figure 3.2

The burning platform illustrates graphically a condition where change has to be made, no matter how uncertain or frightening it is. Major change is always costly, but when the present situation is even more expensive, or in this very extreme case life-threatening, 'burning platform' conditions exist. Typically, people need some convincing of such a compelling need to change, and the assessment of the costs - comparing the cost of the status quo with the cost of changing - is a business imperative for change managers.

One of the problems that most perplexes managers in implementing change is that problems can appear in unexpected quarters. Staff who are normally the most dependable, experienced and hard working, the most committed to the success of the organisation, may be the ones who exhibit all of the classic signs of resistance to change. They may feel they have more to lose or are more cautious about changing a structure that they think works well. It may be that they feel they lack a compelling need to change, but, whatever the motive, the key position of these staff makes their behaviour a serious threat to the success of the change programme.

To help understand change better, change managers have turned to clinical psychologists for advice. As in the 'burning platform' example, it is helpful to consider the most extreme situations to demonstrate the principles of people's reaction to change. In fact the reaction to the announcement of a major change programme is almost exactly the same as the reaction of a patient who is given bad news about a terminal illness, a serious injury, or chronic illness involving permanent disability or change in lifestyle. As a result, approaches developed in clinical psychology can enhance understanding of the best way in which to encourage a positive response to change. These show that, with careful management of the announcement and of preparing the way for change, it is possible to manage negative responses, achieve acceptance and then work with people to build continuous commitment to change in the future.

Yet, even a positive response to change - where there is general agreement that the change will be beneficial to the organisation and the staff involved, may lull managers into a sense of false security. Moving through the cycle shown in Figure 3.3, it can be seen that there is a risk area. As implementation proceeds, people may begin to develop doubts, perhaps because a problem emerges or timescales slip. If such doubts are expressed publicly, managers can react to them. More dangerously, the doubts remain as private ones. Unseen by management, people begin to lose impetus, and instead to resist the change they had previously accepted.

Successful managers recognise this risk and are constantly on the alert for signs of opting out, reacting quickly to bring the change programme back on course. Resistance is seen as an inevitable part of major change and the aim is to restore a mood of hopeful realism, from which to build informed optimism and finally to achieve satisfaction and completion of the programme.

More commonly, however, the emotional response to major change is depressingly negative as shown in Figure 3.4. This is a world with high levels of stress and tension. Aggressive and destructive emotions are unleashed and change may seem impossible to achieve. Managers may weaken and shrink back from the brink if they do not understand themselves what is involved and take steps to counter it. Research in clinical psychology shows a series of emotional

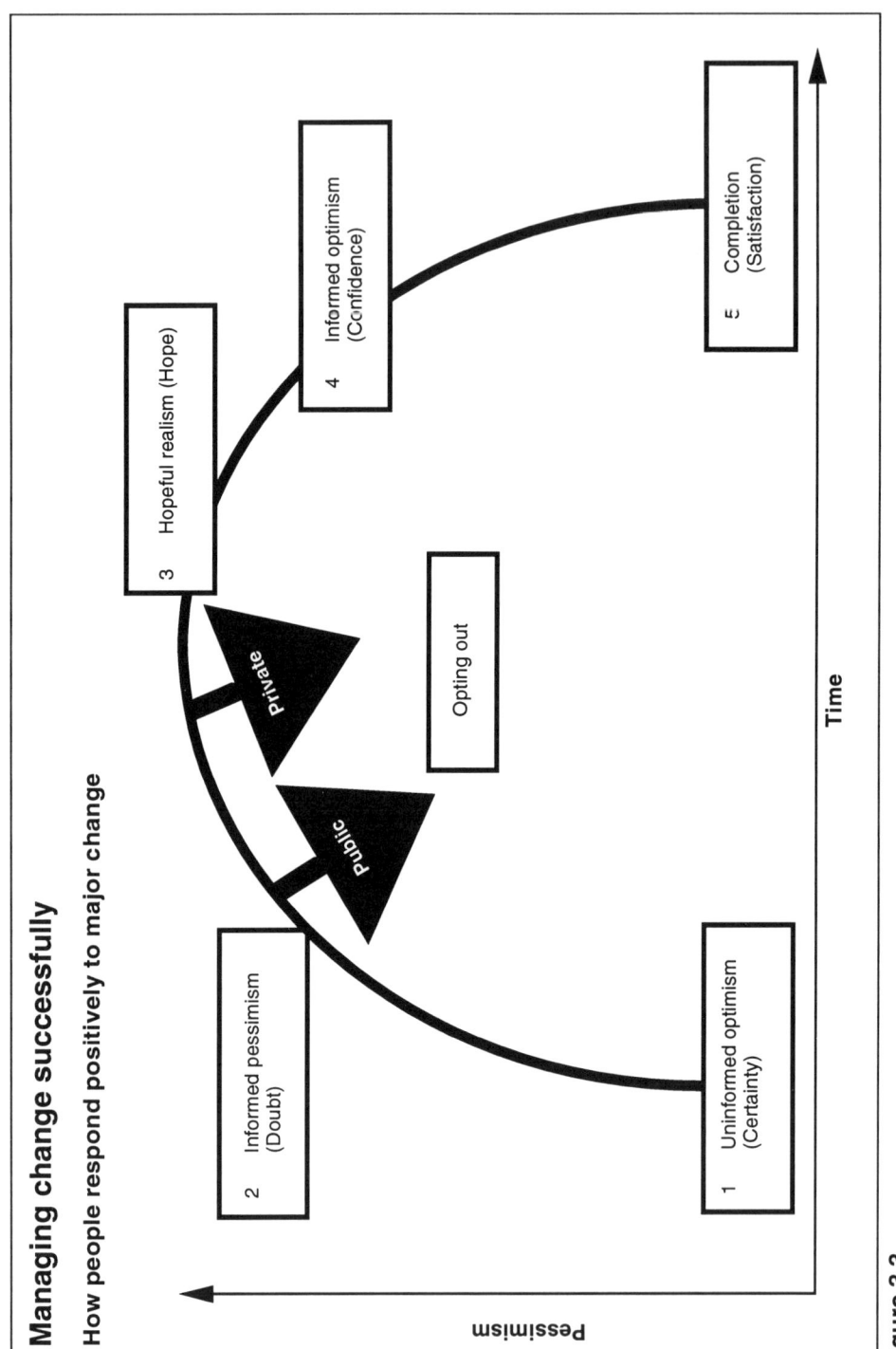

Managing change successfully
How people respond positively to major change

- 1 Uninformed optimism (Certainty)
- 2 Informed pessimism (Doubt)
- 3 Hopeful realism (Hope)
- 4 Informed optimism (Confidence)
- 5 Completion (Satisfaction)

Opting out

Private

Public

Pessimism

Time

Figure 3.3

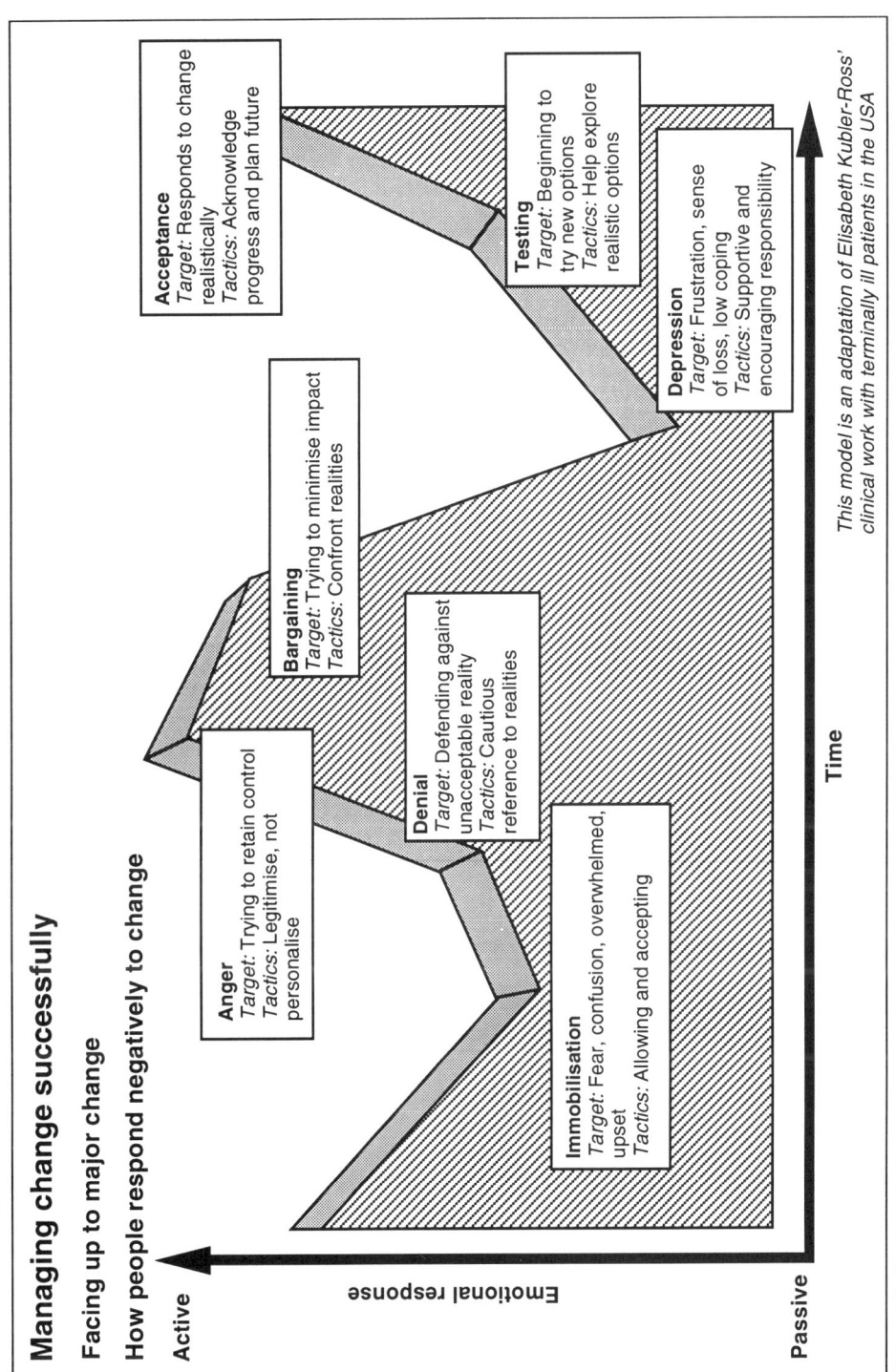

Managing change successfully

Facing up to major change

How people respond negatively to change

Anger
Target: Trying to retain control
Tactics: Legitimise, not personalise

Bargaining
Target: Trying to minimise impact
Tactics: Confront realities

Denial
Target: Defending against unacceptable reality
Tactics: Cautious reference to realities

Immobilisation
Target: Fear, confusion, overwhelmed, upset
Tactics: Allowing and accepting

Acceptance
Target: Responds to change realistically
Tactics: Acknowledge progress and plan future

Testing
Target: Beginning to try new options
Tactics: Help explore realistic options

Depression
Target: Frustration, sense of loss, low coping
Tactics: Supportive and encouraging responsibility

Active

Passive

Emotional response

Time

This model is an adaptation of Elisabeth Kubler-Ross' clinical work with terminally ill patients in the USA

Figure 3.4

responses, many of which are a familiar part of many other events and experiences in other settings. Just to understand the emotional range they are experiencing is often enormously helpful to people, particularly when they discover that their reactions to change, their fears, emotions and negative views, are all perfectly normal.

Time and time again, all that has been needed in breaking the ice that has formed in the manager-staff relationship, is to raise the level of awareness among individuals. They begin to realise that the fear of change and the pain caused by uncertainty are not unique to them. Often there is a visible relaxation of tension when people realise that there are ways of addressing their fears, and a sigh of relief that the strain being experienced has been recognised.

There may be also occasions when opposition to change is based on a real detriment to the people involved which may not be necessary or intended. It may arise because the consequences of some decisions have not been understood by those who made them. Managers in these circumstances should refer back to the decision makers and ensure that the unpleasant side effects are essential rather than accept decisions as immutable when they might not be.

The issue for management is to anticipate, recognise and manage the differing stages and moods of anger, denial and depression that their staff are experiencing, and to tailor their response, raising the level of understanding and gaining acceptance for major change. Yet even if people have a better understanding of their response to change, they may remain obdurate, hostile and cynical. More must be done to win over staff and build their commitment to change, and specialised change management tools and techniques have now been developed to assist with this process.

Building commitment to change

In the early stages of the process in particular, communication is vital. In the context of reorganisation this needs to challenge rumours and misinformation as well as convey positive messages about the changes in hand. However, even where managers have made a real effort to communicate widely with the workforce, to explain what is intended and to gather a fair degree of commitment to it, things can still go wrong. Without constant effort from the managers leading the change programme, the initial commitment begins to wane. The reality is that commitment is a multi-staged process. People cannot commit to major change without progressing through a sequential process of testing and validating change. Resistance is only one part of the commitment process. Successful change managers need to take charge of all of the stages. Careful structuring of processes to recognise the multi-stage nature of effecting major change is essential.

Figure 3.5 shows the principal stages involved in building commitment to change. Each stage involves close coordination, teamwork and excellent communications if progress to the next stage is to be achieved successfully. As part of this process, it really does become possible to build up the capacity of employees not just to

Managing change successfully

Building commitment

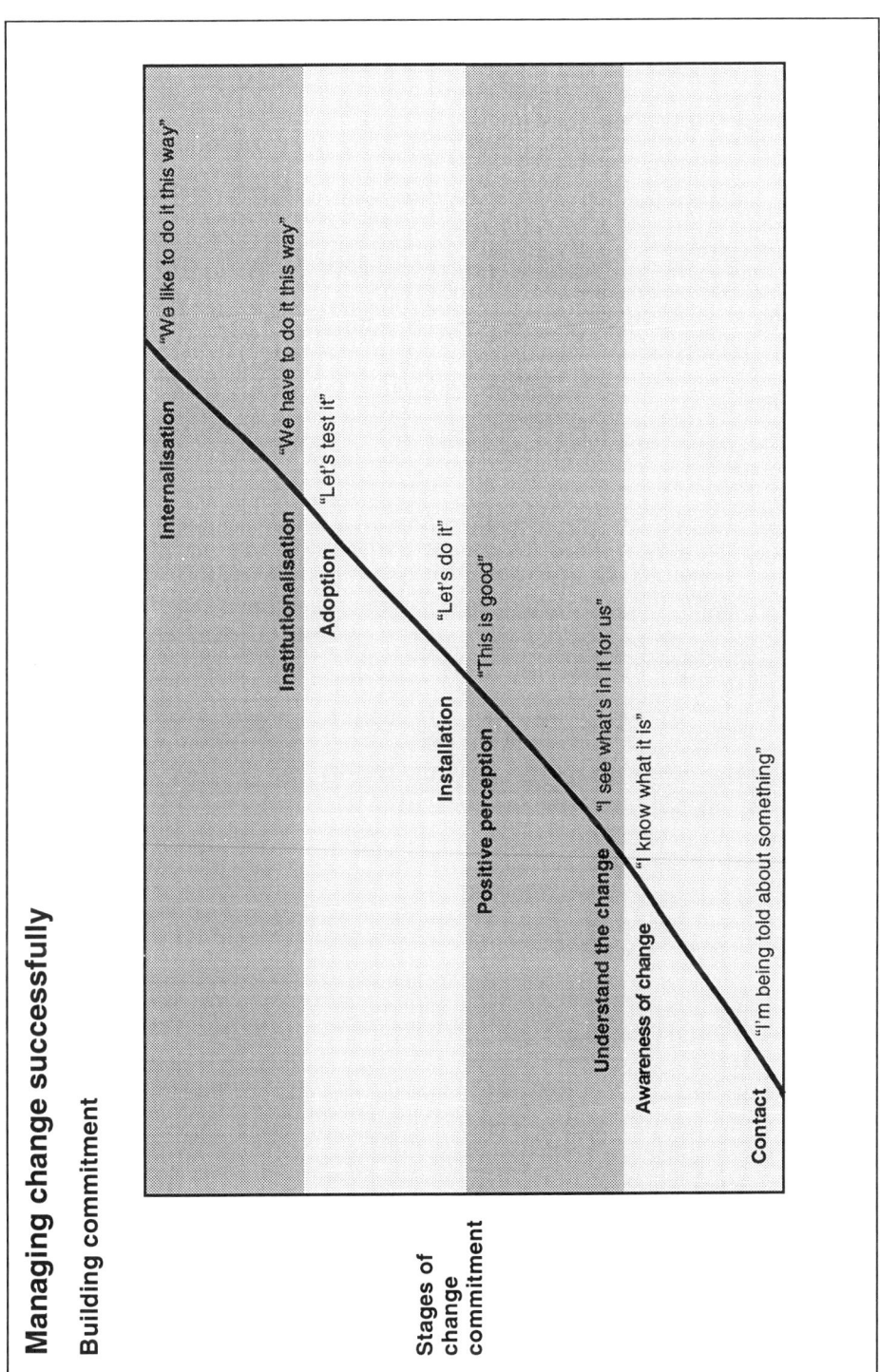

Stages of change commitment

Contact — "I'm being told about something"

Awareness of change — "I know what it is"

Understand the change — "I see what's in it for us"

Positive perception — "This is good"

Installation

Adoption — "Let's do it"

Institutionalisation — "Let's test it"

Internalisation — "We have to do it this way"

"We like to do it this way"

Figure 3.5

41

live with the effects of change, but to develop a positive long-term view of change as an important benefit, and part of obtaining greater job satisfaction.

This can be described as building resilience. People who are resilient to change bounce back from the personal disruptions caused by change quicker than others. It is a frame of mind, an attitude to life which means that staff can accept change and make it work for them. The main attributes of a 'resilient' employee are:

- **positiveness:** displaying a sense of security and self assurance that is based on their view of life as complex, but filled with opportunity - their glass is half-full, not half-empty

- **focus:** having a clear vision of what they want to achieve

- **flexibility:** demonstrating a special pliability when responding to uncertainty - they don't give up at the first sign of difficulty, but press on and look for new ways forward

- **organisation:** developing structured approaches to managing ambiguity and uncertainty - they plan logically to minimise emotional, 'knee-jerk' reactions to proposed change

- **proactiveness:** engaging change rather than defending against it - they stop seeking a period of stability and build the change programme into their jobs

Building resilience is important because less time and money will be wasted in change. People will adjust more quickly, resist less often and maintain performance levels more evenly. By developing individual resilience the organisation's capacity for change will be enhanced. Managers can help individuals to build on positive responses to change, manage negative responses and gain acceptance and support for change programmes. This is a powerful means of building continuous commitment.

Taking charge of change

It is important to understand the key roles in a change programme but also to emphasise that people move between roles. The technical terminology used by change management specialists identifies four main groups, as shown in Figure 3.6. These are called change sponsors, change agents, change targets and change advocates but this should not be taken to imply that change is something one fixed group of people (change agents) does to another fixed group (change targets). This week's targets can turn into next week's sponsors, agents or advocates.

TAKING CHARGE OF CHANGE

Change managers and change roles	Those involved
Change sponsors - commitment and involvement at the top is essential if a change programme is to be truly successful and enduring.	**Chief executives and heads of functions** - this is not a task which can be delegated to more junior managers who are told to go away and come back when they have succeeded.
Change agents - the doers and facilitators of change, using tools and techniques to manage the change process, these are key people who provide the engine of change, the motivators with a specific remit to use all the tools and techniques at their disposal to drive on the change programme to success with enduring benefits.	**Senior managers and rising 'stars' with career development potential** - they must be chosen from amongst the very best staff with breadth of vision, energy and determination - they are needed to set the example for others to emulate and to help provide the optimism and determination to succeed which the change programme will require.
Change targets - the whole workforce, the people whose commitment is essential if change is to be implemented successfully.	**The whole workforce** - the people who, if things go well, can themselves become sponsors and cascade the commitment to change all the way down the organisation.
Change advocates - people who energise and motivate others to change, but who do not have the organisational power to make change happen.	**Specialists, advisers, consultants** - internal or external influences, people whose views and judgement staff can understand and respect.

Figure 3.6

Each role has an important part to play in the change process and an essential first step in the change programme is to define these roles and explain what is expected from them so that all involved are clear. Then it is necessary to select people to fill these positions to start the process in a way which suits the culture and organisation of the authority.

Whatever the role an individual fills at any given time, teamworking is a vital part of achieving change. Most successful change programmes use cross-functional teams to drive the programme forward. In assembling these teams, successful change managers are seeking access to a range of different perspectives; perspectives that can be brought together within the change programme, giving staff exposure to different skills, helping to enhance the capability of every team member and provide the prospect of a real 'buy-in' to the change process from a wide range of employees.

Sadly, many groups never fully realise these benefits because they fail to form effective teams or to operate around a common agenda and set of goals for change. Or the sponsors, agents and targets participating in the teams fail to generate real interdependence between each other to permit the creation of genuine momentum towards the goals of the change programme. The teams formed become destructive in their development of ideas or find themselves unable to go forward, failing to deliver the synergy which the team was intended to deliver.

Thus team building, team leadership skills and self-managing team work are all techniques at the heart of change management programmes. By working together, they produce synergies where the total achievement is greater than the mere sum of the parts. Furthermore, experience suggests that change programmes rarely work well without the support of some external inputs. These generally are brought in to work with staff in facilitating change processes and to transfer essential skills to internal managers and staff. As Figure 3.7 shows, the independence of external advisers has a real contribution to make in breaking down barriers, and helping to start discussions and the exchange of ideas.

Change agents - Little thistles grow to big thistles

Dr Ian Preston CBE, the Chief Executive, Scottish Power has led a major programme of change to transform a large, centralised public sector, technically driven electricity company into a lean, decentralised and diversified private sector company accountable to shareholders with a strong commercial focus, whilst at the same time raising technical quality standards and developing a more responsive customer service ethos. Scottish Power has made major savings in costs and manpower whilst increasing turnover and profitability. In his view, change cannot be generated effectively without some external facilitation at the outset - providing a different perspective to help staff reassess their roles, break down barriers and overcome resistance to change. (Presentation at Latimer House, 1 October 1993).

Figure 3.7

In striving to improve high quality two-way internal communications with their staff, senior managers often encounter 'black holes'. Black holes are a common cause of change failure. They occur when initiating sponsorship is not cascaded down the line resulting in inadequate sponsorship results. Similarly, messages moving up the line from the workforce to senior managers are lost in the black hole. The power of this group is so strong that information sucked into it lacks the power to leave and is trapped, never to see the light of day again.

All too often the black hole can be found at the middle management level - where key managers may not be communicating. Messages about change then fail to reach their targets and employees lose confidence in management's ability to effect change. They do not believe managers are listening to their views even if they seem to be constructive and supportive. This is not a statement about physical remoteness - it can apply just as much to junior staff in main offices, as to staff remotely located at the edge of the local authority's area.

Using tools and techniques actively to address this communications block and eliminate or avoid the black hole is an important part of the change management process, as is ensuring that the right people are chosen with clear roles as agents or advocates of change.

Managing change successfully also requires adoption of a framework for change. This involves three groups of interrelated methods and techniques, illustrated in Figure 3.8. These are used:

- to determine and sustain a change vision; an assessment of what needs to change, and why
- to assess behavioural risk factors and plan processes to overcome them
- to ensure rigorous programme management through project management techniques and disciplines

Creating the change vision for the local authority is the catalyst, the vital first step in establishing the key factors which will transform the management of local government. It needs to accommodate the requirements of structural change, as well as transformational change, assessing a wide range of options appropriate to the new authority's external circumstances and to the view it has of the way it wants to operate. The change vision therefore needs to identify and codify:

- the authority's vision of itself as 'community leader'
- what needs to change
- what will promote change and what may constrain it
- behavioural and other risk factors

The change vision process should be recognised as genuinely important. It is too easy to pay lip service to it and write off the visioning process as too high flown or theoretical. In reality, it should be about commonsense, hard edged matters such as key policy and strategy issues for the authority, including resource allocation matters, use of assets, as well as key values. For example, a new unitary authority which inherits from predecessor authorities widely differing policies in, say, housing management, will need to balance a concern

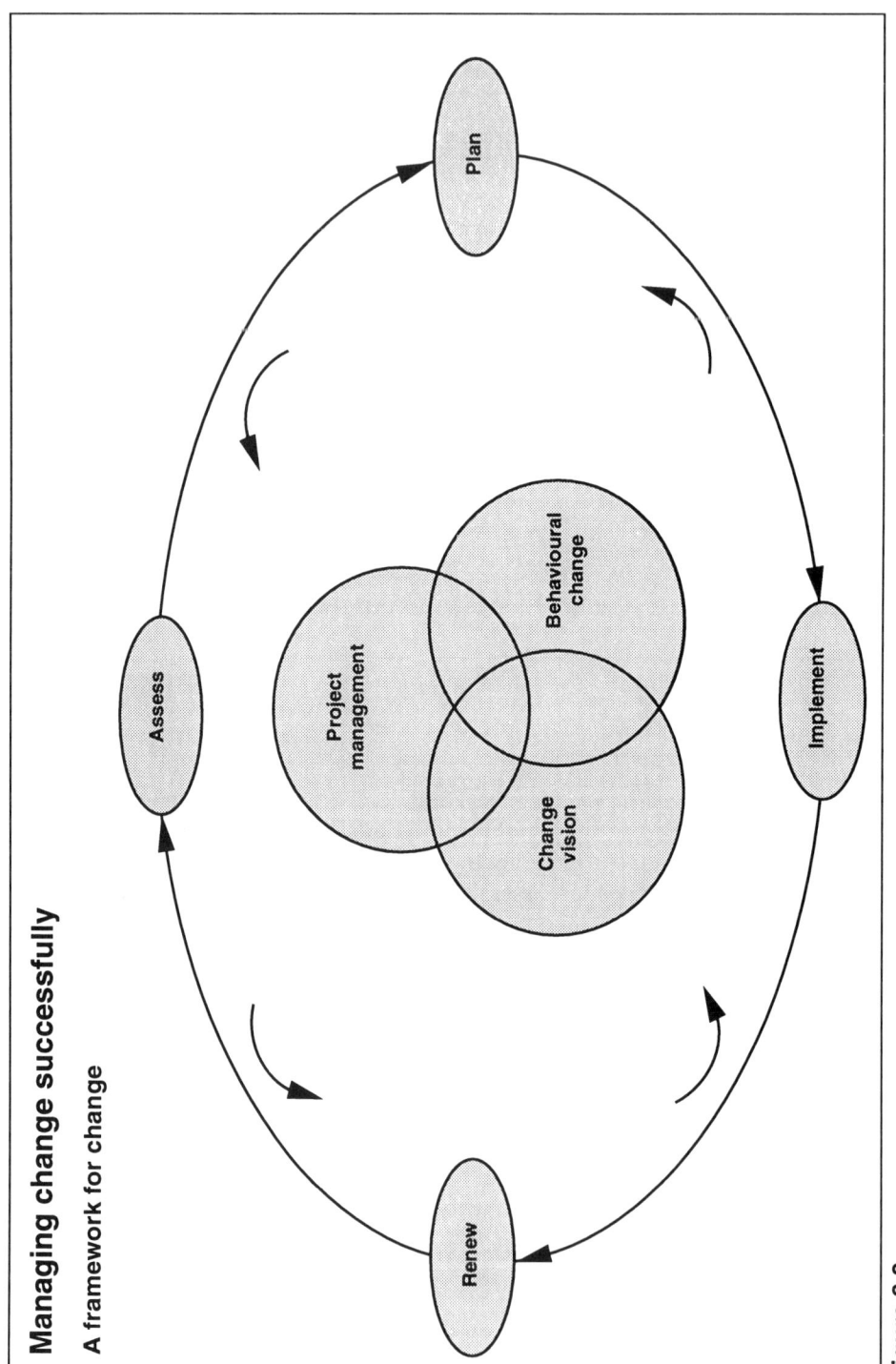

Managing change successfully

A framework for change

Figure 3.8

with achieving common standards in a mainstream service, with its commitment to valuing diversity and allowing local choice.

The change vision also needs to look towards the wider horizon, as sketched out in the previous chapter. It is an opportunity to look beyond more obvious short-term problem areas and extend the authority's perspective. It should be outward facing, covering the external impacts on the organisation and recognise the consumers of local authority services as drivers of change. And it also needs to consider the key issues of internal management and style identified in the previous chapter. Some useful tools and techniques designed to achieve this are introduced in Part II.

The second element of the framework for change is the application of behavioural change diagnostics and methods to assess behavioural risk. These focus on developing insights into the way people respond to major change, embracing the key issues in effecting major change and the means by which they may be addressed to achieve a successful outcome. The tools and techniques used must take account of the risk factors: where are people likely to resist change? And, regarding the opportunities that present themselves, where and how can people be encouraged to embrace change? Behavioural risks and opportunities are rarely fully evident at the start of a change programme; indeed, it is those that managers are least aware of that can cause the most problems. As they emerge during the change programme they require continuous diagnosis and discussion between the change managers, sponsors, agents and targets of change.

The third element is effective programme management, through which the change vision and behavioural change elements in the change programme can be brought together to control the resources needed to drive successful implementation. This component draws on classical project management techniques to structure, phase and control required inputs and outputs. It is about establishing the principles of accountability and responsibility for specific aspects of change, and about setting clear objectives and targets as an essential part of 'taking charge'.

There is no secret ingredient here; rather it is a practical approach using well-tried and tested techniques to keep the change programme on course. It is designed to ensure that a realistic timetable is prepared, with targets and milestones set in advance, and that those involved in managing change are provided with project management training skills. In effect, the overall aim is to build a new organisation and culture, using techniques similar to those used to build any other new structure or system. A continuous process is required through which change is assessed, planned, implemented, and renewed, as illustrated at Figure 3.8.

This is how change management can be seen as a means of changing the culture of the local authority in its totality becoming a project in its own right and, in doing so, providing an important enabling support for the range of different subprojects that will be required to achieve structural change satisfactorily to the official schedule, and to implement long-term change in accordance with the authority's wider vision of its community's needs.

Conclusion

Experience in other sectors, and indeed in the reorganisations of 1974 and 1975, suggests that local government will not succeed in implementing radical and comprehensive change on the scale required without proper recognition of the human and behavioural factors involved. But understanding these factors is not enough, active management of their consequences is also essential. A 'change management' approach, applying the thinking set out here, has real potential to assist local government in responding to the challenges it faces, avoiding black holes, 'bottlenecks' and other pitfalls, which might prevent or reduce the threat of failure, and maximise the chances of success. New tools and techniques are available to underpin the achievement of structural and transformational change.

The next chapter identifies the key issues involved in managing the transition to new authorities and in beginning to identify and lay the ground for a long-term, more permanent vision of change. The fifth and final chapter of Part I will explore in greater depth the main areas on which politicians and senior managers will need to focus if that vision is to be successfully put into practice.

4

ENDINGS AND BEGINNINGS
Transition to the new unitary authority

Mergers, takeovers and breakups

Much of this book is about grasping new opportunities and making new beginnings. This chapter, however, looks first at endings: at the challenge of winding down authorities which will cease to exist, and at the process of the transfer of responsibilities. It then goes on to look at the issues involved from the perspective of new unitary authorities.

The reorganisation and transition process involves a very considerable task which must be started as soon as possible once decisions are made about the future shape of local government in any area. Preliminary work on setting up new authorities will inevitably have to be carried out by existing authorities, whatever their own fate. Members and officers will have to ensure that services are maintained and that the ground is prepared for the new authorities. Without positive and sensitive management, there is a real risk that services will suffer, and that information and experience essential to the success of the new authorities will be lost. Lessons can be learnt from previous reorganisations e.g. the Institute of Local Government Studies (INLOGOV) study on the aftermath of the abolition of the Metropolitan Counties (Leach et al 1992).

In some cases, reorganisation will mean that authority areas are to be broken up into smaller units. Generally this will occur where county or regional councils are being replaced by a number of unitary authorities. In other cases, authority areas will be combined to form larger units, usually districts being brought together to form a new unitary authority. Often both division and combination will occur in the same area, with new unitary authorities being smaller than the existing county/region, but larger than existing districts. In England, the possibility also exists that it will be decided to retain an existing authority, either a district or county, and for that authority to take over functions from the other tier. For example, in the Isle of Wight, on which the Local Government Commission made its first decision, the County Council is being merged with the existing two District Councils. In any of these scenarios, there may also be boundary changes further to complicate matters.

In addition, timescales for change are short. As far as England is concerned, all decisions are due to have been made by the end of 1994 though this must depend on the extent to which the Government refers back the commission's initial recommendations for further consideration, as has been the case for Derbyshire, Durham and Gloucestershire, and the extent to which authorities themselves seek to challenge final decisions in the courts. For example both Avon and Cleveland sought judicial review during 1994. Nonetheless, it is still envisaged that implementation will have been completed by April 1997 in England, and that all new authorities in Scotland and Wales will come into being in April 1996.

All this makes the exercise of setting up new authorities, and transferring responsibilities to them, in many ways more complex than in other reorganisations. There will be no shortage of advice on the technical matters to be dealt with in reorganisation, though as yet much is in draft or has still to be issued. Indeed, the main problem may be finding adequate time to read all the various publications, and pick out what is important. Figure 4.1 lists some of those sources currently available for England. But because of this complexity, and the very short time allowed by the Government for implementing the transfer, it is essential for existing authorities to work together in a structured way, on an agreed programme of tasks. The first part of this chapter sets out a process of co-operation among existing authorities, between them and new authorities in shadow form, and discusses the management issues involved in winding down.

Co-operation between existing authorities

In many parts of the country, officers and sometimes members from various authorities within an appropriate area have already been meeting on a regular basis to exchange information and monitor progress. Once decisions have been made, it will be necessary to put these arrangements on a more formal footing. Figure 4.2 illustrates the groups and sub-groups which will be required, and their principal tasks. Responsibility for steering the process should rest with a Members Steering Group, supported by a Chief Executives Joint Working Group. Detailed work will need to be done in functional and service officer sub-groups.

Groups will be needed for each successor authority. This will mean that where the functions of an authority are being transferred to more than one successor, there will be a need for its members and officers to participate in more than one group. Joint meetings will also be required to discuss the division of assets and other resources of the authority. Alternatively, groups could subdivide to provide advice to each successor authority. But even so, it will probably be necessary in the period immediately before transfer of responsibility to split groups

Principal sources of technical advice (England)

- **Department of Environment advice and regulations**
  - *Local Government Changes for England Regulations 1994* (covering continuity of matters, shadow authorities and certain points on planning, charter trustees, fire and police disciplinary matters, the registration service, sheriffs and coroners - already published)
  - associated consultation paper covering proposals on residuary body
  - consultation paper and draft regulations on transitional operation of finance system, including:
    - administration of local taxes
    - arrangements for grants
    - transfer of funds (other than superannuation funds)
    - budgeting and tax setting
    - closing accounts of old authorities
    - audit
    - transitional arrangements for compulsory competitive tendering
  - consultation paper on housing finance
  - consultation paper on arrangements for 1994/95 reorganisation costs
  - advice on transfer of contractual rights and liabilities (awaited)

- **Local Government Staff Commission for England**
  Advice available or awaited on:
  - filling of early vacancies and creation of new posts and structures
  - staff transfer and recruitment
  - terms of compensation for loss of office
  - code of good practice on issues concerning transfer of personnel
  - arrangements for appeals
  - compensation for detriment
  - role of Monitoring Officer on staff issues

- **CIPFA**
  - *Financial administration implications of the Local Government Review* (A handbook of essential tasks to be undertaken by the finance function)
  - Code of Practice on Prudential Approach to Financial management prior to Local Government Reorganisation (awaited)

- **Audit Commission**
  - *Time for Change* (May 1994)
  Also plans to publish a series of papers for:
  - councils at different stages in the reorganisation process
  - technical and management issues (identifying best practice and providing comparative performance data)
  - information exchange on issues relevant to authorities undergoing reorganisation

- **Local Authority Associations**
  - advice on wide range of issues associated with review

- **Other professional bodies**
  - technical aspects of reorganisation from an individual service perspective

Figure 4.1

Co-operation between existing Authorities

(prior to the creation of Shadow Authorities)

Group and membership	Tasks
Members Steering Group Nominees from existing authority	• overview of policy issues and plans • advice to successor authorities • discussing matters of common concern
Chief Executives joint working group Chief Executives from each existing authority	• advice to steering group on policy issues and plans • agreeing strategy for winding up • monitoring and co-ordinating work of sub-groups • discussing matters of common concern
Sub-group for: • Finance • Personnel • IT • Property • Each of the services (or groups of services) Officer representatives from each existing authority	• detailed work on specifying information needs • providing required information • discussing transfer arrangements of staff and property • other issues of common concern • reporting to Chief Executives and to Members Steering Group

Figure 4.2

permanently to ensure that each Shadow Authority has its own advisers. Establishing the groups will also require other issues to be addressed including:

- political balance of representation

- terms of reference and constitution

- support service requirements

- information sharing arrangements

There will be a need for some contingency planning at this stage - it may not be clear what sort of control the new authority will be under, and different approaches may be necessary depending upon the outcome of the first election to the new authority.

Establishing shadow authorities

Shadow authorities are likely to be set up for all newly created unitary and two-tier authorities. However, the Government has stated that, in cases in England where a district or county takes over the functions of the other tier without any significant boundary change, the inheritor authority will not be considered a new authority, and there therefore will be no need for a separate Shadow Authority - the existing authority will perform this role. Where a new authority is to be set up in England, the order establishing it will provide for a 'shadow phase'. This means that elections to the authority will be held some time in advance of the actual reorganisation date probably in May of the year before. In Scotland and Wales all new authorities will have shadow authorities. In Scotland elections to these will be on 6 April 1995 and on the 4 May 1995 in Wales. Shadow authorities will be expected to prepare for taking over the actual operation of services on the reorganisation date. They will elect a chairman and vice-chairman, select leaders of the political groups, establish their chosen committee structure and in general, determine how the new authority will be managed.

The Members Steering Group set up to prepare the way for the new authority will need to prepare a report for the Shadow (or inheritor) Authority on the issues it has addressed, and set out the advice it wishes to give on policy issues as well as matters relating to the transfer. The report will need to be discussed and accepted in an appropriate forum, for example, the first new council's meeting, after which the Shadow Authority will then take over the lead in setting up the new authority. The Officer Working Groups from existing authorities should continue to operate, since they will still be the primary source of advice to the new authority at this stage; however, once chief executives designate have been appointed, advice should be given through them, as shown in Figure 4.3.

It will then be for the Shadow Authority to begin the processes of structural and transformational change which are the primary focus of this book. The first meeting of the new council will be critical, since it is then that the new councillors will have the first opportunity together to consider their vision for the new

Co-operation between existing Authorities and Shadow Authorities

Group	Tasks
Shadow Authority	• policy decisions for new authority • agreeing transfer of assets with other Shadow/Inheritor Authorities • budget for new authority • staffing of new authority
Chief Executive and other Chief Officers designate	• advice to Shadow Authority on above • setting up new departments
Chief Executive's joint working group	• final stages of strategy for winding up • advice to Chief Executive designate and Shadow Authority
Sub-Groups as before	• final stages of information exchange • advice to Chief Officers designate and Shadow Authority

Figure 4.3

authority, and, in that light, to reach decisions on the key areas of internal management identified earlier. Such decisions are very much on the 'critical path' of setting up the new authority, since senior appointments will depend upon organisation structure and committee structure, and this will in turn depend upon the overall philosophy of the authority. The more radical the approach, the more there will be a need to involve the new council in full in agreeing appointments and determining staffing policies.

It is critical that new authorities can consider a range of well developed options, together with their implications, very early on since the decisions required of them at this time will be both fundamental and time critical. There will be a need for good, robust decisions to be made quickly.

In planning the transition process, it is all too tempting to concentrate exclusively on the needs and priorities of the new authority, and assume that existing arrangements will simply carry on until it is time for them to stop. But there is also a need to consider how to manage the winding down of outgoing authorities, and how to handle the problems they are likely to encounter.

Winding down old authorities

The members and officers of an authority to be wound down have two primary roles. The first, as set out above, is to provide advice and information, and facilitate transfer of assets, to the new authority. The second is to keep their existing authority running smoothly, representing the interests of their community and maintaining the provision of quality services.

There is, however, a risk that the needs of the old authority will be overlooked in the concern to set up the new. On a personal level, individual members and officers will be concerned for their futures, and as politicians and professionals they will also be concerned about the future of their community and its services. Some will be involved in setting up one of the new authorities, as well as running down the old and some senior officers may be moving to new authorities geographically and/or culturally distant from their existing employer. Most staff will be expecting some kind of role in a successor authority, and as the transfer date gets near, they will know what that role will be. It is therefore natural that they will tend to concentrate on the new authority. Others will be leaving local government on reorganisation, willingly or not. They may start to lose interest as the end draws near, and the result may be an apathetic approach to decision making, and less than full commitment to managing continuing day-to-day problems.

In order to ensure that all necessary steps are taken to meet the needs of the outgoing authority, and to provide a focus for people's efforts in a difficult situation, it will be important for the chief executive of the authority to take control and establish a strategic view of what has to be done to wind down the authority in good order. Each element should be expressed in terms of specific targets and timescales, and indicate which officer is responsible for achievement.

The chief executive should expect to receive regular monitoring reports on progress against these targets from those responsible. The principal areas to be addressed are:

- maintaining effective services throughout the transitional period

- ensuring that the authority continues to protect and represent the community's interests

- keeping staff and the public informed about the changes

- providing successor authorities with information

- assisting in the strategic planning of the new authorities

- managing the transfer of assets and liabilities

- protecting staff interests

- preparing schedules of existing contracts and commitments

- managing the final handover and associated ceremonies

These are shown in more detail in Figure 4.4. All staff should be made aware of the plan, and of the importance of achieving the targets. It would also be helpful to discuss it with other chief executives in the joint working group described above.

The politics of winding down will also need to be addressed through this plan. Even where there has been no co-operation during earlier stages, it is unlikely that this will persist once final decisions are made, since co-operation will be the only way that existing members can influence the new authority. When the GLC was abolished, for example, even those authorities fiercely opposed to it politically received full co-operation from those involved in handling the transfer of responsibilities.

In the immediate period before the previous reorganisation of local government in 1974 and 1975, many outgoing authorities tried hard to provide the best possible facilities for their area, and there was a rush to create capital receipts by selling surplus assets and then spending those receipts on new schemes. Every effort was made to obtain permission to fund new buildings, and many new arts and sports centres were build at that time. It was then left to successor authorities to fund their running costs and service the loan debt.

With current very tight spending constraints, there will be considerably less opportunity this time to do the same thing, but it is perhaps a natural tendency to want to leave behind something positive. It should nonetheless be possible to reach joint agreement between authorities about what capital schemes are needed, and what levels of balances should be handed over. Whether 'fair shares for all' are achieved will inevitably depend to some extent upon negotiating ability and political clout. And the Government may in any case place formal restrictions on the extent to which outgoing authorities can make long-term

Strategy for winding down

- **Maintaining effective services throughout transitional period**
  - ensuring that proper plans and budgets are drawn up for the closing period of operation
  - monitoring achievement of those plans
  - stressing the importance of continuing good management procedures (target setting, performance monitoring, staff appraisals, budgetary control and closeness to customers)
  - maintaining links with business community and voluntary sector
  - maintaining an overview on the process of transition

- **Ensuring continuing protection and representation of community's interests**
  - ensuring that community's needs are not overlooked
  - continuing to represent community in European and national fora

- **Keeping staff and public informed about changes**
  - drawing up plan for internal and external communications
  - continuing good practice two-way communications with staff (consultation meetings, team briefings, newsletters etc.)
  - working with successor authority/ies to inform the public about proposed changes

- **Providing successor authorities with information**
  - working with other authorities to determine initial advice and briefing on key transition issues for successor authorities
  - supplying successor authorities with information as requested throughout transition period e.g. through participation in co-operation arrangements and through undertaking service audits
  - supplying successor authorities with details as required of management and operational policies and practices
  - highlighting areas of good working practices

- **Assisting in strategic planning of new authorities**
  - working with other authorities to identify and meet planning requirements
  - providing advice and assistance as required on formulation of plans and policies including joint working options

- **Managing transfer of assets and liabilities**
  - drawing up schedules of property and current use and condition
  - dealing with non-tangible assets such as data, intellectual property
  - providing information as required on all other assets and liabilities

- **Protecting staff interests**
  - developing information base of staff and personnel policies and practices
  - ensuring that staff are aware of employment and severance opportunities open to them
  - ensuring staff are fairly treated in job offers by successor authority/ies
  - maintaining channels of communication for staff concerned about their future
  - maintaining appropriate dialogue with trade unions

- **Preparing schedules of existing contracts and commitments**
  - providing information about present and planned third party contracts and commitments
  - scheduling existing grant giving and other relationships into the voluntary sector and developing protocol with new authorities about their continuation
- **Managing handover and associated ceremonies**
  - planning in detail for final months
  - ensuring key staff are able to provide information for continuity after handover, especially in relation to final accounts
  - formulating and funding appropriate handover and closure ceremony

---

Figure 4.4

contracts or commitments (as will be the case in Wales and Scotland and is advocated by the Audit Commission for England).

A further lesson from this period is that some policies agreed in the early days of new authorities rebounded upon them later. For example, many combining authorities agreed an explicit policy of 'levelling up' all service standards to that of the highest. But, for some, finding the resources to achieve this proved very difficult, and different service standards persisted for many years. This illustrates the importance of a very careful process of taking stock, and a realistic approach to planning subsequent change.

Managing the wind down

Change is always unsettling, as Chapter 3 has indicated. But change involving the loss of an authority's identity is particularly difficult. Paradoxically, the better job an authority has done in motivating its staff to believe in it, and feel positive about working for it, the more difficult it will be for staff to accept its demise. Staff will be aware if the authority has lost a fight to survive - many authorities have involved staff in supporting them during the decision making and consultation process - and an adverse decision will be a bad shock. Indeed, there may be a last ditch attempt to reverse the decision, for example through a challenge to its legality.

Eventually, however, reality will need to be faced, and there may be a period of considerable anger and sadness. This needs to be openly acknowledged and managed, if it is not to be destructive, and the previous chapter sets out ways in which to handle this kind of response. If a state of acceptance can be achieved, real progress can be made. Staff who worked for the former GLC until the end, for example, remember the peculiar sense of both sadness and relief which marked the closing months of operation. But once over the initial shock, they were able to hand over to London Boroughs and other bodies, and close down the authority, with very little adverse impact on services. Indeed, at the end there was almost a party atmosphere! Experience in other organisations also demonstrates how anger and grief early on can turn to pride and determination to end on a high note. The announcement of the closure of Chatham Dockyard, for example, initially produced depression and reduced output. But this gradually changed to a wish to succeed, and to deliver the final refit project as a piece of good work completed on schedule.

In general, therefore, there should be a policy of 'business as usual', and a drive to continue to provide quality services. There will also be considerable extra work preparing for the change and meeting the new authority's needs. This means continuing to set performance targets, carry on with staff appraisals, and continuing with team briefings and staff consultation. If at all possible, the scope should be explored for additional remuneration or bonuses in recognition of extra work and excellent performance, preferably explicitly related to the targets set in the plan for winding down the authority.

A key requirement is good, accurate and prompt communication. When the shape of the new authorities is known, the chief executive should communicate the outcome to all staff as soon as possible, and let people know how the transition process will be managed. This will cover the old authority's role in providing information to help the new authority to become established (*see* below) and also cover matters to do with the personal future of each member of staff. Everyone will have concerns about his or her future, and it is important to follow up the initial notification with a detailed report on how staff appointments and transfers to the new authorities will be handled, together with information on terms for possible redundancies, compensation schemes and early retirement.

Some staff, including those in senior positions, are likely to be unsure of their future position for a considerable period of time. Indeed, even the chief executive may feel considerable personal uncertainty since all senior posts will all be filled by open competition. Staff will need to voice their concerns, and feel that they will be supported in negotiations on future staffing arrangements. There will be particular problems in those situations where some authorities are continuing to exist, and others abolished. In such cases there is likely to be a fear that incumbent staff in existing authorities will be given preferential treatment, and a sense that others will have lost out. Guidance from the various staff commissions on the policies to be adopted during the transfer (described in more detail below) should help to avoid this. It will be necessary for existing authorities to look after the interests of their staff, handle industrial relations issues and trade union consultations and ensure that correct policies and procedures for transfers and appointments are followed.

External communications

Just as staff may be concerned about the transfer, so some recipients of services will be concerned about how they might be affected. This is particularly important in the case of vulnerable groups. It will therefore be necessary for the existing authority to reassure its customers and clients, and inform them how their needs will be met under the new arrangements.

New authorities will not initially be staffed to handle their own publicity, and will therefore have to rely on PR departments of existing councils to handle their communications. Agreement will need to be reached on what messages are to be conveyed, and by whom. In some cases joint press releases, consultation meetings, and written communication will be needed (*see* Part II, Chapter 15).

Concerns may also be expressed by other local bodies with whom existing authorities have established relationships. For example, voluntary bodies relying on existing authorities for grant income, private sector companies with whom authorities do business, and other claimants on authorities' funds and resources will all have specific concerns. Consultation and communications arrangements will need to be put in hand as early as possible to ensure that other local organisations such as these are kept in touch with the transition process and have an opportunity to discuss particular issues which affect them.

Finally, even during the last period of operation, it will be important for the outgoing authority to continue to be aware of issues of concern to the area, and to speak for the community on these issues as necessary. Communications with the European Union and with other government agencies will continue, and outgoing authorities will need to speak for their communities, in effect on behalf of new authorities, on plans and grant claims for future years.

Lowering the flag

Outgoing authorities will wish to mark the occasion in some way, particularly where they have a long history and wish to demonstrate, for example, by raising the profile of their achievements, that their hard work was not in vain. Appropriate ceremonial is an important part of managing loss. For the most part, however, a seamless transfer of responsibility will be required, so that, in practice, there is scarcely perceived any difference, at least as far as the public are concerned; offices and facilities will close on 31 March, and reopen on 1 April 'under new management'.

Setting up new authorities: twin-tracking change

The immediate concerns of the Shadow Authority will be to continue to progress the smooth transition of responsibility from existing to new authorities. But, as suggested in previous chapters, the process of developing a longer term vision for the new authority needs to begin as soon as possible. New authorities have thus to 'twin-track' change from the outset. On the one hand, they must deal with the practical and technical issues involved in taking over their responsibilities from outgoing authorities; on the other, they must define for themselves the kind of authority they want, and need, to be. These questions are, of course, interrelated. As suggested above, appointments cannot be made to key positions until internal management issues have been considered; plans cannot be made for medium-term income and spending requirements until a clear view is reached on future policy and strategy for the locality.

The time before vesting day is therefore a period above all for 'taking stock': understanding the current position in services, management, performance and changing needs in the constituent authorities, and of assessing likely opportunities and problems. The scope of such an exercise is potentially very wide, crossing the full range of what present authorities do, and how. The key areas to be covered, and the issues to be addressed, are set out later in this chapter.

In addition, it is during this period when certain specific practical actions need to be taken:

- agreement on division and transfer of property (buildings and other assets)

- agreement on transfer of staff

- agreement on disaggregation and transfer of information

- agreement on certain financial matters

Key points on these areas are set out below. There then follows a brief section on how preparations for Compulsory Competitive Tendering will interact with the process of establishing the new authorities before the issues involved in 'taking stock' are addressed.

Transfer of property

The main thrust of the Government's proposals is that all matters relating to the transfer of property should, as far as possible, be settled by agreement between the various successor authorities. Although a national Residuary Body will be established (in England), it is hoped that it will only need to be involved in relatively few cases where there is an irreconcilable dispute. The role of the outgoing authority will be limited to the provision of information and advice, and it will be for the new authorities to reach agreement on the actual division of property between them.

Where an authority is being combined with others to form a new authority, it will usually be a matter of transferring all property to that authority. Where an authority is being split up into several new authorities, each of its properties will need to be transferred to one of the successor authorities. Up to date property records will be required with information on the use and location of each asset, so that the receiving authority can be identified.

In the first instance, it will be for the joint officer sub-group of property experts to tackle this task, in consultation with the relevant services, and to advise the shadow (inheritor) authorities. Points of disagreement will require negotiation so that decisions can be reached before the transfer date. If agreement is not reached, the property will transfer in England to the national Residuary Body in the first place, who will then decide on future ownership and transfer it accordingly. In Scotland, there is provision in legislation currently under consideration for 'one or more residuary bodies' if the Secretary of State thinks these will be necessary, and also allows him to set up a Property Commission if required.

There will also be a need for identification of any surplus property. The English regulations currently in draft provide for the sale of any such property, and for the divisions of the proceeds between successors. It is likely that the actual sale would take place after reorganisation, and would be handled by one authority on behalf of its successors.

Transfer of staff

Smooth transfer of staff is essential to the success of new authorities and to helping existing authorities maintain services during the transitional period. The Government has established in England the Local Government Staff Commission to advise on staff matters. Its policy objectives are:

- to reassure staff affected, as far as possible, by the provision of fair and equitable arrangements to safeguard staff interests

- to give new authorities sufficient discretion on choice and numbers of staff to achieve economic, efficient and effective local government

- to ensure minimum disruption to local government functions during the transition from one structure to another

- to avoid unnecessary expenditure on severance and recruitment, by retaining existing staff where this would be compatible with efficient and effective local government

In Scotland and Wales there will be staff commissions with similar remits.

These objectives set the tone for the transfer process, although each new authority will need to consider its approach in more detail. Of course a prior step will be for the new authority to reach a view on structures and staffing levels, and therefore on the numbers and nature of posts to be filled. Outgoing authorities may make recommendations on this through the processes described earlier in this chapter, but it will be for new authorities to decide their own arrangements.

The English Staff Commission's paper on Staff Transfer and Recruitment (*see* Figure 4.1) requires authorities to identify staff in three categories:

- posts where there is to be automatic transfer of employment from existing authorities

- posts where prior consideration is to be given to staff from existing authorities before open competition

- posts where there is to be open competition

It gives detailed advice on how to identify them. Staff in the first group should be able to be told their future without delay. For those in the second group, procedures will need to be set up to ensure fair competition between all existing staff, especially where some staff are in an authority which is to continue to exist, while others work for authorities which are to be abolished. The third group is expected to consist mainly of senior management (Chief Executives, Chief Officers or equivalent) and this group will need to await the Shadow Authority's decision, following competition. Similarly, in Scotland it is likely that senior posts will be subject to open competition with more junior staff simply transferring. The legislation for Scotland places the burden of preparing a staff transfer plan on the old authorities who will then have to seek the agreement of the new authorities.

Particular management issues may arise as a result of this approach since it is likely that most members will have previously served in the area of a new authority but the most senior posts may be filled by people new to the area. They may therefore bring new ideas into an environment with a history of different ways of operating.

The English Staff Commission will also be providing guidance on how to ensure uniformity of treatment between authorities of staff being made redundant, for whom there will be a national scheme of compensation, or taking of early retirement. There will also be advice on how to handle appeals, and on compensation for staff who cannot obtain posts in new authorities without taking a reduction in earnings ('compensation for detriment'). There will need to be a channel of communication for members of staff in existing authorities to air any personal issues or grievances. It is expected that similar guidance will apply in Wales and Scotland.

The Staff Commission for England will also issue advice on the handling of vacancies arising for other reasons during the run-up to the transfer date. Filling such posts immediately on a permanent basis could be difficult because of uncertainty about the outcome of decisions on structures and staffing, and could create longer-term problems also. Premature loss of staff during the transitional period was a problem at the time of the abolition of the metropolitan counties, and may affect this reorganisation also because of implementation at different times in different areas. The commission, therefore suggests alternative approaches, such as temporary cover, use of consultants, fixed term contracts, extending retirement dates, or filling posts through recruitment from the same review area.

Transfer of information

Information to be transferred will include a wide range of data, held both on manual and computer records. The task of disaggregating this, especially where large authorities are to be broken up, should not be underestimated. Where information is held on computer records, particular attention will need to be paid to the method by which the data is to be transferred. Splitting existing databases will need careful planning, having regard to the compatibility of hardware and software and to the design and capacity of the receiving systems. Indeed, it may be preferable for one or more of the successor authorities to continue to maintain some of the existing databases at least for the initial period, making information available to all who need it. Similarly, where different authorities are coming together, the new authority may need to operate more than one system in the short term, until a satisfactory combined system has been identified. Devolved local systems, where they exist, may be easier to transfer. But new networking arrangements may be needed to share data with other parts of the new authority.

A first step will be to identify what information is held for each service area and function, how it is held, who will be likely to need it in the new authorities and what format it should be collected in. At the technical level, details of use, location and type of existing hardware and software will also be required. Priority will need to be given to operational systems such as payroll, accounts, rent collection, libraries, student grants etc, but some early consideration of higher level management information needs in the new authority will also be required. Information Technology specialists from existing authorities will need to work closely with service specialists in managing the process of transfer, and further delegation may be required to individual project groups to handle specific problem areas. Their plans will need to take into account the need to implement compulsory competitive tendering for computer services within 2 years of the inauguration of the new authority. This is discussed further in the guidelines on information strategy and management (Part II, Chapter 11).

Financial matters

There are a number of important financial issues to be considered during the period prior to the transfer. These relate first to the budget for the operation of the Shadow Authority, and how it is to be financed. Second, there are questions related to the transfer of financial assets and liabilities of existing authorities, in particular:

- the level of balances, provisions and reserves to be transferred
- arrangements for transfer and management of loan debt, unused capital receipts, and various funds and provisions
- transfer of creditors, debtors, collection funds, etc.
- treatment and management of any superannuation fund

In England, the draft Transfer of Property Regulations require authorities to 'use their best endeavours' to reach agreement on transfer of assets and liabilities. Failing agreement, assets and liabilities of an abolished authority will transfer to the 'designated authority' named in the Government Order on the reorganisation.

Third, there is the question of the new authority's income and expenditure base, its initial budget, and longer term financial plans. This is by no means straightforward. It will include:

- establishing the base budget linked to information on staffing numbers, facilities etc.

- calculation of the Standard Spending Assessment/Grant Aided Expenditure and grant base of the new authority (central policy guidance will be needed on this)

- preliminary assessment of the levels of Council Tax

- forecasts of income from other sources, including fees and charges

- forecasts of other expenditure, including transition related

- access to capital investment funds (credit approvals)

Forecasts will need to be based in the first instance on current authorities' plans, service-level assumptions and contractual arrangements. Later there will be judgements to be made about the extent to which changes can be made from the outset, particularly where there are significant differences in the approaches taken by different combining authorities. The politics of this process have already been touched upon, and these issues are discussed further in subsequent parts of this chapter on 'taking stock' and 'laying the ground for long-term change'.

Finance staff in particular, but also to a lesser extent service staff, must expect to spend a considerable proportion of their time in providing advice and information to the new authorities, and participating in the preparation of its first budget. Since such staff will either transfer to the new authorities, or leave at the end of the final year of operation, one of the successor authorities will be required to take designated responsibility for drawing up the final accounts of the outgoing authority for audit. It will be necessary for finance staff from the old authority to be available to give advice in this work, even where they have transferred, as their first hand knowledge of the accounts will almost certainly be needed.

A considerable amount of official advice and regulations on financial issues is in course of preparation (*see* Figure 4.1). Much of this is already published in draft form, and final versions are expected soon. Chartered Institute of Public Finance and Accountancy (CIPFA) guidance will also be available which will cover a wide range of financial issues in some detail including banking arrangements and financial systems implications.

Preparation for Compulsive Competitive Tendering (CCT)

Authorities that will be subject to reorganisation will only have 18 months, in some cases less, to implement the requirements of current CCT legislation. Current exemptions that will apply to new authorities will allow contracts for manual services let under the 1980 and 1988 Acts to be extended until 6-18 months after changeover. White collar contracts will be required to have been let after 18 months following changeover. This timetable means that each incoming authority will have a significant task in preparing its approach to CCT.

The new authority may inherit a complicated web of contractual arrangements for procuring services. This may involve the whole or part of an in-house Direct Service Organisation (DSO) plus one or more contractors, all providing essentially the same service. These arrangements are likely to have been set up on different bases with different specifications and may have different end dates. The structure of existing DSOs will require review and consideration will need to be given to operational issues such as the use of depot space and equipment.

Outgoing authorities will need to assist new councils in their task by providing detailed information on existing contract arrangements and user requirements. This will enable incoming authorities to more quickly:

- review the existing contract arrangements

- define their contract strategy

- develop specifications of service requirements across the new authority.

In completing these tasks account should be taken of:

- the future needs of customers (both internal and external) and arrangements for monitoring customer satisfaction

- how to benefit from the 'best of' former arrangements and developing best practice (*see* Part II, Chapter 9)

- maximising productivity and competitiveness in advance of the tendering process.

In addition new Councils will need to be aware of any cases where outgoing authorities may be entering into long-term contractual arrangements which they may consider to be inappropriate and which may prove expensive and difficult to break.

Putting substance to the shadow - 'taking stock'

It will be evident from the above that Shadow Authorities will need a significant volume of information about, and from, their predecessor authorities, to achieve several simultaneous objectives:

- where disaggregation of an existing authority is involved, to determine what should be transferred, and to whom, as described in the previous section, and ensure a smooth transition of responsibilities

- to determine the nature and extent of the new authority's future resource base - financial, human, material, and indeed information itself - and its strengths and weaknesses

- to enable the new authority to understand the aspirations, needs and expectations of its locality and of the communities within it, and the current and future demands that are likely to be made upon it

It is through a comprehensive process of 'taking stock' that the authority will begin to develop a vision of itself as community leader, and to start its transformation to enable it to discharge that role effectively, as well as ensure that structural change happens smoothly and on schedule. The scope and focus of this process is summarised at Figure 4.5. In particular, the authority will need to gain an understanding of two key issues: firstly, the opportunities and risks likely to present themselves, and secondly, the relative starting positions of its constituent or predecessor authorities, over a wide range of issues.

Both opportunity and risk may be broadly characterised as either controllable, or unpredictable. Opportunities within an authority's control will primarily relate to internal resources and management capabilities, and may be readily assessed using, for example, Strengths, Weakness, Opportunities, Threats (SWOT) analysis. For example, where two or more authorities combine, there may be opportunities for greater economies of scale; better strategic planning in land-use and transport; access to specialised services; efficiencies in support services; or a higher public profile with external organisations.

Areas of internal risk may include the risk of failure inherent in the management of the transition process, given the climate of uncertainty and many differences in culture. It may also include risks associated with financial exposure and service related risks, for example, failure to address problems in services for vulnerable groups, such as children in care, or the emergence of substantial disparities in service standards and provision across the new authority. In this last context it will be important that all old authorities are open about these risk areas so that new authorities know about them and can plan to manage them.

External opportunities and risks will tend to be more unpredictable and, therefore, more difficult to define in advance. They will arise through changes in the competitive environment, in policy and legislation, and in consumer and wider economic trends. Here scenario planning can help to identify possibilities.

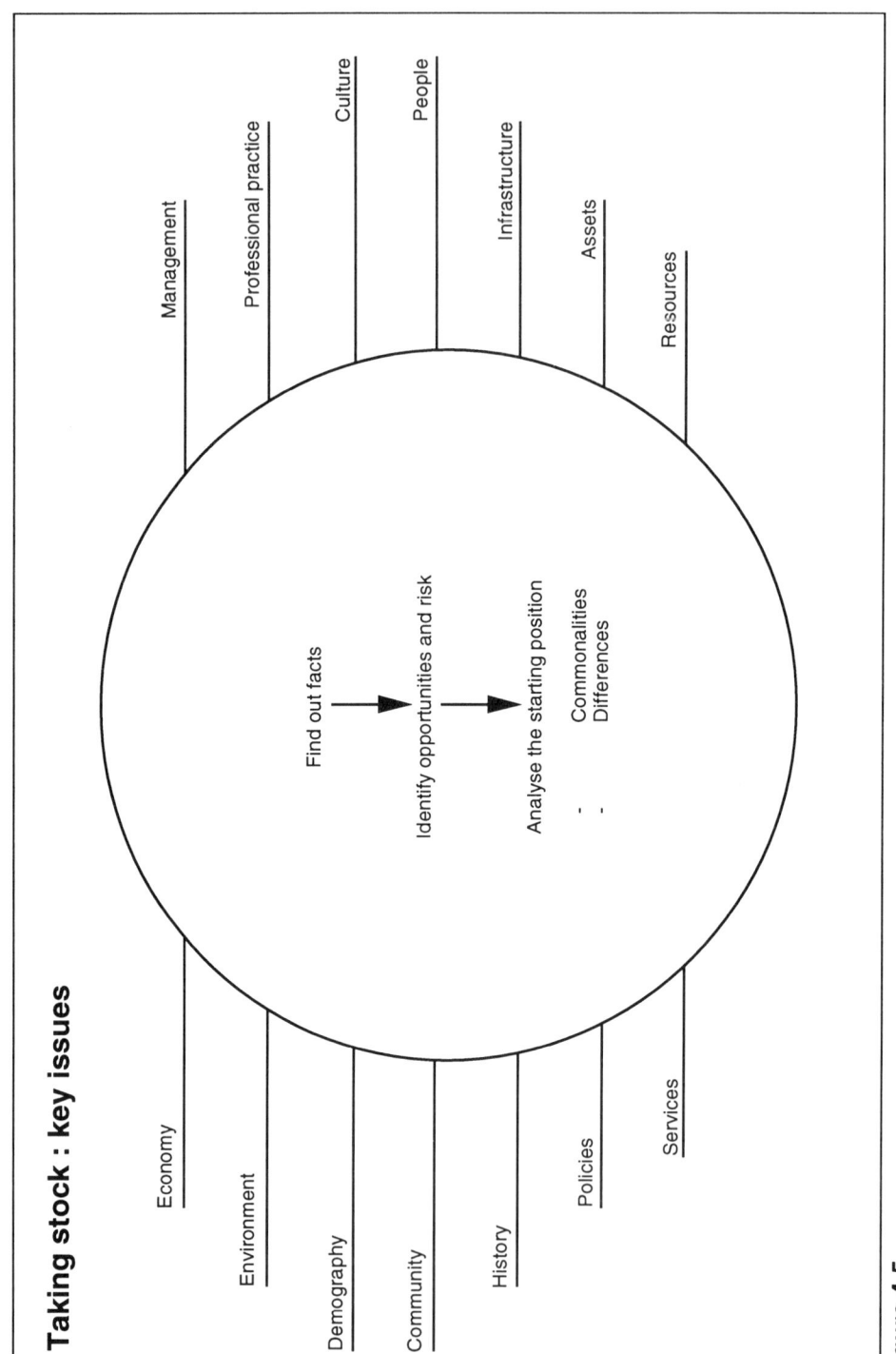

Taking stock : key issues

Management

Professional practice

Culture

People

Infrastructure

Assets

Resources

Economy

Environment

Demography

Community

History

Policies

Services

Find out facts

Identify opportunities and risk

Analyse the starting position

Commonalities
Differences

Figure 4.5

The new authority also needs to form an initial view of the similarities and differences between its predecessor authorities, in relation both to policy questions and to management issues. This will be particularly important where there have been differences of view between existing authorities about options for reorganisation in the period leading up to a final decision. It will be important to recognise and value the diversity of the constituent parts of the new authority, in order to avoid falling into the trap of adopting a 'lowest common denominator' approach, or, at the opposite extreme, pursuing a 'highest standard' approach come what may, however unachievable. A pragmatic approach to standards and operational practices is more likely to be effective, which prioritises action in the areas of greatest disparity and/or where public attention is most likely to be damaging.

In defining its requirement for information at this stage, the Shadow Authority will therefore need to consider data in relation to:

- external factors having an impact on its locality and on local communities

- key facts about the scope, scale, standards and modes of operation of services for which it will be responsible

- internal issues, including the extent of political and policy differences and key aspects of the way in which constituent authorities have been managed

- assets and liabilities, covering property, information and financial issues, as described above

Examples of likely areas of information need are listed in more detail in Figure 4.6. Wherever possible, data should be collected on a common basis across constituent authorities, reflect standard definitions (for example, from the Audit Commission or other external bodies) and relate to the area of the new authority. In broad terms, a 'due diligence' approach will be required: it will be the responsibility of the new authority to ensure that, so far as possible, it has relevant, timely, accurate and verifiable data on which to base its future planning and decision making. In doing so, it will of course rely closely upon existing authorities, as discussed earlier.

The information gathering process itself also may generate a number of useful by-products. As officers and members work together to determine information requirements, collect data and analyse results, closer working relationships can begin to develop. Ideas and options for the future strategic development of services and internal management may emerge. A wide group of staff at all levels can be involved, especially once future staffing issues have been resolved, and the opportunity taken to build on individual and collective knowledge to arrive at a consensus view on key issues for the new authority, and building allegiance to it. In this sense it can lay the ground for successful merger of the constituent parts of the new authority, and for building confidence in it.

The Shadow Authority will therefore want to create the most productive climate for the operation of the groups described earlier in this chapter who will be collecting and analysing information. Some of the problems inherent in the transitional stage have already been touched upon. Recognising the diversity of cultures and allegiances of individuals involved, and in view of the inevitable uncertainties of this period of change, it will be important to lay down ground rules which:

- recognise problems arising from the different sizes and origins of constituent authorities

- allow for differences in political complexion

- emphasise co-operation and merger (rather than takeover)

- encourage groups to focus on objective data (rather than subjective opinion)

- encourage equity across communities, and avoid parochial interests

- give equal voice to individuals, whatever authority they represent

- provide for sensitive handling of controversial issues, competing agendas, and self-interest

- establish a clear arbitration route in the event of disagreement

Detailed schedules of information requirements will need to be drawn up, identifying content, format and data definitions, and a timetable for production outlined which relates to the timetable of the transition process as a whole. Information on less tangible aspects of management (such as cultural issues) may also require such interventions as internal opinion surveys, and cross-authority focus groups.

The output from the process will be a detailed action plan, setting out the tasks to be achieved in the run-up to vesting day, and a longer term, more strategic assessment of areas for change. Where key facts are uncertain, not known, or cannot be obtained for whatever reason, contingency plans will be required.

'Rebadging'

Finally, as vesting day approaches, the Shadow Authority will also need to consider matters of external presentation. Repainting signs, vehicles and other facilities, redesigning stationary and other corporate material, and providing good directories of 'who does what' and how they can be contacted are important components of building a positive image for the new authority, and thus of

Taking stock: Information needs

External factors
- local economic trends: general, and those having an impact on local authority services
- environmental issues
- demographic trends, particularly among key client groups such as children, young adults, the elderly and the vulnerable
- socio-demographic issues and the composition of communities
- current and likely legislative developments nationally and internationally

Service issues
- scope
  - breadth of service function
  - statutory requirements
  - discretionary services
- scale
  - user numbers, groups and trends
  - staff numbers, levels, qualifications and experience
  - numbers, location and condition of service delivery points and other facilities
  - involvement of external agencies; existing contracts for provision of services or supplies
  - levels and trends of income and expenditure
- standards
  - performance data, especially statutory performance indicators
  - customer satisfaction data
  - standards of service specified in external contracts and internal Service Level Agreements
- modes of operation
  - formal delegations and decision-making processes
  - organisational structures
  - operational policies, guidelines and procedures
  - working practices
  - performance management processes
  - information systems

Internal management
- strategic management processes, including planning, decision-taking, and financial management, and formal statements of policy and standing orders
- organisational and operational structures, and formal hierarchies
- professional practices affecting working practices and management
- people management, including recruitment, retention, appraisal and promotion policies and information
- cultural issues: values, standards of behaviour, internal working relations, consultation and communications procedures and approaches

Infrastructure, assets and liabilities
- property (buildings, equipment, vehicles etc.)
- information (databases, hardware, software etc.)
- finance (balances, provisions, reserves, debts, receipts etc.)

Figure 4.6

71

creating a new identity for the authority in the public's mind. It will need to be accompanied by a communication strategy, both internal and external, which takes over from that employed by the outgoing authority, as described above, to introduce and explain the philosophy and approaches which will characterise the new authority.

The new authority: laying the ground for long-term change

Whether large or small, all new unitary authorities will involve merging functions, staff, assets and operations from at least two predecessor authorities. New authorities will from the outset be faced with a wide range of tasks as all aspects of management and operations are brought together, against a background of continuing public need for quality services. The primary need, both in the run-up to vesting day, and for a time thereafter, is to approach these tasks with the aims of building confidence in the new authority, and ensuring continuity of service delivery.

The main reason for this emphasis in the short term is to enable the new authority to build its new identity on a secure foundation, laying the ground for the more comprehensive transformation to come, while giving the authority the information it needs to plan the process of change and especially, to assess the pace at which real change is likely to be possible. An initial assessment will already have been made of the gap between predecessor authorities in, for example, performance standards, service philosophies, resource levels, or managerial and political culture; and of the extent of specific risks and opportunities, during the process of 'taking stock' described earlier in this chapter. A priority for the new authority, once it is up and running will be to look at these issues again in the light of practical experience.

As Figure 4.7 illustrates, the larger the gap in culture and practice, the greater the likely behavioural risk and the more thoroughgoing the processes of change management required to achieve change successfully will need to be. For each new authority, there will be in effect a breakpoint, at which the emphasis on cautious management of the merger process may be superseded by more radical and rapid change. Such a point may or may not happen before the more mechanistic aspects of merger have been fully implemented. But if genuine transformation is to be achieved, identification of the breakpoint will be an essential part of planning and monitoring the process of change.

The whole of this initial period for the new authority will be a difficult balancing act between the present and the future. Everyone involved, members,

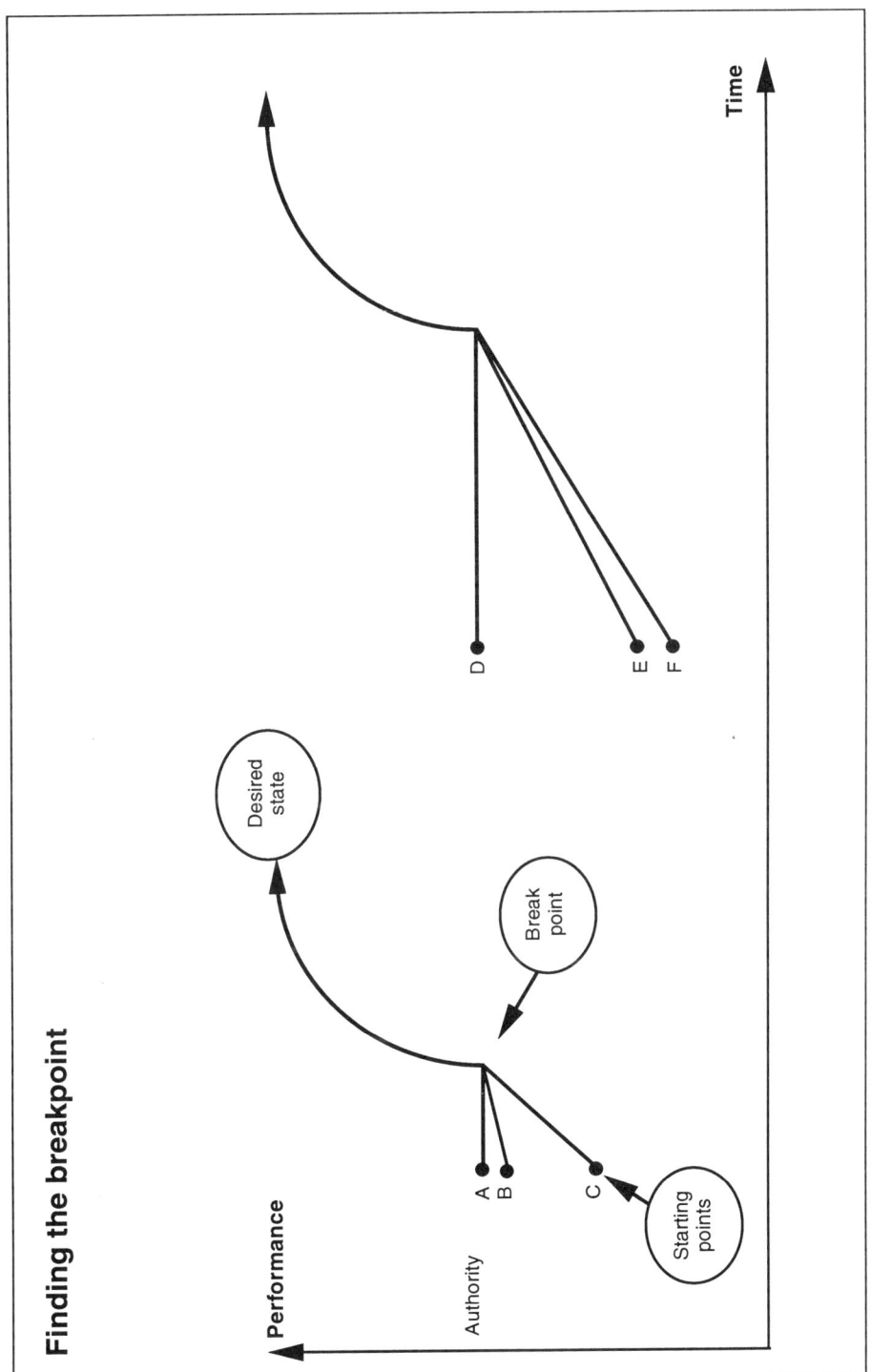

Figure 4.7

officers, contractors and the public will be looking to the new authority to make the most of the opportunity presented for improvements and innovation. It will be essential to provide reassurance that these will follow, while at the same time keeping the pace of change manageable and avoiding unnecessary risks by going too fast. But this is the period when the ground is being prepared for longer-term change, and every opportunity must be taken to establish the authority's identity and build consensus, both internally and externally, about the authority's longer-term vision.

During these early weeks, requirements for many changes are likely to be identified. Some of these may be able to be introduced easily, others will require substantial technical, practical, and behavioural change. The authority will need to develop a comprehensive change programme, as identified in Chapter 3, and stick to its implementation. But it will also need to ensure that this is capable of pragmatic adaptation to respond to changing external circumstances.

Building confidence

Much of what is involved in merging authorities will be task-based. Given the relatively short timescales between final decisions on reorganisation and its implementation, there will inevitably need to be solutions adopted to particular problems in this early period which are pragmatic and which may fall some way short of the new authority's developing vision. It will be essential to monitor these closely to ensure that they do not become entrenched in the processes of the new authority, and so that staff remain confident that real improvements will follow. It is this that will be the real challenge of following the 'twin-track' of structural and transformational change referred to in the previous chapter.

Processes of building an understanding of change, and a commitment to it, will therefore be the key to longer-term success. Because of the circumstances of this reorganisation, initial support from all those involved cannot necessarily be assumed. In particular, staff goodwill cannot be taken for granted. Confidence will need to be developed within staff groups that transition, merger and longer-term change are being managed effectively and that their effort is being properly and correctly focused. Success in achieving key tasks will further help to build confidence; as will effective internal communication before and after vesting day.

As certainty builds about the way in which the new authority will be managed, new problems are likely to arise. There may be people disappointed with their new roles, inappropriate staff in place in the new structure, mismatches of staff numbers and skills, and personality and culture clashes. Other staff may be over-enthusiastic and keen to make their mark. Many of these issues will not be within managers' control, at least in the short-term, and will need sensitive management.

This is also a period when effective risk management will be of vital importance. The new authority will have identified through the process of taking stock those problem areas inherited from its predecessors, for example, as a result of under-investment, changing demographic factors, or bad management. But there may also be new risks arising directly as a result of reorganisation, for example, widely differing service levels, unfilled senior or key operational posts, or unclear political priorities. Identified risk areas will need to be tightly managed over the interim period of transition and merger, until they can be properly addressed within a comprehensive and strategic framework for change. Regular monitoring will be necessary in the meantime to ensure that progress is achieved in containing and reducing potential problem areas.

How these risks are managed will depend upon how critical they are assessed to be in achieving the authority's objectives. For example, one authority may consider financial risk reduction as the priority, whilst another may put greater emphasis on reducing risks to service delivery. Some difficult choices will be necessary, but, as a general rule, an effective risk management strategy should focus first on areas within the control of the authority, and assess relative probability and potential impact.

Maintaining services

Building confidence in the new authority externally will depend not only on the avoidance of problems but also on the maintenance and stabilisation of service delivery. This is likely to involve managing a high degree of diversity in terms of staff attitudes and approaches, as well as service levels. A new authority inheriting widely differing standards of service across its area, or very different operational approaches, especially in high profile or politically sensitive activities, is unlikely to be able to resolve these differences in the short-term. This is likely to give rise to both practical and political difficulties. Resource constraints are likely to prevent universal equalising upwards to highest levels, at least in the short-term, but any other form of equalisation may thus be seen to create losers and will require careful planning and presentation. The emphasis is likely to be on maintaining a steady-state, correcting only the most glaring disparities, until the authority has been able to conduct a full policy and strategy review, and has agreed its long-term priorities.

Service standards are particularly vulnerable to poor staff morale, to management distraction and to conflicting priorities. There may already have been a tendency, during the transition period with all its potential problems, to focus internally at the expense of service delivery and customer relations. If public confidence is to be developed and maintained in the new authority, this tendency must be actively resisted. In the short-term it will be essential to emphasise continuity; but equally it will be important to manage people's expectations where longer-term change is likely, so that they understand what is happening and what the authority's plans are. This will apply both to service users and to staff, and indeed to any intermediaries or third parties involved in service provision.

Other issues likely to arise during this period which may endanger front-line service delivery include poor support services and accommodation and infrastructure problems. Support functions are likely themselves to go through major upheavals with many staff transferring and having to form new working teams. The services they can provide may be limited for human or technological reasons. For example, a recently fragmented education IT support team may be trying to help set up a new departmental budgetary control system, revise networking arrangements for school computer systems, and ensure teachers get paid, all from a new office rapidly converted from a previous function.

Other accommodation and infrastructure issues may arise where specialist resources (for example, social work teams) previously based centrally within a county or region are broken up and reallocated to successor authorities. It may be difficult quickly to find them adequate accommodation with proper access to the records and other support facilities they need. They may also see any change in their role, from very specialist to more generic, as a threat to their professional status. Also, new staff groupings may initially be based far apart without the necessary IT or other infrastructure support, making communication and co-ordination difficult.

However well planned and managed the transition process, some practical problems of this nature are bound to occur. High levels of tolerance will be required, and a real commitment to customers required to protect them from the knock-on effects of such difficulties. Day-to-day management will need to be highly customer-focused, to ensure that difficulties are identified and addressed as quickly as possible. Monitoring of customer satisfaction will be an important priority during this initial period, partly for strategic reasons, partly to ensure that operational problems are brought rapidly to light, and partly to reassure customers that well-planned changes are being actively considered, whatever may be the short-term problems. An overt focus on identifying 'best practice', from the customer's viewpoint, can be used to demonstrate the authority's intention to ensure that longer-term changes are soundly based.

From transition to transformation

The processes of transition to new unitary authorities described in this Chapter are complex, and will involve a great many people working closely together. Summarising, the main stages are as follows:

- co-operation between existing authorities to start the process off once decisions are taken

- establishing Shadow Authorities which will then take over the lead from existing authorities

- agreement between existing authorities and Shadow Authorities as to the transfer of responsibilities, resources, assets and liabilities

- Shadow Authorities beginning simultaneously to develop a vision for themselves as community leaders through 'taking stock'
- old authorities winding down in parallel
- following vesting day, a period during which new authorities build confidence and maintain services, whilst planning longer-term change
- following vesting day, a period during which residual matters of transition and transfer are finally settled

But the process of 'transformation' which is at the centre of this book does not end there, indeed, in a sense, it has only just begun. Transformation proper goes beyond mere merger, beyond short-term change, beyond even the questions of 'levelling-up' or 'levelling-down'. It aims at achieving major change in culture and style, to sustain a new kind of local government, and bring a new vigour to local democracy. The final chapter of Part I sets out the main areas on which senior members and officers will need to focus in order successfully to achieve this fundamental change.

5

TRANSFORMATION
From restructuring to renewal

Implementing the vision

The theme of this book has been the twin challenge of structural and transformational change facing local government. At a minimum, there is a programme of specific reorganisation of responsibilities and areas to be carried out to a planned timescale. But beyond this, it is argued that local government has to create a new vision of community leadership, which emphasises a strategic perspective of communities' needs, focuses on users' interests and makes a tangible commitment to encouraging active representation and participation, and which is able to deliver consistently high standards of performance in every aspect of activity and management.

In tackling this agenda, new unitary authorities have the advantage over existing authorities in that they can start afresh in determining vision, strategy and internal management, over the full range of local government's functions. But they also face the substantial task of taking over from their predecessors different people, resources, and physical assets. A key factor in establishing themselves rapidly as successful and robust institutions will be the extent to which they are able to build a truly unified and integrated approach, going well beyond initial merger.

Laying the ground for longer-term integration starts at the outset of the short-term transition process. Interestingly, it is still possible to find active traces of their antecedents within some authorities created at the time of the previous reorganisation 20 years ago.

Authorities not affected by the reorganisation are of course spared the immediate preoccupations of achieving structural change. But the demands of responding to a rapidly changing external environment are no less challenging for them, in terms of the need for active change management. Instead, they have all the potential difficulties of any existing organisation attempting to bring about substantial change from within.

For both new and existing authorities alike, however, the aims of long-term change must be to:

- agree a mission and goals for the authority focused on achieving its vision for its communities, and providing an effective response to the circumstances of its area and the issues facing local government

- create a unified decision making process and management structure fully committed to, and involved in, delivering this vision

- develop an organisational culture committed to serving users in the community and focused on encouraging their involvement in decision making

- promote new and demanding standards of performance in every aspect of activity, and ensure full accountability for achieving those standards

- have in place fully integrated systems, operations and infrastructure in support of these aims

Unlike the specific, one-off, tasks involved in achieving structural change, a process of 'transformation' has no defined end-state although it has a well defined direction. It involves a pattern of continuous reassessment of the authority's situation and vision and a commitment to continuous improvement. Culture and style must therefore positively enable further change and innovation, through encouraging greater flexibility and responsiveness. Inspiration comes not only from within - it will be important for authorities to challenge a natural tendency for introspection, drawing only from local government, and instead to seek out relevant experience from elsewhere in the public sector and the private sector.

How then is this desirable state to be achieved? As Chapter 3 has emphasised, diligent and systematic application of programme and project management skills and techniques are essential, starting at the top, with dedicated sponsorship of the change programme, and extending throughout the authority to every member of any project team involved in planning and implementing an element of the programme. Within this, however, it is possible to identify five key areas of active change management which will each be critical to achieving success:

- **Leading and directing** - defining the tasks leading members, chief executives and senior managers should undertake to 'take charge of change'

- **Achieving cultural change** - implementing the change process by changing people's behaviour and facilitating an improvement in the quality of their working environment

- **Monitoring best practice** - keeping a watching brief on the performance of other organisations, measuring practice and progress against recognised benchmarks, using the experience of others to achieve success and avoid common pitfalls

- **Concentrating on essentials** - identifying the most important practical projects to facilitate change; for example, rationalisation and redeployment of assets, or developing improved infrastructure

- **Focusing on improved performance** - emphasising continuous improvement and ensuring that mechanisms are in place across the authority to create real accountability

This chapter considers each of these areas and concludes Part I. Part II of the book then introduces particular tools and techniques likely to be most helpful to local authorities embarking on change, and describes their principal characteristics in more detail.

Leading and directing

The leadership of the authority, which includes leading members, the chief executive, and other senior managers - will have a crucial role in achieving change. They will be responsible for defining the change vision, for communicating it and the change programme associated with it, and for ensuring that it is carried out. They must make sure that the overall style of leadership of the authority sets the right tone and that the authority is managed in accordance with the highest standards of corporate governance. Finally, they are the prime change sponsors (*see* Figure 3.6), fully involved in, and committed to the objectives of the change programme, driving on the implementation of their vision and being seen to do so by their staff.

Communicating vision and strategy

Defining the change vision for a new authority, and initiating the change programme, starts as soon as the members of the leadership team have been identified. But it does not ever really stop. The leadership team will need to build on their initial vision as they learn about their community and about the resources they have available. In particular, they will need to focus attention on, and inject energy into, further strategy development and implementation as soon as they are confident that the authority is firmly established and the risk areas of day-to-day management are under control. The issues they have to face are then similar to those of any authority seeking to achieve significant change.

An important aspect of effective implementation of change is clear communication, both internally and externally, of key aspects of vision and strategy, for example: service policies and priorities; performance standards; and the authority's policies on the ways in which services will be delivered, whether in house or through a third party. There is now considerable scepticism about the impact and relevance of 'mission statements', strategic goals and statements of objectives for organisations. Nonetheless, world class companies continue to take the external manifestations of their vision and strategy very seriously indeed. Where they are clearly driven by top management, and where consistent and supporting policies are in place, they have considerable benefits in communicating the company's objectives to the workforce, to customers and suppliers, and to shareholders, and in demonstrating the company's strength of commitment to its strategy.

Much the same arguments apply in local government. The authority's workforce, their suppliers and other third parties, the consumers of the authority's services and their electorate all want and need to know what the authority is committed to achieve and what its priorities are; and the authority will find it easier, in the long run, to achieve its aims if there is public understanding and support. Rising customer expectations of public service standards, through the Citizen's Charter and other mechanisms, and emphasis on encouraging public accountability, continue to press for public statements of the authority's plans and targets and, more importantly, for vigorous attempts to communicate these initiatives to all those who have an interest. This can only assist leaders in keeping the authority on course in the direction they have charted.

Emphasis on accountability also needs top level focus on promoting and maintaining the highest standards of conduct. There is renewed interest in this in public and private sectors alike, with the Cadbury Report's recommendations on corporate governance and wider concern about business ethics in general (Cadbury 1993). There are of course already well established standards for the conduct of public services and the stewardship of public money. But, as more and more commercial relationships are established, for example as a result of compulsory competitive tendering, in addition to existing commitments for contracting and purchasing, it will be important to define the basis on which the authority will carry out its business and will manage its relationships with key suppliers. More fundamentally, if the public is to maintain confidence in its elected representatives and in public administration, it is essential to be able to show clearly that high standards are being set and achieved, and where they are not, to have systems in place to identify problems and put them right as quickly as possible.

Setting the tone: leadership style

Most leaders know that they are expected implicitly to act as role models for the entire authority and should, therefore, set the tone of change. There are many different models of leadership. The military style, like that of Montgomery or Schwarzkopf, for example, relies on well defined and essentially unquestioning hierarchies, where strong characters can impose decisions within a clear framework. A business leader, like Lord Hanson or Sir John Harvey-Jones, must also be able to stand back and set a clear strategic focus for the organisation, but this ability often has to be combined with a willingness to roll up sleeves and get hands dirty. Rigid hierarchy and remoteness are not acceptable traits for either the workforce or the shareholders. This makes the task of knowing when to stand back, and when to 'muck in', an immensely difficult one. Figure 5.1 shows some of the attributes that chief executives in the corporate sector think are important for business leaders, and these apply no less to local government.

Ranking of important leadership attributes by successful Chief Executives

1. Ability to take decisions
2. Leadership
3. Integrity
4. Enthusiasm
5. Imagination
6. Hard working
7. Analytical ability
8. Understanding of others
9. Ability to spot opportunities
10. Ability to meet unpleasant situations
11. Ability to adapt to change
12. Willingness to take risks.

Source: John Adair *Effective Leadership*, Pan 1988.

Figure 5.1

Experience suggests that successful implementation of major change tends to require in particular:

- **accessibility** - using not only an open door policy or even greater 'openness' in decision making , but also a willingness to meet all of the staff regularly face to face, speaking to them directly at meetings and when visiting the places where they work

- **teamwork** - adopting a non-hierarchical approach with a strong commitment to teamwork, consulting, counselling and coaching staff in reaching decisions

- **active sponsorship** - being fully and proactively involved and committed to change and being seen to be so, leading the project management of the change programme

- **empowerment** - making a firm commitment to devolve more decision making to more junior staff within clearly defined guidelines and accountability structures

- **responsibility** - accepting that the buck stops at the top

- **communication** - establishing better two-way communication links with the key stake-holders in local government, including the consumers, the workforce and the elected members

In local government's situation, it is also important to achieve clarity about roles. Relationships between leading members and officers are not always straightforward, and in a new authority in particular it will take time to develop and build effective ways of working together. If the change programme is to succeed, however, it will be essential that the leadership team, both members and senior officers, are seen to be working together, and to have a united view of the authority's vision and long-term goals.

Sponsoring change

As part of the vision they create for the authority, the leadership team plays a central role in establishing a compelling case for change, a case that all employees, not just the top team, can believe in and commit to. This leadership is a critical part of the successful change process. The sponsorship of change by the most senior levels of the organisation demonstrates to the workforce that their leaders believe in the change and are committed to seeing it through to full implementation. The resolve necessary to sustain successful change only happens when the change vision and strategy are clear and the benefits of change outweigh the costs, where the costs of taking the 'do nothing' option are clearly seen to be higher than changing. Provided people throughout the authority see it in that way, then the pain of change can be overcome and the change process completed successfully.

The sponsorship of the change programme also requires considerable involvement in project management techniques. In sponsoring change, it is the leadership team which must take responsibility for:

- **organisation** - ensuring that the right structure is in place for managing and implementing change with clear roles and responsibilities

- **planning** - that clear objectives and targets are established and that a well defined project timetable with project milestones has been prepared

- **control** - that regular reporting arrangements are in place and action can be taken to bring the programme back on course whenever it falls short of the planned objectives

- **direction** - holding key people in the project to account and ensuring that the change programme continues to reflect the authority's planned goals

If a change programme is to be successful, these sponsorship functions cannot be delegated although sponsorship of a less formal kind should, if the programme is successful, begin to spread throughout the authority. The leadership team must communicate top-level involvement and commitment. They must also ensure that the programme does not become detached from the authority's real needs.

Achieving cultural change

The importance of effective and active management of behavioural change has been an important theme running through the processes of chapter change described in the previous chapters. Change management processes will of course continue to have an essential contribution to make to creating a unified and fully integrated approach within new authorities, and more generally in building commitment to change. In particular, continuous and effective internal communication is essential.

Creating a common culture

The consistency and strength of corporate culture are constant themes in achieving change successfully. An organisation with a strong culture, consistent with the cultural impact of the change proposed, is more likely to achieve successful implementation. Culture change can be a powerful lever of change, or a deadly barrier to it. Cultural change costs the organisation in terms of time and resources even when it is running comparatively smoothly, but major resistance to change will increase these costs. Where specific changes and existing culture are in conflict, this is very likely to happen. Because the change is seen by staff to run counter to their existing beliefs and values, it is usually the planned change that is rejected.

When people are required to change, they can quickly reach overload point unless the change is managed to help them assimilate it. Changing the deeply ingrained habits of a strong existing culture may put staff under considerable stress and they may even be disruptive, slowing the change programme and delaying the achievement of a common culture. Change management tools and techniques help optimise people's capacity for change - their assimilation resources. Using these resources wastefully, by managing change poorly, or taking on too much change at once, may cost the authority dearly as staff respond negatively to the cultural change and disrupt the process: use too little and an opportunity to press on to make changes may be missed and disillusionment and apathy set in because of the lack of effective progress.

The need to create a common culture hence is a major risk factor in any process of cultural change, and will therefore be a particular issue for new authorities. Change must be structured to avoid the blocking effect of negative cultural influence, and to harness whatever cultural forces exist to promote positive change. A common culture involves more than gaining the support of the workforce for the authority's mission and goals. It involves embracing the different cultures that have been combined to form the new authority, and melding them together, at a pace which people in the authority can live with. Achieving this single entity will require behavioural change from everybody. It will mean defining and putting into practice a clearly defined set of core beliefs and values which are clearly linked with the authority's vision, and which are well-communicated, understood and shared.

Building commitment

Extending the scope of effective teamwork, and empowering staff to work out solutions to problems for themselves, is an essential part of building commitment to change. Levels of commitment do not change overnight, but the use of strong teamwork can help to accelerate the process and lay down the foundations for new ways of working in the future. Teamwork thus has an essential role to play from the outset in planning and setting up new authorities, as well as in taking

---

Obtaining buy-in

Following strategic assessment of a new authority's needs and resources, a council highway depot is identified as surplus to requirements. It is decided in principle that it should be closed. Through recognised consultation and communication procedures, staff affected are made aware by top management of the decision, and are given the opportunity to debate the issues before final authorisation of the decision. They respond to being told openly about what is planned, even if they do not like its potential impact on their lives - the depot is to be merged with a neighbouring depot, previously from another of the new authority's predecessors. In discussion, a positive perception is created and understanding achieved - the depot to be closed was poorly constructed and obsolete, the nearby depot is modern and well equipped, job losses will be small and on a voluntary basis, and many staff will be offered comparable positions at the remaining depot. Staff at both depots are invited to help plan the move and discuss how it might be carried out effectively without disrupting services - they agree to try and carry out the work as quickly as possible. The decision is confirmed and timetables are agreed. A process of counselling gets under way to identify those staff willing to take voluntary redundancy. Finally, the decision is accepted and institutionalised - the plan is agreed, the closure implemented, and the move achieved with the minimum of disruption.

Figure 5.2

the change process further. If team membership is carefully considered, it can also make a major contribution towards promoting effective integration.

The objective is for managers and staff to take charge of change together, and to help develop personal 'resilience', the capability to adapt to change (see Chapter 3). Invariably, individual effectiveness within the authority will be enhanced by greater team effectiveness. By working more closely together in effective teams, people skills are enhanced, different perspectives are brought together and shared and people are more readily able to buy-in to the vision, and support a common culture. Through teamwork, real synergy can be created, in that what is achieved in terms of solutions or methods is greater than the sum of the individual parts.

Building commitment involves many stages (Figure 3.5) and a great deal of work is required to sustain the initial momentum for change. To obtain 'buy-in' takes time. A case study at Figure 5.2 shows how it might be undertaken.

Communicating

As this illustrates, it is essential to continue throughout the change programme to communicate with all those who are directly affected by the changes. High quality two-way internal communications should continue as a permanent feature. For the sponsors of change there are prizes for persistence - messages addressed to staff directly avoid the 'black holes' referred to in Chapter 3. As the change process gathers momentum and begins to show success, the risk of 'black holes' should decrease. Furthermore, it is essential not to see communication only as a 'top-down' procedure. Structures and processes within the authority should also include arrangements for messages and feedback to travel upwards from junior staff to senior management, and inwards from the periphery to the centre.

Communication must also be sensitive to people's concerns, if it is to allay fear of change and assist in building resilience. Signing up for the shared vision will be influenced among other things by issues of job reductions and rationalisation, and the communications structure must anticipate any new or recurring fears. External support similarly will be more likely to be forthcoming if public concerns are recognised.

Local authorities, like many large organisations, have not always been good at communication. This is improving but, particularly given the scale of the various changes about to occur, it is essential that these improvements accelerate and become embedded in the culture of each organisation.

Innovative methods can help. Although conventional newsletters, notices and circulars and consultations with staff representatives will continue to have an important place in the communications system, these can be supplemented with considerable advantage by low cost initiatives that refresh and revitalise links with the whole workforce, and also with the authority's consumers and electorate. These might include:

- **roadshows** - speaking to the public or to the workforce direct, for example at council offices or other larger premises, with an opportunity for questions and answers

- **group discussions** - talking to smaller groups of staff or users during visits to operations in the field with an opportunity for dialogue, question and answer sessions

- **team briefings and 'cascades'** - ensuring that messages communicated to heads of functions are passed on to more junior staff in a series of briefings or messages cascaded down to them

- **videos** - transmitting messages direct from elected members or top management staff as a supplement to regular messages on important occasions.

Monitoring best practice

A focus on best practice has a key contribution to make in facilitating the integration of previously separate authorities and, more generally, in creating the momentum for continuous improvement. There are a number of sources for identifying 'best practice', all of which need to be actively taken into account in identifying appropriate standards and practices:

- those in other authorities and other sectors offering comparable services

- in a reorganisation situation - those found in predecessor authorities

- those expected and required by service users

- those defined nationally through legislation or professional bodies.

The idea of 'best practice' has potentially wide application throughout every authority's activities. It can apply not only to front-line services, but also to decision making processes, resource management, personnel management, systems development, indeed to every aspect of the way the authority does its business. Defining 'best' will be at the heart of the authority's vision and strategy. It will need to respond to local needs, meet national standards where required, and focus on issues of cost, quality, timeliness and customer satisfaction.

Some techniques for identifying 'best practice' are outlined in Part II, Chapter 9. These generally involve a combination of internal and external sources. Within new authorities in particular, it will be important at the earliest opportunity to set up 'best of' groups to review standards and approaches employed by predecessor authorities and, in general terms, take the best of what was done as the basis for the new authority's approach. This method can be very effective not only in exposing differences from which people can learn, but also in creating a positive environment in which people focus on collaboration and co-operation.

But it is also important for the authority to look outwards. External 'benchmarking' compares what is done in other comparable organisations, in the public or private sector, to gain new insights and identify opportunities for improvements based on tried and tested solutions. External information can also be provided through market testing, depending upon the authority's policy in this area. Most importantly, however, information about past achievements and future hopes received directly from the users of the authority's services, and from other parties involved - for example, voluntary sector groups and other local associations - will be a key source of 'best practice' feedback. This in itself will be an important way of encouraging greater participation in the authority's planning and decision making processes.

The aim should be to establish a database of current 'best practice' in key areas, and to implement specific operational and management changes focusing on the achievement of such standards. The database then should be regularly reviewed and updated, both by internal discussion and by external fact finding. For the exchange of information within the authority, quality circles drawn from different functions and departments can be helpful and effective ways of maintaining best practices under regular review. In effect these are a permanent continuation of the 'best of' approach.

Staff sit down together on a regular basis and exchange ideas on ways in which they could perform their tasks to a higher standard, or more effectively and efficiently and agree on actions they can recommend to senior management or, most importantly they can implement themselves. The quality circle tries to eliminate phrases like 'we've always done it this way' and to ask instead 'is this the best way of doing this?'. If the answer is still 'yes', the quality circle goes on to ask 'can we innovate and think of different ways of doing this?'.

Concentrating on essentials

An essential component of the change programme will be a series of specific projects addressing practical aspects of change required by the authority in order to implement its vision. Possible examples are:

- **implementing local devolution** - putting into practice the authority's approach to the way in which it wants to involve local communities in decision making

- **removing disparities in service levels and eliminating risk areas** - the short-term solutions adopted in the early days of a new authority to overcome obvious disparities and manage risk areas will require more permanent changes in line with the authority's vision and strategic priorities

- **improving information systems** - new information technology or management information systems may be needed to replace patched, merged or outdated systems (a new information strategy may be required by the authority)

- **changes in staff skills and numbers** - the change process, if it is being implemented effectively, will underline areas where new skills are required to support new ways of working; adoption of 'best practice' may expose excess staffing capacity as more efficient and effective working practices are adopted, or it may identify a mismatch between current skills available and future skills needs

- **rationalising and redeploying assets** - initial decisions on holdings of physical assets may need to be reviewed because different ways of working and slimmed down management structures mean, for example, that assets are in the wrong place, or there is excess capacity

- **improving structures and processes** - the need to make changes to organisation and decision making structures and processes should always be kept under review, especially where, with experience, it becomes apparent that the initial approach adopted by the authority is obstructing or endangering the change process

It is in making changes like these that project teams of more junior managers can often assist by undertaking design and development work, and in managing implementation. The more people who can be involved directly in components of the change programme, the more its aims and objectives are likely to be communicated and understood, provided they are well-managed. Such projects should, where appropriate, also involve consultation with people outside the authority - local user groups, experts, and other public sector bodies with a policy or service interest. Again, the way in which these projects are done, as well as their actual objectives, plays an important part in communicating and institutionalising the authority's vision and chosen way of doing business.

Improving performance

A focus on performance is an essential aspect of the new style of local government. Performance is of course about achieving required standards and maximising efficiency. It is also about 'best practice', as discussed above. But in the terms meant here, it goes beyond this to achieve continuous improvement, where the local authority is not afraid to innovate and experiment, if that is what the electorate and the consumers demand, and where there is a continuous search for better ways of doing things.

An essential component of the change programme is therefore a performance management system which supports new philosophies of service innovation, and creates incentives for further improvements in the future (see Part II, Chapter 10). Support will be needed at every level of the authority, from the top down, if innovation and continuous improvement are to be encouraged. Any performance management system in this context must include:

- **reporting** - ensuring that performance information is reported in a comprehensible and relevant format

- **measurement** - ensuring that the right approach is in place to assess fairly the important performance targets, or behavioural attributes, ensuring achievement and compliance, with non-compliance addressed promptly by remedial action

- **reward** - ensuring that career development and reward packages are organised to recognise and support performance and innovation.

That improved performance can be measured is often only an implicit assumption. The issues here are that many so-called 'soft' performance targets - for example, in relation to customer care and the way services are delivered in practice are less readily measurable than hard targets to do with cost and time. This means that such targets must be set carefully and monitored sensitively to ensure that the data gathered are of sufficient quality. For example, where satisfaction surveys are sent to housing tenants after major repair works these surveys should be held at the most appropriate time after the work has been done and should be prepared in the best format.

Although in one sense people may fairly be expected to view quality and continuous improvement as normal objectives in performing their jobs in line with their job descriptions, it has to be recognised that in any really effective performance management system, the reward system must be seen fully to support and reinforce the achievement of higher levels of performance. Continuing financial constraints of course create difficulties and there are many who agree that a traditional private sector approach to performance related pay is not appropriate in local government, but a priority within the change programme should be the development of innovation in the career development and reward packages that are offered to staff.

The corollary of this is that authorities must also be seen to be tough on non-performance. Too many barriers to this form of action may have been instituted in the past, for example, union agreements may have made it difficult, or the sanctions available have little impact. Nevertheless, it must increasingly be seen as normal that not only is good performance rewarded, but also that those who do not achieve the performance targets set for them are identified and their problems addressed, through appropriate retraining and counselling, or in extreme cases, by disciplinary measures. If good performance is rewarded, and poor performance is seen to be addressed in a constructive and supportive way, this should be encouraging for all staff. It is to be hoped that the best staff will themselves wish to play a part in helping poorer performing colleagues to raise their standards as a normal part of teamwork and co-operation.

A focus on effective performance management is not, of course, restricted to individual members of the authority's own staff. Such disciplines have a key role to play in the management of internal relations between different parts of the authority, and between the authority and its external suppliers. Service level agreements and external contracts will require overhaul to ensure that what the authority is aiming to achieve in terms of service standards, or public participation, is included and monitored.

Making accountability real will be a key role for members. This will require some clear thinking about information requirements and methods of performance reporting, as part of the change programme.

Getting it right

Perhaps the hardest message of all, however, is that, if change is to be implemented successfully, none of these areas of change is optional, and none of them is enough on its own. Even the right strategy will be useless without effective implementation, and effective implementation depends on getting everything right. Any changes in the authority's activities will require consequential and reinforcing adjustment in other areas - everything must be looked at as one integrated whole.

The interrelationships are illustrated at Figure 5.3. If different elements of the change programme are not consistent with one another, this will communicate mixed messages within the authority, to the public, and to other bodies with whom the authority deals. Performance will fall short of the authority's goals, in one way or another, and external perceptions of the authority's suitability and credibility as community leader will be damaged. If, however, the authority can demonstrate consistent, and continuous, improvement across its many functions, and through all its many internal and external relationships, this will make a substantial and lasting contribution to renewing local government's importance.

The stakes are high, and the investment and energy required from leading members and senior officers especially will be substantial. But the ideas, approaches, and techniques set out in this book are intended to assist them in rising to the challenge they face, and, ultimately, to ensure that local government and local communities will be the gainers. Part II looks at key tools and techniques which can be used to help achieve both short-term and long-term objectives and indicates at what stages in the change process each might be most useful.

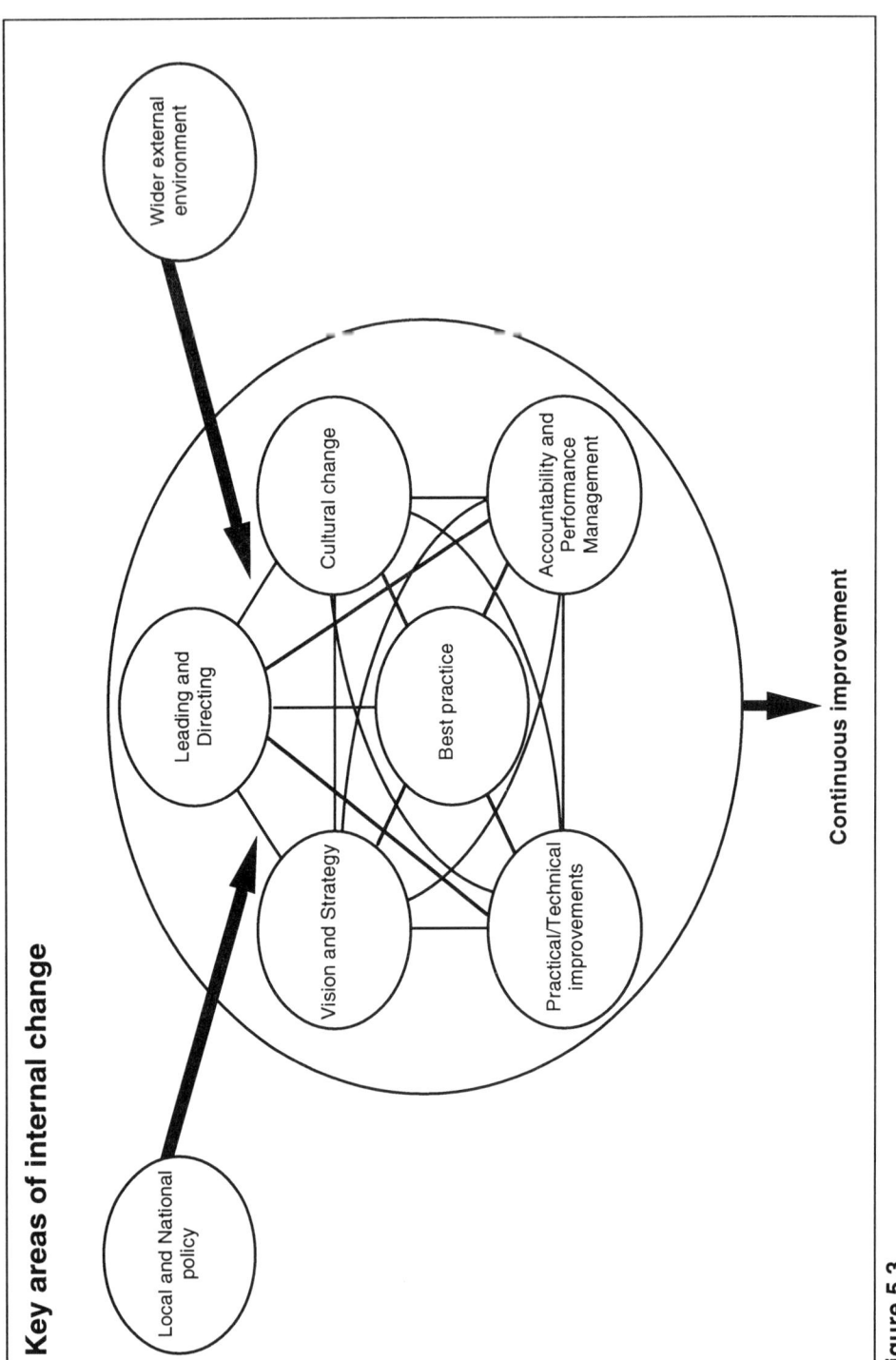

Key areas of internal change

Wider external environment

Local and National policy

Cultural change

Accountability and Performance Management

Leading and Directing

Best practice

Vision and Strategy

Practical/Technical improvements

Continuous improvement

Figure 5.3

PART II

Doing it Well and Getting it Right : Key Tools and Techniques

6

INTRODUCTION

In Part I, a major programme of change was identified for local government. All authorities continue to face a demanding legislative programme, including the requirements of Compulsory Competitive Tendering (CCT), but more significantly still, face the challenge of renewing local government as a vital part of the country's system of government. Those authorities affected by the Government's reorganisation in addition face the task of managing a process of structural change to a very tight timetable.

There will, of course, be many practical and technical problems to be dealt with, and guidance is already forthcoming from a range of bodies on some of these aspects (*see* Figure 4.1 in Part I). But a particular theme of this book has been the importance of managing the human and behavioural aspects of change - all too often ignored by policy makers. As decisions are made, and the process of change is better understood, good managers (whether elected members or officers) will increasingly want and need to know more about the ways in which they can get out and actually do something to ensure that things go smoothly. They will need many different tools and techniques to help them achieve their task.

Part II introduces particular tools and techniques that are likely to be most useful to local authorities in implementing structural and transformational change. Some of these are directly relevant to the particular needs arising from the specific circumstances and nature of the changes facing local government:

- developing a vision and strategy for new authorities

- integrating and unifying within new authorities staff and other resources from predecessor authorities

- the need for new authorities rapidly to establish public confidence in their ability to manage services and respond to the problems they face

- the need to deliver improved performance in services and in customer-client relationships, based on 'best practice' and user needs

- developing information strategies and systems

Others focus predominantly on the need to develop the ability, both of an organisation as a whole, and of the individuals within it, to plan, manage and respond positively to change. This involves a wide range of tools and techniques which fall into five main categories:

- enabling the change management environment to be properly analysed and surveyed

- well-established project management techniques to plan, control and implement a change programme

- assessing and developing individuals' skills and competencies to undertake change management

- applying and implementing change management processes

- supporting communications tools

Certain tools and techniques, particularly those concerned with developing individuals' and organisation's ability to manage and cope with change, will be relevant throughout the period of structural change and beyond. Others will be more relevant to specific points in the change process. Each of the nine chapters which follow begins with an introduction which identifies the tools and techniques described in that chapter and the stage in the change process at which they can be used. The three key stages identified are: 'Taking Stock' (understanding how things are); 'Merging and Building Confidence' (putting the mechanisms for change in place); and 'Transformation' (achieving change).

7

STRATEGY DEVELOPMENT

Introduction

This chapter contains details of five techniques which can be usefully applied by people in authorities which are either choosing to change their strategic approach or being compelled to do so as a result of reorganisation or other externally imposed change.

The five techniques covered and an indication of when they may be appropriate are shown in the table below:

Table 7.1 Strategy development

Tools/techniques	Taking stock	Merging and building confidence	Transformation/ achieving change
1 Strategy workshop	Identify need for change	Agree action/team building	Problem solving/ identify future goals
2 Assessing customer satisfaction	Identify need for change	Monitor achievement of stability	Measure achievement
3 Risk assessment and management	Identify risk	Manage risk	
4 Cost benefit analysis	Preparation of options	Ranking of priorities	Annual budgetary/ options evaluation
5 Data gathering and analysis	Establish priorities	Rank priorities	

Tool/technique 1: Strategy workshops

Context

Once decisions have been made about reorganisation, there will need to be a review and appraisal of the key objectives and aims of the new authority. The existing strategies for service provision of predecessor authorities may not fulfil the needs of the new organisation and, indeed, may even be counterproductive. There will be many new circumstances to respond to and established views of services may no longer be appropriate. New circumstances will almost certainly include:

- a different political framework at the local and possibly national level
- new external contexts of operation
- new internal operational constraints
- different groups of people working together
- different group cultures and behaviours

The overall direction of the authority will be set by the political framework, but the identity of the authority and its culture will be unformed. The development of a strategy to move towards the desired political objectives will be essential if the transition is to take place successfully and services are to be provided which meet the customers' needs.

Members and managers of the new authority will need to respond to these challenges by developing a 'new and shared vision' of the transformed organisation. This vision can be achieved by identifying and evaluating strategic alternatives and implementing the necessary changes. The changes will need to include:

- skills
- people
- systems
- behaviour and attitudes
- structure
- methods of service provision, and
- management style

Many staff within the new authority will be uncertain of the way forward and will need to be shown a new direction which has the commitment of the authority's leadership and top management will need to build consensus among senior managers to cascade the new vision to the rest of the organisation.

An effective technique to develop this unified view of the authority's future is that of strategy workshops. This is a technique, often used in business planning, which examines and evaluates the strategic options available to move the authority forward to its desired state.

Strategy workshops

During the process of change which the authority will be experiencing, there will be a frequent need for the leadership team to remove themselves from the melée of everyday tasks and concentrate on the longer term organisational objectives. The strategy workshop provides the occasion for top managers in organisations to think freely about the vision for the authority.

A strategy workshop consists of a group of individuals taking time away from the routine of day-to-day issues to develop and test the ideas which will shape and fashion the authority's future. Ideally the group would comprise:

- leading members and the senior managers of the new authority, who will have the in-depth knowledge of the main issues for the authority as well as practical experience of the development of strategy

- an external contributor from the commercial world who will bring novel and unusual perspectives to the process of strategy development and will challenge ideas from a radically different viewpoint

- an external facilitator from outside the organisation with strong knowledge and understanding of the issues being discussed but with equally strong skills of group facilitation, to ensure the workshops function effectively

The total number of people involved in these workshops should ideally be less than 12. This permits the facilitator to chair the event effectively, allows the formation of smaller groups for specific areas of group work and is a small enough number for all participants to contribute.

Each workshop usually consists of at least one and sometimes two days away from distractions. For this reason they are often held at hotels or conference facilities and not at senior managers' normal place of work. The facilitator is briefed as to the aims of the workshop and develops a programme for the event accordingly. The programme could include brainstorming, scenario planning, SWOT analysis and other tools and techniques which focus thoughts on key concerns.

The workshop should promote a supportive and non-threatening environment where the participants are encouraged to be free-thinking and creative without any fear of criticism or comment, and where innovation, testing and consensus building can occur, (all of which are essential for the successful management of change).

This does not mean, however, that workshops simply act as talking shops for senior managers. They should be tightly focused and should result in constructive outputs or plans which can be carried forward and implemented by the participants. A useful focus can be to find a solution to a specific problem. This concentrates the minds of those participating at the workshop and produces tangible results.

The key factors for success in strategy workshops are:

- the group should have a mix of skills, backgrounds and experience to ensure that all strategic possibilities are examined

- the facilitator should be experienced in workshops and in the general subject area

- the subject matter should have been thoroughly prepared in advance to ensure common understanding (use should be made of appropriate market research, issue papers and risk assessments)

- the external participants should be well-versed in this type of approach

- outputs should consist of clearly identified actions for specific individuals.

Using the workshops

During the initial stages of the changes which the organisation will be experiencing there may well be a need for regular strategic workshop events to be held. The uncertainties of the staff will be reproduced in most managers and workshops can provide a structured framework for resolving problems.

Workshops are not only useful in setting up the new authority and planning change. They can be highly useful as a regular part of the strategic planning process to examine the success of previous initiatives in achieving corporate objectives and to develop new strategic responses to new and existing needs. In the commercial world these workshops are often used for new ventures or products, and, during the regular reassessment of objectives during the strategic planning cycle.

Advantages of using strategy workshops

The main benefits of using strategy workshops in the formulation of the new and shared organisational vision are:

- They provide an opportunity for senior managers to develop ideas and build consensus in a non-threatening environment

- Specific issues can be addressed within a focused framework

- A greater knowledge of issues can be built up

- Common understanding between Management Team members can be quickly generated

- A clear framework for decision making can be agreed.

Tool/technique 2: Assessing customer satisfaction

Recent initiatives such as the Citizen's Charter have emphasised the importance of the customer, i.e. that members of the public are entitled to expect high quality public services which are responsive to their needs and provided efficiently. Feedback from clients and customers regarding their level of satisfaction with services can provide valuable insights into the effectiveness, strengths and weaknesses of services.

Regular customer feedback is essential at every stage of reorganisation. In the context of merging services this feedback can help highlight similarities and differences and assist in developing future strategy. It provides a means of assessing whether a baseline performance is being achieved across the new authority. Customer feedback should also be an important element of developing best practice, measuring the progress being made in achieving the transformation of services and the introduction of new standards. Finally, it will form an important source of information for those services preparing for CCT.

What is customer satisfaction?

Customer satisfaction can be defined as the difference between quality perceived and quality expected by a customer. If the two are balanced the customer will be satisfied. If the perception exceeds the expectation, the customer will be impressed. If, however, the perception of service is lower than the expectation, the customer will be dissatisfied.

Customers' expectations of service quality will be based on their past experience of:

- services previously provided by the authority's predecessors

- similar services provided by other organisations (whether in the public, voluntary or private sectors)

For different types of services, different factors will be more or less important. This is illustrated in Table 7.2 for a range of industries and services, based on Gallup surveys examining sources of complaint.

The Citizen's Charter initiative has developed six principles of public service. These provide a useful starting point for considering what are likely to be the key customer satisfaction factors for local authority services. The key factors will, however, vary from service to service (for example, comparing leisure facilities with homecare for the elderly). The six principles are:

- publishing clear service standards

- information and openness

- choice and consultation

- courtesy and helpfulness
- putting things right
- value for money

How do you measure customer satisfaction?

There are a variety of approaches to measuring customer satisfaction. Some of these approaches are outlined below:

- customer surveys
- customer focus groups
- observational research
- complaints procedures

Which approach (or combination of approaches) is most appropriate in any particular circumstances will depend on a number of factors. These will include the extent to which the feedback needs to be comprehensive or representative, the timescale available and the level of resources which can be devoted to the process.

Customer surveys

This is perhaps the most common approach to measuring customer satisfaction. Customers surveys can take a wide variety of forms, for example:

- questionnaires sent through the post
- telephone surveys
- face to face interviews

The sample size will need to reflect a representative range of customers and be of a sufficient size to produce a statistically significant result.

Customer focus groups

These are groups of approximately 6-12 people who are brought together with a trained facilitator in order to discuss a product or service. This approach to market research is becoming increasingly popular in the private sector.

The facilitator needs to be independent, familiar with the nature of the service and able to steer a group discussion. The facilitator starts by asking open questions to encourage participation in the discussion. He or she then directs the discussion to focus in on the specific issues that will provide the most useful customer feedback.

In order to create the right atmosphere, the meeting should be held in reasonably pleasant surroundings. Participants will need to be reimbursed for any costs they have incurred in attending the session.

Table 7.2

Customer satisfaction: different customers value different factors

Service / Factor	Car service	Bank	Insurance	Hospital	Airline
Effectiveness and accuracy	***	*	*		
Fast(er)	*	**	**	**	
Cheap(er)	**		*	**	
Friendly staff		*	*	**	*
Qualified staff		*	*	*	*
Courtesy		*		*	**
Effective scheduling					

Source: Gallup Surveys, based on sources of complaint

Observational research

Useful feedback on customer perceptions can be obtained by using staff or independent researchers to observe the provision of service and the interaction with customers. For example, some large corporations get staff as part of their training to pose as customers - in order for them to experience first hand the quality of service and be able to observe other customers' reactions more closely.

It may be difficult for staff to achieve the same level of anonymity in a local authority setting that can be achieved, for example, in a retail chain with a large number of outlets. However, complete anonymity is not essential to the process, particularly if the emphasis is on observing customers' reactions. This could be done by staff, independent researchers, or perhaps by officers from other authorities who are willing to participate.

Complaints procedures

Clear complaints procedures are encouraged by the Citizen's Charter. For some services, they are also a statutory requirement - for example for Social Services since the introduction of Community Care. While complaints are by their nature negative and complaints procedures may seem to be a 'necessary evil', they can nevertheless be a valuable source of customer feedback, particularly if the complaints are appropriately followed up.

One clear advantage of monitoring the level of complaints over the other approaches described above is that it enables trends to be identified over time. Analysing the pattern of complaints is also important. Only a very small proportion of dissatisfied customers make the effort to complain, perhaps less than 5%. Hence, the complaints received are likely to be representative of the feelings of many others.

Tool/technique 3: **Risk assessment and management**

The inescapability of risk

Strategic risk management is a response to the uncertainties and risks faced by organisations. Uncertainties and risks are heightened during periods of major change - such as merging authorities, winding down old authorities or transforming existing services.

In order to manage the risks, it is crucial that they are identified as early as possible, and that consideration is given to how they will be monitored and controlled. Risk assessment will be particularly important in the process of 'taking stock', described in Chapter 4 of Part I and of managing services through a period of change.

There are three key issues:

- stages in the process of controlling risk

- risks associated with merging authorities

- risks associated with winding down authorities

Stages in the process of controlling risk

The stages involved in assessing and managing risk are set out below.

Stage 1: establishing objectives and priorities

In order to establish a risk control strategy, it is first necessary to identify and clearly understand the objectives, both the objectives of the organisation as a whole and the objectives of the risk control process. Establishing the objectives will enable priorities to be set in terms of:

- the sources of risk to be examined (e.g. political, financial, legal, projects, personnel)

- the relative importance to the organisation of the various implications of risk (e.g. potential effects on financial resources, staff morale, public opinion, project timescales, service delivery, quality)

Establishing this framework for risk assessment and management at an early stage will enable appropriate time and resources to be targeted at monitoring and controlling the key risk areas.

Stage 2: identifying and assessing risks

The first part of this stage involves identifying the risks faced by the authority. This can be achieved by performing a top-down review of the organisation. Staff carrying out this review need to be encouraged to think creatively about potential risks and their implications. At this stage it is not necessary to assess the severity of the risks, the aim is to produce a comprehensive list of sources of risk.

Once this list has been produced and agreed, the next step is to assess the various sources of risk in accordance with the priorities and framework established in Stage 1. Assessing the risks requires consideration of the following factors:

- the probability of the risk occurring

- how severe the impacts would be if the risk does occur

- the degree to which different risks are dependent on each other (and therefore need to be considered together)

- the period of time during which the level of risk is greatest.

Risks can be assessed by assigning probability, impact and tractability scores. Tractability scores reflect the extent to which a risk can be managed or controlled. Greatest management effort can then be targeted on those risks which are more probable, would have a significant impact and are capable of being controlled by the authority.

Stage 3: managing risks

The first step to successful management of risks is to ensure that responsibility for monitoring and controlling is clearly allocated. This can be assisted by listing the risks identified in Stage 2 in a format that can easily be updated. Such a monitoring report might include a description of the risk, the scores assigned to the risk, the name of the key manager responsible and an outline of the control strategy. The control strategy should indicate how the risk area is being monitored and what controlling mechanisms are in place. If there is a significant area of risk which is outside the authority's control, it may also be appropriate to outline the contingency plan or fall back position.

In order to manage risk effectively during a period of rapid change it is necessary to introduce a regular monitoring cycle. This will help ensure that risks are being properly monitored and the report is being kept up to date. It will also provide a mechanism for new risks that develop to be included in the process, and for risks which have now been superseded to fall out. For new authorities which have been created by merger, it is likely that a significant level of risk will exist for the first 18 months to two years. An appropriate frequency for the monitoring cycle might be as follows:

- monthly during the first six months

- bi-monthly or quarterly until all significant risks have reduced to an acceptable level

Clearly, there is no benefit in creating a risk monitoring process that is unnecessarily cumbersome or bureaucratic. The level of detail in the monitoring report and the frequency with which it is updated should be the minimum sufficient to facilitate effective risk management. The key objectives are to:

- ensure all significant risks are identified and managers are aware of them

- ensure responsibilities are clearly allocated and gaps or duplication of effort avoided

- ensure progress is being made and action taken where required

- improve the overall effectiveness of day-to-day management

Risks associated with merging authorities

The nature and level of risks associated with merging authorities will vary according to the nature of the authorities and services being merged into the new organisation. The risks will also be affected by local political factors, as well as the management style, organisational culture and approaches to resource management and service delivery of the previous authorities. Examples of risk areas which may be significant are provided in the following figure.

Merging authorities: examples of risk areas

Political/Cultural

- The overall political complexion of the new authority may cause resentment in some areas of the authority which effectively experience a change of control.
- If a larger authority merges with a smaller one, it may feel more like a takeover to staff in the smaller authority. This may lead to resistance if it appears that the previous practices and procedures of the larger authority are being imposed across the board.
- Some problems with services that existed prior to reorganisation (skeletons in the cupboard!) may come to the attention of the public during reorganisation. This may cause the perception that the changes are having a negative effect on services.

Financial

- Where a former county or regional service has been split, there is a danger that the share of resources and of ongoing revenue support inherited by the new authority do not allow the service to be delivered in the same way and will result in the 'levelling down' of services.
- The variety in previous expenditure patterns, possibly coupled with incomplete information from predecessor authorities, will make the first year's budget difficult to establish. This may increase the risk of budget overspends.

Projects

For example:

- Projects to implement new IT for the new authorities may be delayed by a number of factors, e.g.:
  - the need to fit in with overall IT strategy which may still be developing;
  - difficulties with a limited numbers of software providers trying to support implementation in a number of authorities at the same time.
- Projects to create unified databases or registers of information may be delayed by factors such as:
  - gaps in the information provided by former service departments;
  - incompatibility in the format of data provided by former service departments.

Figure 7.1

Risks associated with winding down authorities

The figure below indicates some of the risks associated with winding down authorities.

Winding Down: examples of risk areas

Political

- The allocation of the resources of a county/region between successor authorities may be problematic, since both the distribution of resources and the pattern of need across the area are likely to be uneven. Also some service facilities may serve a wider area than the boundaries of the new authorities.

Financial/legal

- The allocation of debt between successor authorities may be problematic if records regarding the original purpose of the debt or legal records regarding associated property are incomplete.

Personnel

- Given the short-term nature of the work, there may be problems with staff recruitment, motivation and morale. If the work is delayed, additional cost will be incurred.

Figure 7.2

Tool/technique 4: Cost benefit analysis

Cost benefit analysis is a traditional technique for assessing whether an individual project should be implemented or for comparing the costs and benefits of different projects. Its use is straightforward when the costs and benefits can be measured simply in financial terms. However, for most projects/activities this is not the case. Indeed, the benefits and costs of a project may be so many and varied that an objective analysis is very difficult if not impossible.

The concept of cost benefit analysis is, however, a useful aid to decision making as it involves full consideration of the implications of a course of action. This is particularly important in a local authority because decisions have an impact not only on a wide cross section of people and other organisations but also on the environment.

By reference to a local authority's objectives and priorities cost benefit analysis can assist in the comparison and ranking of projects and in identifying projects for which the cost/benefit ratio is particularly high.

Cost benefit analysis will not on its own demonstrate whether an objective is being achieved in the most efficient and cost effective manner. Nor will it result in the development of radical new ideas for service provision. Its contribution to the transformation of local authorities will, therefore, be limited. However, it will continue to make an important contribution to the process of democratic decision making.

Tool/technique 5: **Data gathering and analysis**

Before merging services or authorities, it will be necessary to 'take stock' of the position of the predecessor services and authorities. This will be necessary for the following reasons:

- to understand the relative scale, similarities and differences between predecessor services

- to help formulate a practical action plan for merging operations or organisational structures

- to establish a budget for the first year of the new authority

This section considers some of the issues that will need to be addressed when taking stock, in order to ensure that adequate information is available to inform the decisions that will need to be made within what will inevitably be a limited timescale. The following issues are discussed:

- establishing priorities

- data gathering techniques

- quality of information

- making sense of the data

Establishing priorities

Before commencing with a data collection and analysis project, it is important to establish clear objectives. What information is needed and why? Without clear answers to these questions it is likely that much time and effort will be wasted.

The depth of information required also needs to be considered. For example, in different circumstances the following levels of information may be necessary:

- strategic level (overview management information)

- operational level (detailed records)

- financial perspective (budget breakdown and supporting assumptions)

At the taking stock stage, the main requirement will be for a combination of overview management information and budgetary information. Once the priorities have been clearly identified, it will then be necessary to consider how to approach the collection and compilation of the data.

Data gathering techniques

There are a number of possible approaches to gathering information. The most appropriate method will depend on a number of factors, including the volume of information to be collected, the level of detail required, the available resources and the timescale. Some important data gathering techniques are listed in the table below, together with some of the principal advantages and disadvantages.

Whatever combination of techniques is adopted, it is important as far as possible to gain the co-operation of those people supplying the information. Their co-operation will generally speed up the process and improve the quality of data collected. The following actions should help encourage co-operation:

- explaining clearly what is required, why it is needed and what it is going to be used for

Table 7.3 Data gathering techniques: advantages and disadvantages

Techniques	Advantages	Disadvantages
Interviews	Flexible: allows time for probing questions, discussion and clarification	May be time consuming, especially when preparation and follow up time is included
Questionnaires	Once prepared, can be widely distributed. Ensures everybody is asked the same questions. Allows respondents time to think about issues	May not generate the exact information required. Responses may need to be checked. Responses may not be received quickly
Requests for copies of reports or standard computer printouts	Relatively quick and easy for both parties	May end up with large volume of information only partially relevant and with inconsistent formats
Direct interrogation of systems or databases	May provide opportunity to specify precisely the information required and to manipulate data into an appropriate format	Some systems/packages will be inflexible. The process may be delayed by a need for specialist assistance

- giving people realistic timetables for pulling together the necessary information

Quality of information

Where data are collected to support important decisions, it is necessary to ensure that they are of a suitable quality. Quality of information can be assessed against a number of criteria, including:

- accuracy
- completeness
- relevance to the issues being considered
- significance (relative importance)
- compatibility with information from other organisations

Another important factor is timeliness. It may be necessary to some extent to compromise on quality in order to ensure the data is provided quickly, for example where key decisions have to be made to a timetable dictated by external requirements. However, as far as possible, where information has been gathered from a variety of sources, it should be checked and reviewed with the following questions in mind:

- Have we answered the original question?
- Have we got our facts right?
- Is any data missing?
- Is further data required?
- Does it make sense?

Making sense of the data

At the taking stock stage, the data compilation and analysis work to be performed is unlikely to be particularly sophisticated, though for budgetary purposes it will need to be very clearly thought out and robustly presented. The main analytical tools will include comparison and modelling.

Methods of comparison allow similarities and differences in the current position of the authorities to be identified and investigated. Comparison may include, for example:

- comparing performance statistics, financial indicators or levels of service provision in the various predecessor authorities
- comparing these statistics with other similar local authorities
- examining local trends over the last few years

Modelling allows possible future scenarios to be investigated. For example:

- What if standardised salary levels and remuneration benefits are introduced across the new authority?

- What will be the effect of changes in the rate of inflation or fluctuations in interest rates?

In a model, the appropriate base data regarding the service area or cost centre are established. Then certain factors are varied in order to see the overall effect on operational performance or budget. This is often more easily done using a spreadsheet package, which will automatically recalculate all the figures each time a variable is changed. Care needs to be taken since research has shown that over 90 per cent of spreadsheets larger than 150 rows contain at least one significant mistake. Any spreadsheet model being used to support major decisions should be checked to ensure the following:

- the arithmetic is correct (input values have been correctly entered and formulae correctly constructed or copied)

- the model is logical (the logic of the calculations matches the assumptions of the model user and has no significant gaps)

- the presentation is comprehensible (the spreadsheet is clearly laid out and indicates what data have been input and what has been calculated).

8

PROJECT MANAGEMENT

Introduction

This chapter focuses on the key technique of project management. The table below shows the main stages of the process and the three main stages of the change programme.

Table 8.1 Project management

Tools/techniques	Taking stock	Merging and building confidence	Transformation/ achieving change
Project management	• defining scope and objectives • defining roles and responsibilities • allocating tasks • scheduling activities • estimating resources and costings	• Monitoring and controlling (activities and costs) ---------------	------------->

What is a project?

The main factor that separates a project from day-to-day routine work activities is the concept of a discrete set of activities aimed at a predetermined objective within a finite timescale.

In practice, there are many weaknesses in the above statement as a definition of what actually constitutes a project. However, defining what is and what is not a project is not as important as the question: will the application of a particular set of working tools and techniques assist in achieving a particular objective? In the context of reorganising local government, major 'projects' are:

- establishing a new unitary authority, or

- redefining the role of local government within the existing single tier or two tier framework

Within this, there may be many other specific changes, as examples of more typical projects:

- the building of a new service facility

- relocating the finance department

- computerising tenancy records

- contracting out the security services

The main criteria which would group these activities as projects are that they:

(i) result in a measurable change

(ii) have specific composite goals and objectives

(iii) are unique

(iv) are limited in time and scope, and

(v) require a variety of inputs and drivers which need to be managed

One point that is apparent even from this relatively short list is that there are broadly two types of project:

(i) Technical - those that involve changes in technology

(ii) Procedural - those that aim to change culture or working practices

It has become increasingly important in modern project management to recognise that however technical an activity may appear there will always be a procedural element. Failure to recognise this fact (for example, not communicating to the workforce the benefits of the new system) may easily undermine the success of the project.

Within procedural activities especially, goals and objectives may conflict. An example of this is the trade-off between quality, time and cost. Potentially more dangerous are the incidents of covert objectives or hidden agendas such as project managers seeking to use the opportunity to extend their span of influence. Careful project management can never guarantee success, there will always be unknown factors, but it will drastically reduce the probability of failure.

In response to this, the concept of Goal Directed Project Management has been developed - in effect, project management as the management of change.

Successful implementation of a project plan will result in moving from a current position to a desired position (the achievement of the objectives). Every project has task and process elements analogous to the technical and procedural activities defined above. These two aspects of a project are illustrated in Figure 8.1, the project lifecycle. Successful project management depends on effectively managing both the process and the task. Tom Terez in *Managing Change in the 1990s* puts it well, 'Modern management is littered with the wreckage of technically sound programmes that have been crushed by employee resistance'.

While the technical outcomes of change may be clear, it is essential to identify the human and process outcomes. Individuals and groups adapt to change over time and will experience some level of stress during the process.

The effective project manager will provide support throughout the process to address concerns, help groups cope with stress and solve problems arising from the change.

The project plan

The project plan consists of:

    (i) definition of project scope and objectives

    (ii) roles and responsibilities

    (iii) activity summaries and schedules

    (iv) resource needs and costs

    (v) monitoring and controlling progress

There are a number of devices to assist the process of which milestone planning is one.

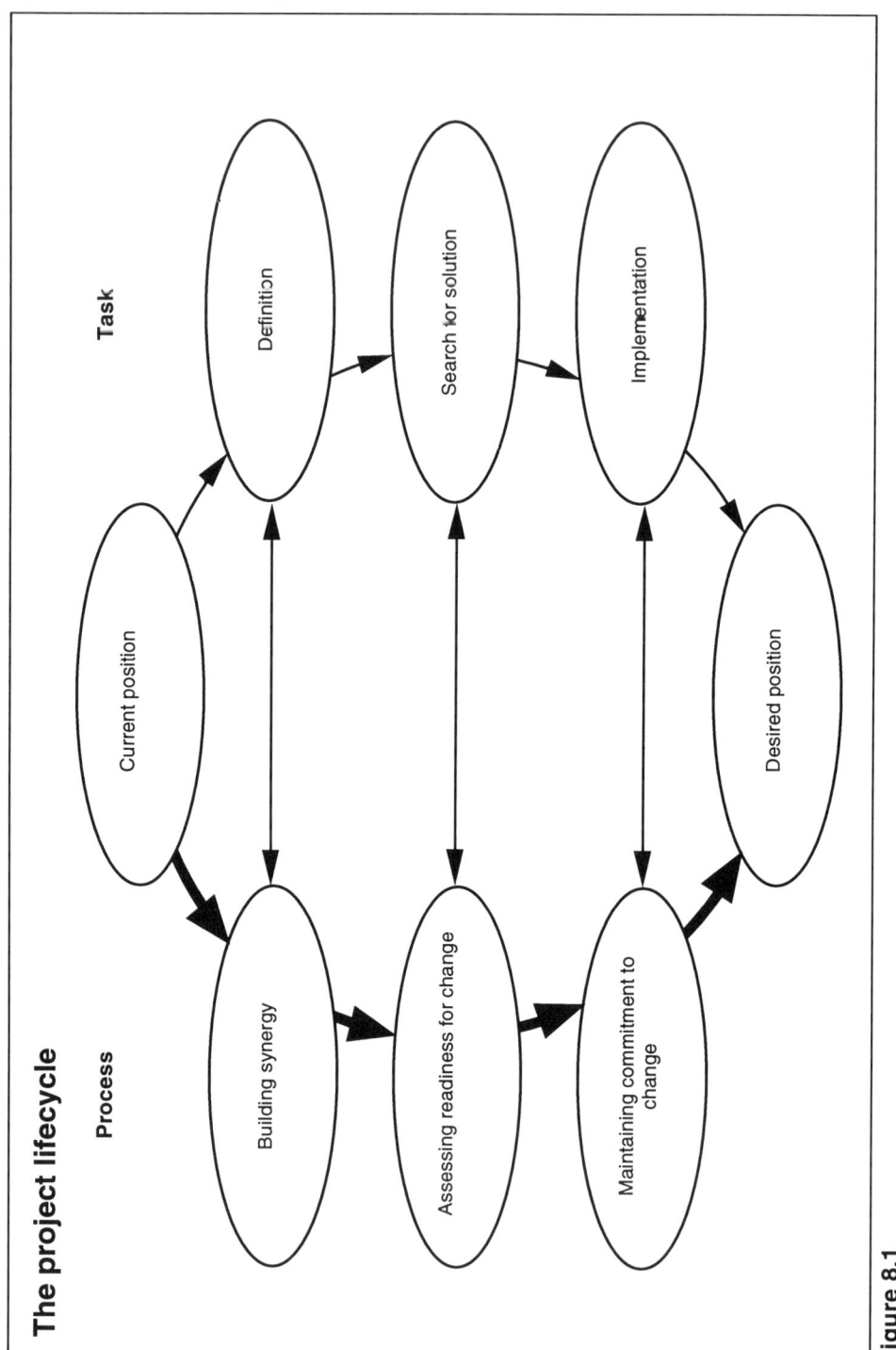

The project lifecycle

Figure 8.1

Milestone planning

The purpose of milestones in the planning context is to enable managers to focus on results. The milestones are the intermediary goals and objectives of the project. By breaking the project down into a series of checkpoints the manager has a mechanism for measuring progress and controlling costs and resource usage. It is also useful for ensuring that emphasis is put in the right places. To be useful, milestones should:

- represent significant stages of the project

- be measurable either qualitatively or quantitatively

- be relatively few in number, and

- be at useful, regular intervals

A typical milestone plan is shown in Figure 8.2. Note from the figure that it is typical to group milestones by similar types of activities, called 'result paths'. The main use of these paths is to help the planner ensure that all aspects of the plan have been considered. Typically, there will be different paths for technical, procedural and monitoring activities.

Defining the project scope and objectives

One can think of many examples of major projects that have overrun spectacularly in terms of time and costs. Worse still are the projects which not only overspend the budget but never actually achieve a satisfactory outcome. The Nimrod Airborne Early Warning system is one well-known public sector example, but authorities are likely to be able to identify others closer to home, particularly in the IT arena where time and money have been expended without achieving any worthwhile tangible results.

In these instances the cause for failure often lies in poor project definition at the outset. There are three consequences of not defining the project precisely:

(i) the goals for the project are imprecise

(ii) the limits of the scope of the project are not set

(iii) the levels of ambition for changes to people, systems and organisation are not in balance with the introduction of new technology

Project management - a milestone plan

Result paths			Milestone:
MIS System SY	MIS Strategy ST	Production Platform PR	

PR0 : Project start

PR1 : When flowcharts for the principal administrative routines have been agreed by production management

SY1 : When the MIS manager has approved for further appraisal a short-list of software systems, selected from a larger survey

ST1 : When principles of vulnerability and security had been approved by the production director

PR2 : When a statement of user requirements has been accepted by the steering committee as a basis for further work

ST2 : When the IT technical constraints have been specified by the MIS department

SY2 : When the methodology for evaluation has been clarified in accordance with company standards

ST3 : When the software development tools have been selected, and tested to the MIS managers satisfaction

SY3 : When the application package to be used has been selected and the further development specified

ST4 : When the operational and system environment has been described and quantified, in accordance with company standards

SY4 : When the development work required has been quantified, including standard sensitivity analysis

PR3 : When the development of the maintenance organisation has been quantified

SY5 : When the project team's recommendations including milestone plan, and project responsibility chart, have been delivered to the steering committee

SY6 : When the steering committee have decided whether or not to proceed

SYO : Project objective

Figure 8.2

120

With Nimrod, a contributory factor to failure was the rate of change of technology. It always seemed attractive to just wait a little while longer to achieve enhanced results with the consequence that goals were constantly changing and control diminishing. To avoid such pitfalls, the project team must:

- define the principles and policies of project work

- define the overt goals and reflect the covert goals

- set the scope of the project

- balance technical and procedural changes, and

- set criteria for success

Project roles and responsibilities

There are three main categories of involvement in any project although, especially in small projects, the same individual may undertake all of them. The roles are:

- Project sponsor

- Project manager

- Project team members

No project will be successful without an effective sponsor - the individual with the vision, desire and commitment to achieve the project objectives. The sponsor of a project to automate housing records might be a neighbourhood housing manager or the director of housing. The sponsor may have a clear objective or just a vague concept of a satisfactory outcome. The main responsibilities of the sponsor are to:

- classify and prioritise the project

- appoint the project manager

- show commitment

- provide adequate resources

- review progress

- approve changes to scope and targets, and

- approve outcomes

The function of the sponsor is a crucial one. Many projects fail due to lack of direction, lack of resources or inadequate priority. Nowhere is this more apparent than in managing cultural change. The change in culture (e.g. to become a more customer-centred service) must be driven from the top. For example, an attempt to introduce staff time accounting to a department in one authority was undermined and finally abandoned because its director would not complete the time account forms.

The project manager is the agent of change. It is for the project manager to harness the resources in order to achieve the desired objective. The main roles of the project manager are to:

- undertake a project feasibility study

- prepare the project plan

- estimate resource requirements

- manage and report progress to the sponsor, and

- produce the outputs

Key activities for the project manager are contingency planning and the management of the sponsor's expectations. The feasibility study should show whether the objectives are realistic. One reason why projects fail is because the sponsor continually redefines the objectives. It is the task of project management to demonstrate the impact of changes in relation to the project goal.

Allocating tasks

There will not necessarily be a specialist team created for all projects. There will be many instances where involvement in a particular project forms only part of the team member's activities. Communication and acceptance of roles is particularly important in these instances.

A 'responsibility matrix' is a useful way to allocate responsibilities to members of the project team (*see* Figure 8.3). The recommended symbols for use in the cells are:

X -   Executes the work

D -   Takes decision solely

d -   Takes decision jointly

P -   Manages progress

C   -   Must be consulted (before decision or action)

I   -   Must be informed (after decision or action)

A   -   Available to advise

T   -   Provides tuition

It will be apparent from Figure 8.3 that it applies not only to team members directly involved in a project but to all individuals contributing to any activity. In other words, the responsibility matrix should set out for the project manager all human resource involvement in the project including the sponsor and any specialist advisers, consultants and affected parties.

The key issues to bear in mind in task allocation are:

- skills and competencies
- the number of people able to work on a task at a given time
- the estimated level of resource required, and
- non-resourced work elements such as quality assurance and reviews

In selecting the project team key issues are:

- aptitude
- reliability
- availability
- career development
- personal preference (when it is possible to consider)

Due allowance must be made for non-productive time such as holidays, familiarisation and training. It is important that everyone understands and accepts their role. This is best achieved through the responsibility matrix referred to above.

Scheduling activities

Once work and resources have been defined to an appropriate level, and once the available resource has been identified, tasks must be scheduled against the project timescale in order to determine start and finish dates. The scheduling of each task must reflect:

- its estimated duration and whether it is fixed or variable

C&L — PROJECT RESPONSIBILITY CHART

Project: Jade feasibility
Chart issue/Date: A-30 Jan
Approved by: KVG
Period length:
Target completion:

Legend:
- X - executes the work
- D - takes decision solely
- d - takes decision jointly
- P - managers progress
- T - provides tuition on the job
- C - must be consulted
- I - must be informed
- A - available to advise

Companies/Departments/Functions

No.	Principle/Milestone name	Production Director	Maintenance Mngr.	Purchasing Mngr.	MIS Mngr.	Project Mngr.	Project Team	Other Production Mngr.	MIS Department	Maintenance Dept.	Consultant
	Principle Responsibility Chart	D	X	X	X	PX					A
	Milestone Plan/Resp. Chart	D	I	I	I	PX	X	I	I	I	A
	Committing Resources	D	X	X	X	P	C				
	Milestone Report	D	C			PX	C				
	Detail Planning										
	- Fix Deadlines	C	C	C	C	PX	C				
	- Select Staff	d	d		d	Pd	C				
	- List Activities					PX	X				
	- Estimate Time/Schedule	C	C		C	PD	X		C	C	
	- Commit Resources	d	d		d	P					
	- Provide Time	X	X		X	P					
	- Implement Activities					P	X				
	Activity Responsibility Chart		C	C	C	PX	C	C	C	C	
	Activity Report					P	X				
	Work Environment Maintenance	D	C	C	C	P	C	C	C	C	

Work cont. D — Period

Figure 8.3

- its dependency on the finish or start of other tasks

- its priority relative to other tasks

The purpose of scheduling is to confirm the viability of completing the work within the given timescale and to 'smooth' the resource requirement, in other words, to ensure that best use is made of the resources by spreading inputs, particularly in relation to limited resources.

Estimating resource needs and costing

Estimating provides the terms of reference for the project, defining time, cost and use of resource. It provides the basis upon which effort, durations and timescale may be derived for control purposes.

The primary requisite for developing accurate estimates is accurate definition of project scope. Accuracy will reflect the level of detail by breaking the work to be estimated down into smaller elements. Resources are estimated in terms of unit times enabling a calculation of total required input to be made.

Difficult to quantify but no less important is the availability or otherwise of particular skills and competencies. It is advisable to consider at an early stage the necessity of buying or hiring specific skills in good time. In this process the concern will be with the actual cost of a project. Assessing and controlling cost is ultimately the responsibility of the project manager, although for larger projects it may be desirable to delegate the activity to a financial controller.

In essence, financial control within a project is no different to any budget activity. Once specific resource needs have been identified, the manager draws up a budget with estimated costs of human resource, materials, technology, accommodation costs and any other costs relevant to project implementation.

Monitoring and controlling

A well thought through plan is a prerequisite for a successful project. Of course, this is not sufficient in itself as the plan needs to be implemented and controlled. Devices which are commonly used to facilitate the control process are described overleaf.

Networks and dependencies

A network is a means to enable a project to be viewed as a whole and at the same time to reveal logical relationships and inter-dependencies between the project activities. It is an activity plan setting out not only the activities to be undertaken but also the order in which they have to be undertaken and the activities whose starts are dependent on the start or finish of other activities.

Using a network produced in this way, together with resource estimates for each activity, enables the manager to establish the most effective sequence of work.

The critical path

Network analysis is the process by which the manager can establish the project's 'critical path'. The critical path through the network is the series of tasks which determines the overall length of the project. Any delay in a critical activity will cause a delay in the project.

Progress reporting

Key questions aimed at ensuring project control are:

- Is progress monitored regularly (at least once a fortnight)?
- Are reports received on the reporting date?
- Do reports highlight variance between actual and planned progress and highlight future variance?
- Do they identify action to correct adverse variances?
- Have work estimates been reviewed?
- Do all activities have tangible end-products for evaluation?
- Does the report include expenditure against budget and adjustments to forecast expenditure?
- Have people affected by the outcome of the project been adequately involved through such activities such as seminars, workshops, newsletter, communications and training events?

9

DEVELOPING BEST PRACTICE

Introduction

This chapter contains details of tools and techniques that can assist authorities in developing best practice in service delivery. It describes mechanisms both for comparing performance and approaches with other bodies in the public and private sectors and for developing a best practice approach to implementation of specific processes such as competitive tendering, outsourcing and contract management.

Table 9.1 Developing best practice

Tools/techniques	Taking stock	Merging and building confidence	Transformation/ achieving change
1 Benchmarking	Identify gap between internal and external practice	Plan for business improvement	Continuous review
2 Best of breed groups	Identify strengths and weaknesses	Implement preferred working practices	Continuous review
Best practice in: 3 Competitive Tendering 4 Outsourcing 5 Contract Management	))) Agree approach/) strategy))	Implement best practice principles	Review and update

Table 9.1 overleaf shows the techniques and mechanisms covered in this chapter and indicates when they might be appropriate.

Tool/technique 1: **Benchmarking**

Benchmarking is a technique used by an increasing number of companies as a tool for obtaining the information needed to support continuous improvement and to gain competitive advantage.

It can be defined as an external focus on internal activities, functions, or operations in order to achieve continuous improvement.

Objectives of benchmarking

The chief objective of benchmarking is to facilitate the achievement of best practice from the perspective of the customer or consumer. It is important to note that these interest groups (known as stake-holders) do not have to be external to the organisation. In the case of interdepartmental services (for example internal provision of IT, legal or financial services) the stake-holder will be another department. With intra-departmental services (for example, graphic design, word processing or administrative support) the stake-holders would be colleagues within the same department.

Benchmarking succeeds best when everyone's interests are understood and considered in the chosen solution.

The technique can focus on roles, process or strategic issues in the pursuit of best practice. The benchmarking activity should be:

- externally focused
- measurement based
- information intensive
- objective
- action generating, and
- geared towards continuous improvement

Benchmarking is the process of comparing business practices and performance levels between organisations (or divisions within them) to gain new insights and to identify opportunities for making improvements. The concept behind benchmarking as a step towards achieving best practice is to learn from approaches used by other organisations that may have developed alternative solutions to shared business issues. These organisations might be in the public or private sector, but the basic premise is that it is easier and of 'lower risk' to learn from other organisations' solutions that have been tried and tested in operation than it is to solve the problems from first principles. This results in faster implementation of change and improves the chance of getting the solution right first time.

When to benchmark

Benchmarking is most often undertaken in response to external forces for change. For example, much of the benchmarking that has been initiated in the public sector over the last five years has been in response to market testing and competitive tendering.

The competitive tender itself could be described as a benchmarking exercise for the letting of service contracts (the client-side responsibility). However, in-house teams bidding for the right to continue to provide a service often seek means of establishing how competitive they are prior to the tender process by various market research and analysis techniques.

Other examples of where benchmarking may be used include:

- quality improvement programmes

- cost reduction

- better value for money

- new ventures

Sources of benchmarking information

There are broadly two types of information which can be used for benchmarking:

- **primary information** - obtained from market research, conversations with industry experts and customers, and

- **secondary information** - obtained from published material, trade magazines, price lists, newspaper articles and attendance at trade conferences

Both types can provide fruitful information. Primary information tends to be more costly and it is essential that any market research or specially designed questionnaires are rigorously tested for fitness for purpose. Secondary information may be less expensive and more readily available but is unlikely to be in an appropriate format and may be out of date.

The benchmarking process

The logical sequence for the benchmarking process is illustrated in Table 9.2. There are 5 main stages which are summarised below:

- identify core issues

- internal baseline data - identify and arrange collection

- external data - identify and arrange collection

- analysis of gap between internal and external practice

- plan for business improvement

Identifying the core issues is not always straightforward. For example, in the case of competitive tendering the primary concern may be to compare costs. It may be tempting to think that competitive pay rates or terms and conditions will of themselves be sufficient in a competitive tender. But this approach overlooks a number of contributory factors:

- organisational structures and ratios of supervisory staff to operational staff

- ratios of administrative and support staff to operational staff

- operational staff productivity

- innovative ways of providing the service (including the use of recently developed technology)

- expected profit margins and shareholder dividends

All of the above will have an impact on costs. Only by ensuring that each of these areas is competitive can overall competitiveness be guaranteed.

The starting point for identifying core issues is a diagnostic review. This requires that every stage of a service is analysed from receipt of order to final delivery (including where relevant both pre- and post-sale customer service) and, at each stage, every sub-activity. For example, service delivery to a customer specification may require access to a transport fleet. This would include such issues as the advantages of ownership against contract hire or leasing. By undertaking the analysis subject to the sensitive criteria of quality of service and cost of service, all the issues critical to successful service delivery can be identified.

Part of the internal diagnostic will be the identification and collection of financial and operational data, on the basis of utility and availability. If the need for key information, which is not readily available, is identified, steps must be put in place to enable its collection.

The key to the benchmarking process is the ability to identify the critical information providing competitor 'best practice'. Bearing in mind the cost of collecting primary information, the manager of the benchmarking process must ensure that the information gathered is relevant, unambiguous and collectable.

Good benchmarking provides quantifiable data so that an analysis of commercial best practice or that of other public sector bodies, provides information on how the authority's current performance compares. Quantifying

Table 9.2

A framework for benchmarking

	Identify core issue	Internal baseline data collection	External data collection	Analysis	Change implement
Input:	• Issue - Unmet customer needs - Performance gap - Problem areas - Strategic advantage	• Overview of process • Current measures • Potential drivers and external organizations	• Benchmark questionnaire	• Compare and contrast Benchmark data	• Implementation plan • Issues
Output:	• Defined benchmark area • Overview of key process to be benchmarked • Selected performance measurements • Identify potential drivers and external organizations	• Process flow mapping • Validated drivers • Benchmark target companies • Short-term operational improvements • Benchmark questionnaire	• External company(s) • Process analysis, performance assessment and measures	• Gap • Process improvements/ Reengineering opportunities • New - Flows - Policies - Procedures • Implementation plan • Outstanding issues	• Plan to close the gap • Actions to close the gap • Recalibrate benchmarks • Additional analysis/ Benchmarking to address issues

performance means that the gap can be measured, and this gives more urgency and direction to the business improvement process.

The 'basket of work' is a simple example of a typical benchmark for a contracting exercise. In this situation, a contractor draws up a specification for a typical range of the products and services supplied. This representative basket is offered to the market for estimates and the contractor can then draw conclusions about competitiveness from the results.

Benchmarking is not just about quantitative measures and outputs, it is increasingly being seen as a valuable means of deriving greater understanding from different processes that are used to deliver variations in performance, for example, the way in which a housing department monitors and brings management information together as well as the level of performance against service standards. As a result, the benchmarking technique is more than a simple way of comparing best practice and effecting continuous improvements. It has more recently become a powerful means of analysing best practice processes which can be used to stimulate step change performance improvements.

The major benefits of benchmarking are derived not from measuring the performance gap between current and best practice, but from identifying how to close the gap, linked closely to the change programme to transform the authority. The benchmarking process involves:

- identifying and measuring the size of the current performance gap

- identifying the processes or structures that need to be changed or redesigned to deliver a step change in performance

- measuring the extent of the performance improvement achieved and to what extent best practice has continued to move on from the original targets

- providing a continuing means of achieving further improvements driven by external best of breed standards

Benchmarking techniques can provide valuable support to the transformed authority - the comparisons made should range over other sectors as well as other authorities to provide a breadth of vision and genuinely transform standards in local government services.

Outsourcing is the transfer of selected functions or services and the delegation of day-to-day management responsibility to third party suppliers. The main arguments for using external suppliers are that the customer can gain access to best practice, a wider specialist skill base with improved cost control, higher service quality and greater flexibility. The customer is then able to concentrate on core activities and reduce fixed costs. Staff transfers are often involved and hence the process can offer significant advantages to staff in services which may be facing an uncertain future or declining workload. This may, for example, be as a result of CCT and the restrictions on a local authority's ability to trade, deriving from the Local Government (Goods and Services) Act 1970.

Cost competition and regular retendering for the business under CCT provides a means of updating the customer on best standards on cost and service quality by the contractors. Obligatory contracting-out required by legislation will provide regular indications of best practice especially through the use of 'benchmarking' in preparation for the full CCT process. However, outsourcing takes the process of contracting out further, so that generally longer-term contracts are involved, and the philosophy is closer to that of a partnership than the conventional customer/supplier relationship of contracting. The possible transfer of staff and greater sharing of risks allow the supplier to closely tailor the service to suit the customer requirements.

Outsourcing is particularly worth considering for services where this partnership philosophy would be valuable. Typical examples of recent outsourcing contracts include facilities management, application maintenance and network management, finance and accounting, legal services, property maintenance and estate management.

In practice, outsourcing is usually achieved through a process which is very similar to standard competitive tendering. CCT has given local authorities considerable experience of this process. While the CCT regulations may not apply directly to an outsourcing process, they will influence the timing of the process and the level of market interest. The Department of the Environment (DoE) guidelines should be taken into account as indicative of best practice and relevant EC directives will need to be complied with. The main differences to a standard competitive process are generally as follows:

- The local authority is committed to using an external supplier. In other words there is no in-house bid, although the local authority need not be committed to accepting a bid in the event that all the tenders received are above the existing costs of providing the service in-house.

- The local authority may require that existing staff are transferred to the new supplier on equivalent terms and conditions regardless of views on the applicability or otherwise of TUPE (Transfer of Undertakings (Protection of Employment) Regulations). This may be essential if staff support for the process is to be obtained, and the transfer may offer significant advantages to the authority. The authority will continue to be serviced by staff with considerable local experience and familiarity with service requirements, thereby ensuring a smooth transition and continuity of service.

- If staff are to be transferred, their co-operation is required. Hence, a process of staff consultation is needed to keep them informed and provide them with an opportunity to influence the tender evaluation criteria. Potential suppliers would normally make presentations to the staff to explain their plans for the future of the service and the opportunities for staff.

- The EC directives are generally less prescriptive regarding the approach to tender evaluation than the CCT regulations. (However, if a contract is to be awarded in-house in advance of CCT, it may be necessary to demonstrate to the auditor that a process of equivalent rigour to CCT had been followed.)

- Given the greater sharing of risks involved between the customer and supplier, the process of post-tender negotiations may assume greater importance. This provides an opportunity for clarification and possibly for enhancing the value for money offered by the tendering exercise. However, any changes envisaged as a result of this process should not materially alter the terms of the specification. This could result in a risk of having to re-advertise.

Care must be taken by management to ensure that control of the service is not lost and that some degree of in-house expertise is retained to monitor the work done and ensure compliance. Provided the relationship is managed in this way, the outsourcing approach to enhanced service delivery and cost reduction may be an attractive alternative to conventional contracting out.

Tool/technique 2: Best of breed groups

Introduction

All authorities will want to ensure that services are delivered as effectively and efficiently as possible. This is particularly important where a merger is taking place and two or more groups of staff have been providing similar services in different organisations. Key questions are likely to be:

- What standards should we set for our services?
- What organisational structure is best for service provision?
- What internal methods of communication and control are most effective?
- Can different approaches to service delivery be effectively rationalised?
- Are different methods appropriate for different elements of service and management functions?

In addition to answering these questions about future services and management there is a great need for services to be stabilised and maintained during the changes which will be occurring. There is a high risk of services being disrupted during the transition period which needs to be managed and minimised.

Services which are currently provided by more than one of the merging authorities will almost certainly need to be physically reorganised but the merger is also an ideal opportunity to examine and evaluate the current methods of service provision to ensure that the service is provided in the most effective and efficient manner within the new authority.

The risk of problems can be reduced, and opportunities for service improvement evaluated, by using the technique of 'best of' groups in the merger phase, in conjunction with other tools and techniques described elsewhere in Part II.

What are 'best of' groups?

'Best of' groups should be set up ideally in advance of the merger of two or more authorities. Their major aim is to examine the current methods of service provision or management employed in the merging authorities and to identify the best methods for the new authority during and after the transition stage.

Groups usually consist of a small number of staff (usually 8-10) involved in currently providing the service. Careful selection of the membership of the groups will be one of the main components of success. Ideally membership should comprise:

- at least one member from each authority

- a cross section of backgrounds and expertise

- a cross section of experience

- a mix of managers and non-managers

- staff with the energy and enthusiasm to effect change

It is often a useful addition to the process to include an external group member who provides a moderating presence to the decisions of the group and can challenge the thought processes of the group to ensure 'group think' does not hold sway. It is useful if the external moderator has experience of the service or function concerned, but is sufficiently analytical and detached from the authority to provide independent advice and guidance.

The groups need to be driven by tight deadlines and milestones if results are to be achieved within the appropriate timeframe. It is important for the groups to be managed in their deliberations by the top management team. This can be achieved by setting a clear timetable for completion, milestones for the accomplishment of particular tasks and reporting structures for the communication of progress. A specific manager should be responsible for each of the areas under discussion.

There is a strong likelihood that there will be many of these groups working simultaneously during the merger phase and co-ordination of these groups by senior managers and the monitoring of outputs by the groups, will be paramount. The 'best of' groups should ensure that the following issues are addressed:

- The evaluation criteria used to assess each method of service provision, or management, should be set at the outset in consultation with customers and senior management to ensure they meet the desired future objectives of the new organisation.

- Current methods should be investigated and documented.

- The strengths and weaknesses of each method need to be evaluated against the evaluation criteria.

- The interrelationships between the different elements of the service or function should be examined to ensure that there is no overlap or conflict in service provision.

- Preferred working practices and procedures will be identified from this process.

The final result of the 'best of' group process should be the emergence of a consensus on the future best methods of service delivery and management. The preferred options will need to be submitted to the management team for the final decision to ensure the interests of the new authority are safeguarded, and are consistent with the standards and best practice that have been identified among other organisations (in the public and private sectors) offering similar services.

Once the preferred methods of service provision have been identified the groups can begin to examine the best way for the merger to proceed while maintaining the service levels required during the changeover period. An incremental approach may be favoured that allows change to be implemented over a given period; or a more radical approach taken providing that the risks to services can be minimised. The method chosen will need to reflect the capability to maintain the service and the confidence of service users.

Some group members may feel that some of their work of the last few years has been undertaken in a less than optimal way. Members of the group will need to put aside these feelings and any preconceived ideas concerning the methods they normally use to provide services, and will need to be open-minded about the opportunities provided by the review process.

'Best of' groups can also be used to act as a focus for benchmarking information. This technique was discussed earlier in this chapter.

Benefits of using 'best of' groups

There are many benefits which can be accrued from using the tool of 'best of' groups during the merger phase of the change process. These are described in outline in the Figure 9.1 below.

Benefits of using 'best of' groups

- Best practice can be identified for the future

- Positive task focused action is stimulated

- Motivation can be enhanced by the involvement of staff in the change process

- Teambuilding can be achieved between staff who will be working together in the future

- Risks can be identified which may affect the performance of the new authority

- The cost of this process can be very low compared to other methods of service development

---

Figure 9.1

Tool/technique 3: Best practice in competitive tendering

Introduction

During the 1980s the Government's programme of compulsory competitive tendering (CCT) was implemented for a wide range of blue-collar services provided by local authorities. Starting from 18 months after reorganisation, new authorities will need to expand this programme to a range of white-collar services. Meanwhile, some authorities have performed voluntary competitive tendering of some service areas in advance of CCT, while others have pursued varying methods of outsourcing a range of services. One thing is sure, new authorities will regularly be undertaking the process of competitive tendering. Their tendering programme will cover a large number of services and represent a significant proportion of their overall budget.

In this context, it is vital that authorities establish competitive tendering processes that reflect best practice, achieve value for money and comply with relevant legislation. This section provides an outline of good practice in the tendering process. It is not intended to provide a detailed or technical discussion of all the issues.

Overview of the process

The process of competitive tendering is illustrated in Table 9.3, where it is analysed into six phases. Phase 1 only applies the first time a particular service is put out to contract. The main part of the process is represented by Phases 2 to 5. A typical timetable would require around six months for Phases 2 to 4 plus a further three months mobilization period for Phase 5, making a total of nine months. The detailed timetable, and in particular the response times allowed to bidders, need to comply with both DoE regulations and any applicable EC directives. The contract commences at the start of Phase 6, and best practice in managing the contract during this phase is dealt with in a separate section.

Best practice in managing the process of competitive tendering is described in Figure 9.2 as a series of 'golden rules'. The 'golden rules' relating to the client role are then discussed further.

Establishing the client/contractor split

The client-side organisation will drive the tendering process and eventually manage the contract on behalf of the organisation. It will need the appropriate expertise to be able to specify service requirements and effectively monitor the future delivery of service. It will also need to establish independence from the in-house bidder in order to demonstrate impartiality in awarding the contract. The time at which the client/contractor split is established during the first round of tendering requires careful consideration.

It may be tempting to establish the split very early to avoid any appearance of co-operation. However, co-operation is likely to be very helpful with respect to certain key tasks - notably that of preparing a workable service specification that does not have gaps. A constructive relationship between the two sides needs to be maintained in order to benefit from the considerable practical experience and local knowledge present in the in-house bidder. The split should be fully established by the time the tender strategy and contract documentation is finalised, so that it can be demonstrated that the key decisions were taken to reflect corporate interests, rather than the interests of the in-house team.

Specifying the service requirements

Producing a clear and workable service specification is crucial to success in the competitive tendering process. The first stage in the process is to examine whether the service currently provided is actually the service users require. There is no point in specifying a service which is inappropriate, out-of-date or not working in the way users would like. A mechanism should be set up to allow representatives of the service users to feed into the development of the specification.

Table 9.3

The phases of competitive tendering

	Phase 1 Getting started	Phase 2 Detailed planning	Phase 3 Specifications and tender strategy	Phase 4 The bidding process	Phase 5 Implementing the results	Phase 6 Ongoing contract management
Client side activity	Set up management machinery	Evaluate proposed activities in more detail	Prepare service specifications and contract documents	Commence formal tendering process	Communicate results	Continue contract compliance
	Make key appointments	Develop outline tender strategy	Identify potential bidders	Bidding processes and presentation of bids	Debrief	Maintain awareness of customer and market
	Establish outline programmes	Provide training for key staff	Identify evaluation criteria	Tender evaluation	Establish future organisation and formalise links	Prepare for next competition
	Establish policy ground rules	Begin market analysis	Finalise contract strategy	Post tender negotiations	Ensure contract compliance	
	Prepare action plans	Select best options for tendering		Detailed evaluation report	Introduce contract regime	
		Get clearance on outline tender strategy				
	-> emerging client contractor split ->		CLIENT/CONTRACTOR SPLIT IN PLACE			
In-house bid team activity		Identify in-house team	In-house team review and analysis	Develop bid strategy	Mobilise in-house service if successful	Manage in-house service to budget
		Formulate in-house team strategy	Development of in-house business plan	Submit in-house bid	Establish client and contractor working systems	Continue to improve performance in readiness for next competition

---

Golden rules of competitive tendering

The client role

- separate the client role from the in-house bidder
- review service levels before writing specifications
- write specifications to encourage competitive pricing
- take care over the tendering strategy
- only allow credible bidders to compete
- use both costs and quality criteria for evaluation
- make sure the contract is monitored effectively
- keep records at all stages

The in-house bidder role

- provide effective leadership for the in-house team
- prepare a business plan to underpin the tender bid
- put maximum effort into tender preparation and presentation
- make sure that cost and quality changes can be delivered
- take steps from the outset to protect confidentiality

Figure 9.2

The specification must tell potential contractors clearly what they are required to provide. A good specification will not be unduly prescriptive about the resources to be employed or the methods to be used but will define the job required in terms of:

- the functions to be performed (scope of service)
- the outputs sought (quantities)
- the performance required (quality)

The specification should not prescribe current processes, practices and methods of working as this will prevent innovation in service delivery by the contractor. It should contain sufficient information to enable contractors to determine and make accurate costings of the service. Contractors should have no doubts about the objectives for the services and what is expected of them. The hallmarks of good specifications are summarised in Figure 9.3 overleaf.

Hallmarks of good specifications

- Document logically structured with no overlap of sections
- Simple language and no jargon
- Terms, abbreviations and acronyms defined
- Words and expressions understandable
- Concise but clear meanings
- Non-repetitive
- Attractive format to encourage reading by contractors
- Each section and paragraph numbered using a logical and consistent numbering method
- Good use of tables, appendices and diagrams if these help to explain the requirements more clearly

Figure 9.3

High level specifications can be appropriate where there exists a high degree of uncertainty or risk, where the authority is looking for novel and contentious solutions without constraining the contractors methodology or broad approach. In some circumstances high level specifications can produce better value for money solutions, since contractors can deliver flexibly and innovatively to minimise costs. Low level specifications are appropriate where the requirement is measurable and has become the basis for output measures of performance.

Existing specifications for similar services are often a useful guide on what to include but should never be used without considering in-depth the services and standards required by the local authority writing the specification.

Finalising the tender strategy

The tender strategy should reflect the review of service requirements, an analysis of current market developments, the level of interest expressed in the contract and the nature of the service involved. Figure 9.4 lists key factors to be addressed in determining the tender strategy.

Where there is an in-house bidder and the service is being tendered as part of the CCT programme, the strategy will be constrained by DoE requirements regarding the scope of work to be included and the contract length. The programme for CCT for white-collar services includes percentage requirements for the proportion of each area that must be put out to tender. Careful analysis is required of relevant work performed centrally and in service departments, both internally and by external consultants, in order to ensure that these percentage requirements can be met. The results of this analysis will need to be summarised in a Statement of Support Service Costs (SSSC). The steps involved in preparing this statement are illustrated in Figure 9.5.

Tender strategy checklist

- Identify the factors which will define the size of the contract (volume of work, geographical coverage, organisational boundaries)

- Assess the advantages and disadvantages of having one or more contracts

- Decide and agree the size and number of contracts

- Determine the type of contract that will best meet the service objectives

- Decide what accommodation or equipment will be offered to contractors

- Determine responsibilities for key aspects such as maintenance, cleaning and repair of accommodation and equipment

- Consider how long the contract period should be

- Assess the range of functions to be put together into a single contract package

- Assess the options for pricing the work required

- Formulate and agree the tender strategy: size, scope, duration, packaging and pricing method

---

Figure 9.4

Safeguarding quality

The importance of good specifications in quality assurance has already been discussed above. Another key aspect to ensuring a quality service is the pre-qualification stage i.e. the production, from those who express an interest in the contract, of a shortlist of contractors who will be invited to tender. This is sometimes seen as mechanical, but provides a valuable opportunity to screen out unsuitable contractors and identify areas of potential concern. Used effectively it can avoid difficulties and problems later.

An evaluation team should be formed to undertake the shortlisting process. A wide range of expertise will be required by the team, including technical expertise of the service being tested and the experience to assess the trading and financial stability of companies. In addition to the financial checks, it may be appropriate to obtain reference enquiries for at least two contracts operated by each applicant.

Evaluating tenders

Once tenders have been received from the shortlisted contractors, a second and fuller evaluation process needs to be undertaken. The three main aspects of this are:

- compliance check

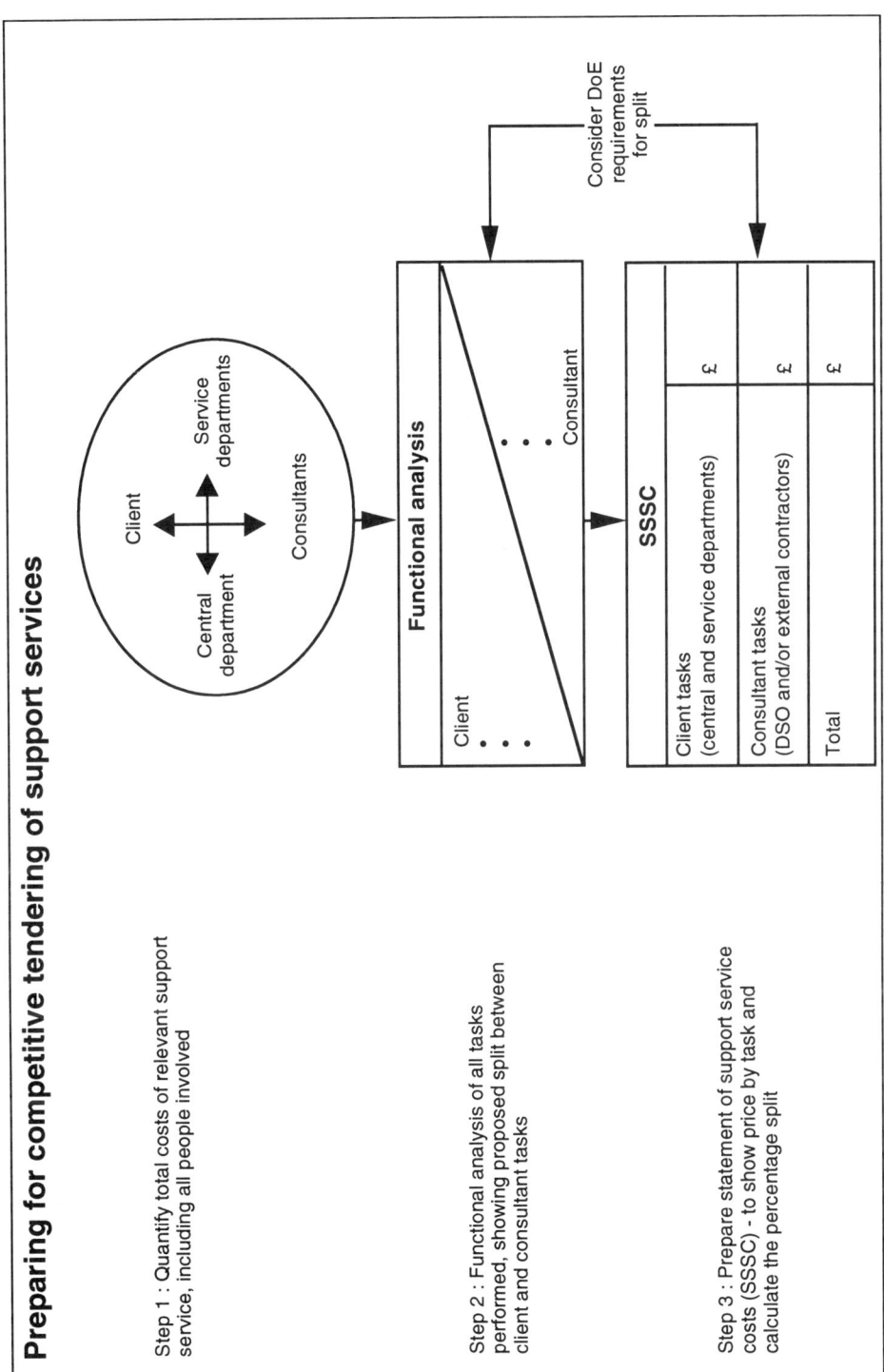

Figure 9.5

- technical assessment

- financial evaluation

The compliance check takes the form of an examination of each bidder's submission to ensure that it complies with the specified tender conditions, such as information schedules, certificates and potential alterations or qualifications. Where a particular submission does not comply, then an assessment will need to be made to determine whether the bid should be rejected at this stage or if there are only minor discrepancies allowed to proceed to the next stage. The evaluation team will therefore need to judge if the degree of failure to comply is sufficient to warrant rejection.

The technical assessment focuses on whether each bidder can meet the technical and operational requirements of the specification and contract conditions. A range of issues will need to be covered and should be related to the information supplied by the contractor. The key areas to be examined should include:

Technical assessment: key factors

• staffing levels/experience	• quality systems
• management arrangements/ experience	• customer care
• company structure	• health and safety
• equipment proposals	• training policy
• materials	• operational plan
• location/accommodation	• ability to deliver
• recruitment policy	• client references
	• current commitments

Figure 9.6

Consideration should be given to ranking contractors in key areas. In this respect it will be essential that the criteria used to judge contractor's submissions are developed in advance. This is particularly relevant where the EC Services Directive applies, as the criteria must be stated in the contract documentation.

The assessment of whether a bidder can deliver the service will be based on the information submitted in his tender. However, there may be occasions when further contact is required to clarify certain issues. Any discussions must be fully documented.

The financial evaluation of bids is a complex process which cannot be treated lightly. The objective is to ensure all bids are compared on an equal basis. This may require adjustment of certain costs so that a valid comparison is made and the full cost of the service is known. It is not a simple one-line comparison.

The detailed financial evaluation will be undertaken by the evaluation team. They should ensure that a valid comparison is made and that any adjustments are fair and equitable. Cost adjustments that may be required include those for accommodation, equipment and redundancy costs, although the latter will depend on the applicability of TUPE.

Following the detailed evaluation, an overall cost comparison will be required which also examines the current cost of the service to arrive at the full financial implications for the department.

Throughout the competitive tendering process it is important to keep full records of the decision process. This is particularly so at the shortlisting and tender evaluation stages. Disgruntled contractors may question the basis of decisions or allege anti-competitive behaviour on the part of the local authority. It is important to keep sufficient evidence to deal with any potential controversies.

Tool/technique 4: Best practice in outsourcing

If an authority is considering outsourcing it is paramount that the options are carefully considered to ensure value for money and to minimise risk. There are many difficult decisions to be taken before proceeding along this route, and, even once it is chosen, there are different ways of outsourcing to be considered. Two of the more common forms are discussed in more detail below. These are:

- transfer to a 'host' company
- management/employee buy-out

Transfer to a host company

This is the process whereby a contract is let by competitive tender for the future provision of a contract for services. Recent examples, even allowing for certainty on the applicability of the Transfer of Undertakings Regulations, have been that staff have generally transferred with the contract.

The hosting route provides a number of benefits:

- the ability to trade in a wider market
- access to commercial and financial skills
- current service base and staff preserved
- potential to achieve cost savings within negotiation of the contract, and
- investment in the systems and expertise of the service providers through access to funds

The level of market interest is likely to be particularly high in advance of CCT coming into force for a particular service. This is because the process may provide an opportunity for the successful company to establish a local government base from which to compete for other work to be put to competitive tender in due course. There are also advantages to the local authority acting in advance of CCT if it decides to pursue the hosting option, as this allows greater flexibility in the contracting process and may help avoid a protracted period of uncertainty for staff. However, it is also possible to pursue outsourcing options post-CCT. This is already happening in some authorities where the viability of the DSO is being threatened by a progressive decline in business. In this case market interest will depend on the type and range of services involved and the size and length of the contracts.

The hosting route potentially offers benefits to both the authority and staff, particular in the guarantee of security of supply of service and through the continued application of the experience and expertise which the authority has built up in that supply. However, it is not a route which should be pursued in isolation - only when a detailed hosting proposal is available can the real benefits and disadvantages be evaluated. As a general comment, a saving on existing service costs can be expected from such an arrangement, at no overall detriment to staff terms and conditions. Again, it is not possible to determine the exact benefits and disadvantages of this option until detailed proposals are received from potential host companies. In the meantime, it is important to continue to develop the in-house service.

Management/employee buy-out

A management buy-out (MBO) is the result of the management, or management and staff of the service establishing a company for the provision of the current services to the authority and potentially to other customers (local authority trading restrictions would no longer apply). It offers a number of possible benefits:

- the ability to trade more widely
- existing skill base is preserved
- potential to achieve cost savings from the competitive process
- the ability to invest in the systems and expertise of the service through access to funds

A management buy-out requires a significant degree of personal commitment from those involved, including a financial commitment, and it can only be fully evaluated if management express an interest in pursuing this course. It is essential to the successful implementation of such an option that it receives the support and possibly the financial involvement of the staff. There are a number of issues which would need to be addressed if such an option were to be pursued:

- the authority would have to demonstrate that competition and value for money had been achieved in the award of a contract to the management buy-out company (although any contract which was in place prior to the implementation date for CCT would not be subject to the CCT process itself)

- the financial markets expect a high rate of return from any investment which they make in a management buy-out - this is higher than for normal company lending as the institutions perceive a higher risk associated with this type of funding

- the MBO company would need to rapidly extend its market if it were to avoid a 'sudden death' situation when its original contract with the authority expired. Even if the contract includes a phased retendering arrangement, thereby potentially removing only certain elements of the work from the contract at any time, there is still a significant risk to the security of employment of staff transferred to the company until a wider market base is established

- a number of MBOs from local authorities have collapsed with very negative publicity. The authority would need to take steps to ensure as far as possible that it was not subjecting itself to the same risks of a collapsed supplier

Although there are risks to the MBO option, it has been successful in a number of cases. This has tended to be where the MBO company has had low gearing (ie a low ratio of debt to equity) and has been operating in a poorly developed market, providing the opportunity to expand its business more rapidly.

Tool/technique 5: **Best practice in contract management**

Once a competitive tendering process has been completed and the new arrangements come into force, the client-side must ensure that the contractor or DSO provides the expected standard of service, in accordance with the service specification. The contractor will generally be looking for ways to improve profit margins during the life of the contract. The client-side must ensure that costs are not being managed down at the expense of performance.

Contract monitoring

The effective control and monitoring of a contract requires a number of tasks to be undertaken by the client-side. These tasks are summarised in the checklist shown in Figure 9.7.

Monitoring contractor performance - checklist

- Ensure agreed procedures and mechanisms are in place to control and monitor the contract.

- Confirm the responsibilities of the authorised officer and notify the contractor who it will be.

- Inform customers and users of the service of their responsibilities with respect to monitoring the new contractor.

- Agree with the contractor the content, format and frequency of its performance reports.

- Arrange monthly review meetings between the authorised officer and the contractor's manager.

- Following the start of the contract, undertake regular but random monitoring of the contractor's performance.

- Follow up customer complaints with the contractor.

- Make payments to external contractors only when the work claimed for by the contractor has been assessed and verified.

- Undertake ongoing reviews of the service levels and service standards.

- Where required, amend the contract or service specification by issuing variation orders.

- Keep comprehensive records and proper files detailing the delivery of the service and recording dealings with the contractor.

- Continuously review user satisfaction and the development of the service to prepare for the eventual competitive re-tendering of the service.

Figure 9.7

Contract monitoring can be divided into five aspects:

- performance - the review of contractor's performance in the delivery of services in accordance with the terms of the specification and especially its performance targets

- progress - the review of the timely delivery of services

- quality - assurance of the quality of work done, through the thorough application of the processes, standards and criteria set out in the contractor's quality plan

- propriety - scrutiny to ensure proper observance of the systems and processes, proper custody and care of equipment, proper use of

Responsibilities of an authorised officer

- Liaising with customers and users of the service and acting as the point of contact with the contractor

- Meeting regularly with the contractor's manager to review the provision of services

- Ensuring that payments claimed by the contractor accurately reflect the services provided

- Certifying payments to be made to the contractor

- Checking that service standards are maintained and that the operation is effective

- Monitoring customer satisfaction and giving feedback to the contractor

- Making sure that all necessary working arrangements are satisfactory

- Co-ordinating the collection and reporting of management information

- Managing the finance and administration of the contract

- Assessing of budgets

- Agreeing variations in the contract with the contractor

- Assessing the services and the value for money obtained with a view to re-tendering when the contract period expires

Figure 9.8

accommodation and facilities, and proper qualification, experience and training of staff

- financial - scrutiny of financial information, particularly the predicted and actual spend and commitment to future expenditure

Irrespective of the size of the contract, or whether it has been awarded externally or to an in-house contractor, the client-side must be organised effectively to manage the contract. This will normally require the appointment of a client manager who, for the purposes of the contract, will be known as the authorised officer. A summary of typical responsibilities is given in Figure 9.8. If there are a number of related contracts and their value is large, the establishment of a discrete management unit may be necessary.

The relationship with the contractor needs to be firm but fair. It is important that inspection does not become adversarial and begin to cause conflict. No contractor can provide a satisfactory service unless their objectives, performance targets and responsibilities are clear and they receive co-operation from the organisation for which they operate. Before the contract starts all customers and users of the service should be told what to expect from the contractor, what their role is in the monitoring process and what facilities and services the contractor will need.

Contractors should be required to provide regular performance reports covering such items as work volumes, achievement compared to the performance measures set out in the specification, complaints received from users and actions taken to rectify problems and progress in implementing any agreed changes, improvements or variations to the service. Authorised officers should keep their own records of performance and complaints.

The frequency and number of review meetings will vary according to the size and complexity of the contracted service. Normally a monthly meeting between the contractor's manager and the authorised officer will suffice, although shorter periods may be needed if problems occur. In addition, a performance review meeting attended by a more senior representative of the contractor should be held every 4-6months to discuss progress, problems and any necessary amendments to the contract. Where a major contract is involved, day-to-day contact between the authorised officer, or a representative, and the contractor's staff may be necessary.

Variation orders can in themselves represent a significant source of business for a contractor. They may cover the following aspects:

- additions or omissions to the contract
- changes in methods or standards
- changes in specification clauses

A variation order commits the client to varying the terms of the conditions of contract or the specification. In most cases, issuing a variation order will mean that payments to the contractor will be revised. The revision to the price basis for the services the contractor is performing is the most important element of the variation procedure. Authorised officers should be set a limit on the value of variation orders that they may issue. Authorisation limits should be set for single orders and for the cumulative value over the year. Variation orders should always be issued in line with the conditions of contract and must be authorised and signed by the authorised officer.

Shortfalls in performance

Where the contractor fails to meet his contractual requirements, there will be a continuum of possible remedies. These will range from a minor infringement of requirements which is obviously a one-off with remedial action immediately promised, through to consistent, and persistent, large-scale infringements of the contract terms, possibly affecting the viability of the business as a whole. In the former case, a formal recorded warning would probably suffice, although the client would need to take particular care with the monitoring procedures over the next few weeks and months in an effort to avoid any repetition, or at least to pick up any early warning signs of recurrent problems.

In the latter case, it would clearly depend upon how the scale and level of infringements had progressed, and how the future relationships with the contractor were viewed. The invocation of penalty clauses might have the desired effect, but in the last resort it may be necessary to set in train legal action leading to termination of the contract, with financial recompense.

The end of the contract

The competitive tendering process relies for its effectiveness upon continuous exposure to competition. Towards the end of the first specified contract, the entire process starts again. Having been through 'the mill' once, certain parts of the process may be less time and resource consuming, but the whole range of activities essential to good competitive tendering still have to be undertaken. Care needs to be exercised to show that the specific needs of service users, which may have changed, continue to be catered for.

10

PERFORMANCE MANAGEMENT AND IMPROVEMENT

Introduction

The UK's economic and political environment suggests that local authorities will continue for the long-term to face considerable resource pressures and constraints. At the same time the Government and the general public will expect to see continued improvements to service standards and customer/client relationships. To deliver these improvements local authorities must clearly define their objectives and priorities and determine the most cost effective means of achieving them. This involves a regular and thorough review and reassessment of service needs, priorities and methods of delivery.

The traditional response to changing expectations and resource constraints is to make marginal variations (reductions and increases) to current service levels. This incremental method of budgeting and resource allocation has a number of disadvantages, namely:

- it involves only a limited review of existing activities with a focus on service variations at the margins

- there is insufficient focus on productivity and methods

- the opportunity for introducing new initiatives is severely constrained

- it often leads to arbitrary cuts to meet financial targets

- it is often viewed with suspicion by managers who fear that they will be expected to deliver the same level of service with fewer resources but with little guidance on how this can be achieved

For newly created authorities the process has another significant disadvantage, that is, it allocates (the majority of) resources according to historic patterns of service provision rather than the service objectives and priorities of the new authority. While this may be inevitable during the period of initial merger it will not lead to the transformation of authorities as envisaged in this book. New authorities must, therefore, learn to use methods of resource allocation and performance improvement which will assist them to deliver their key long-term objectives and priorities efficiently and effectively.

A wide range of methodologies have been developed to assist organisations in the areas of cost reduction, resource allocation and performance improvement. The issue for senior managers and councillors, however, is to decide which methodology is best suited to meet their authority's specific needs.

What follows aims to provide assistance in this area by giving a brief introduction to some of the most well-known methodologies for performance management and improvement and discusses the contribution that they can make to the transformation of local authorities.

The four tools and techniques covered in this section will assist authorities in developing long-term efficiency objectives. In particular these tools seek to combine the review of policy objectives with a fundamental examination of resource allocation and future approaches to budgeting. The techniques covered, and an indication of when they are appropriate, are outlined in the table below:

Table 10.1 Performance management and improvement

Tools/techniques	Taking stock	Merging and building confidence	Transformation/ achieving change
1 Performance management	Identify key performance values	Assess the impact of factors affecting performance	Implement required changes
2 Business process re-engineering	Review structures systems and procedures. Identify cost savings.	Develop set of re-engineering priorities	Implementation
3 Priority based budgeting	Review of resource allocation	Re-allocation of resources to priorities	Continuous review of efficiency and cost effectiveness
4 Activity based costing	Identification of non 'value added' activities and under utilised resources	Benchmarking and cost reduction exercises	Implement Continuous ABM systems

Tool/technique 1: **Performance management**

In responding to the challenges facing local government, performance management helps local authorities to achieve the best possible results from their staff and service suppliers.

For the organisation, performance management should operate at a number of different levels. At a corporate level performance management is concerned with ensuring that the main factors affecting individual performance such as

- clearly stating goals and objectives

- pay and grading

- staff appraisal and development

- skills training and

- human resource planning

are complementary.

For the individual, performance management involves a process of regular review of performance and potential, and based on these, agreeing plans for future development. It also includes reviewing the effectiveness of rewards including pay, conditions, recognition and other key factors which can assist in staff motivation. Individually, these concepts have been embraced by many local authorities over a number of years. Effective performance management requires, however, that a systematic and integrated approach is taken with respect to all key factors affecting performance that will result in the achievement of organisation objectives.

If effectively implemented, performance management has the potential to improve organisational performance by encouraging:

- greater flexibility in the use of staff

- better management and control of resources (*see* Tools/techniques 3 and 4 below on Priority Based Budgeting and Activity Based Costing and Management)

- improved recruitment and retention performance

- a more results orientated approach and

- positive motivation and high morale.

These are not ends in themselves, senior managers will be concerned to see that they contribute to improvements in direct service delivery to the customer.

Implementing performance management

Performance management embraces all of the techniques described above. Many authorities may find the task of implementing performance management in its entirety too demanding. The diagnostic approach described below will assist authorities to

- assess their current activities at a suitably aggregated level and identify areas of strength or weakness

- focus on those areas which offer the most immediate opportunities for rapid improvement

- produce outline implementation plans and establish resource requirements

This approach allows authorities to build on the strengths they have and to make progress at a rate compatible with their requirements.

The approach encompasses three key stages:

Stage 1		Stage 2		Stage 3
Identify key performance values and skills requirements	→	Assess the impact of factors affecting performance	→	Define areas requiring change and prepare implementation plans

Figure 10.1 Diagnostic approach to performance management

Each of these is considered below:

Stage 1: identify key performance values and skills requirements

In order to analyse key performance values and skill requirements the first step is to define clearly what the organisation wishes to achieve and how. This strategic framework may already have been formulated as part of the business planning process (*see* Part II, Chapter 13, Tool/technique 2) and will cover:

- the overall aims of the organisation

- the main objectives and critical success factors

- the purpose and aims of particular departments or units

- the purpose of specific jobs and the targets and measures which job holders are expected to achieve

The links between this framework and the overall management process are summarised in Figure 10.2. With this framework in place it is possible to develop a thorough understanding of the performance and skill requirements needed for each individual in the organisation. Two of the techniques described in Chapter 14, (Leadership Coaching and Change Management Skills Training) will assist in

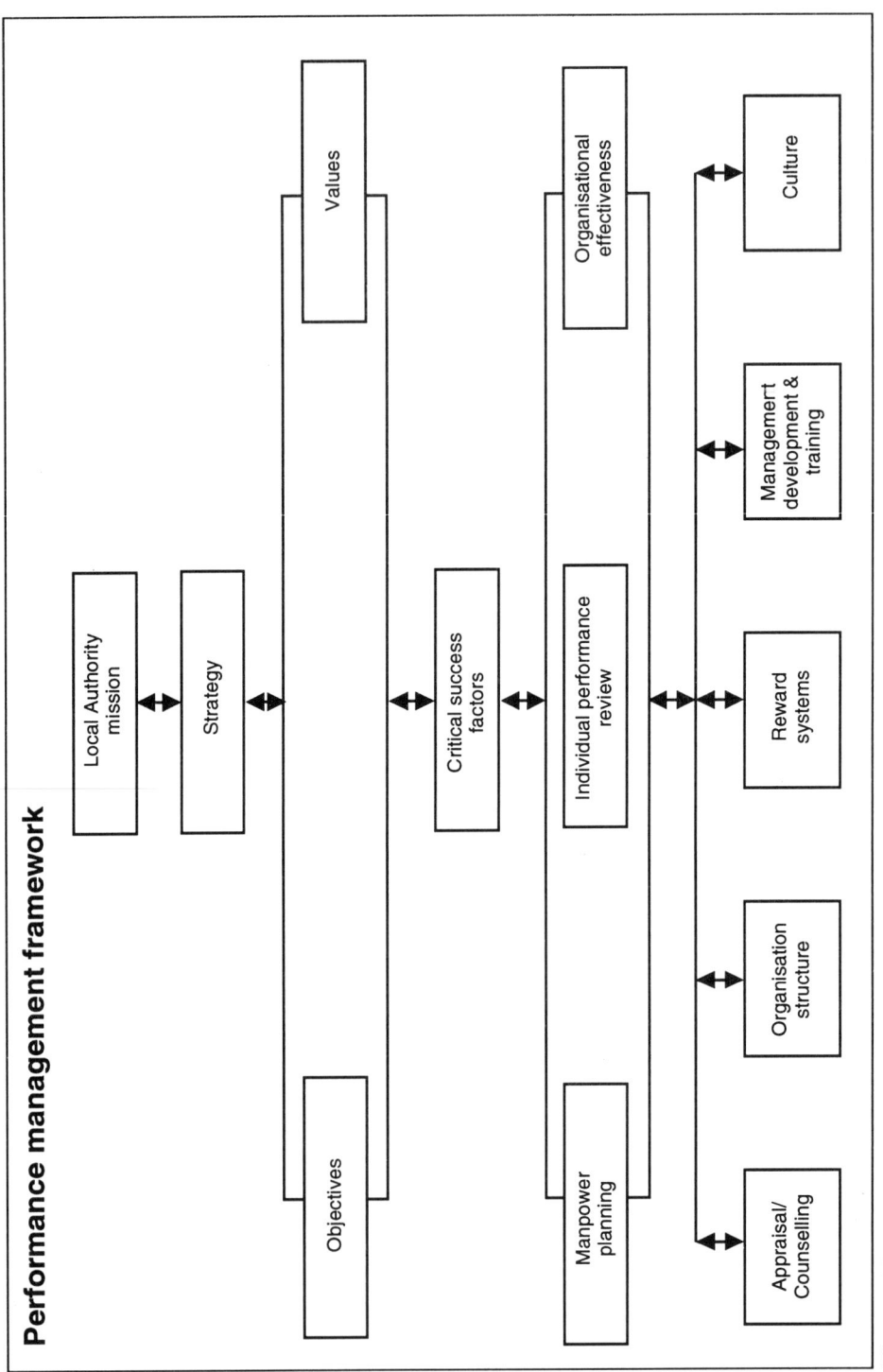

Figure 10.2

this process. It is also important that the overall aims and objectives that are identified within the framework are incorporated into contracts with external suppliers, internal service level agreements (SLAs) and systems of individual performance review.

Stage 2: assessing the impact of key performance factors

Having identified the key performance values and skills requirements for staff the next stage involves identifying the main factors which affect performance and the impact that each of them has. This is the key to the performance management approach.

A wide range of factors may affect individual performance but five factors are likely to be of particular importance. These are outlined below:

- **Staff management and appraisal**   In assessing the present position of the authority, managers will need to consider the effectiveness of staff appraisal arrangements and their relevance to the authority's culture. It will be important to identify the scope for establishing quantifiable targets in line with service or 'business' objectives against which performance can be appraised. It should be ensured that appraisal arrangements are 'action-based' for example, providing useful feedback to staff and highlighting future development and training needs. The effectiveness with which managers review performance on a day-to-day basis should also be explored.

- **Organisation/structure**   In reviewing the impact of organisation and structure on performance it will be important to consider how effectively the authority's structure has adjusted to internal and external changes, and provision for reviewing organisational structure as part of the overall planning process. Clear definition of reporting lines, accountabilities and responsibilities will also be a key determinant of effective performance management.

- **Reward System**   This is an area of increasing interest to local government. The reward system includes salaries, benefits in kind, career development and other intangible rewards such as recognition. The main issues to be considered are: whether the authority is experiencing problems which might indicate an inadequate reward system (eg poor control over pay costs, grading anomalies and recruitment/retention difficulties); and if appropriate incentives are not in place, what scope is there for introducing new arrangements?

- **Management Development and Training**   Effective performance management depends on a clearly defined management development process based on the overall objectives of the authority. Top managers should ensure that a systematic approach to management development is in place that identifies and responds to the need for skills training; and actively manages the careers of potential high performers.

157

- **Culture**   Culture can provide a powerful catalyst for achieving organisational objectives and it can help to focus efforts on critical success factors such as customer service and cost consciousness. The right culture can enhance teamwork and improve communication, decision making and employees pride in their work. Achieving cultural change is examined more fully in Chapter 12, however in this context it is important to focus on whether the existing culture (or cultures in authorities which have merged) fit the organisational values which the authority wishes to pursue.

Stage 3: identifying priorities for change and drawing up implementation plans

Based on the analysis above, the third and final stage of our approach identifies those areas where performance improvements could be most beneficial and considers how best to achieve them. Depending on the factors identified this could involve a range of potential actions including:

- reviewing reward systems

- revising training and development programmes

- instituting cultural change

- re-orientating management structures, processes and systems

- introducing new appraisal or job evaluation schemes

The underlying purpose throughout should be to ensure that the key factors affecting individual performance underpin the key performance values and thereby contribute towards meeting overall organisational objectives.

Tool/technique 2: Business process re-engineering

Business process re-engineering (BPR) is currently attracting considerable attention in both the private and public sectors. It has delivered significant benefits to those organisations which have used it and it may well become the most important business concept of the 1990s.

So what is BPR? In summary BPR is a methodology for 'taking apart' the existing organisation structure, systems and procedures, removing those elements which do not help the organisation to meet its objectives and putting back what is left into an efficient and customer focused whole. It is also a means of increasing an organisation's capacity to change and of creating a culture which reinforces the introduction of improvements.

The transformation of an organisation through BPR cannot be achieved by merely tinkering with what is already in place. That is why the term 're-engineering' is used to describe how organisations should achieve the process of transformation. To the extent that elements of processes are removed through BPR this leads directly to cost savings. Further savings and efficiency improvements also come from having an organisation through which information and actions flow more easily.

Unfortunately, re-engineering an organisation is easier said than done. Success is not guaranteed. As with any other approach to business improvement, an ad hoc and ill thought out approach will at best achieve modest levels of success. At worst, failure, disruption, expense and loss of employees' confidence may result.

The incentive to introduce a well structured and properly resourced programme of BPR comes from the potential for significant and radical performance improvement. Experience has shown that those organisations that 'get it right' produce substantial improvements in unit costs, customer satisfaction levels and service processing times.

So what does it take to be successful in this field? Two overriding factors stand out. Firstly, by focusing on just a few aspects in a business re-engineering programme it is possible to reduce significantly the risk of failure. Identifying how many elements of the organisation can be tackled, and which precise ones and in which order, is critical to success.

Secondly, it is vital for the organisation to focus on re-engineering processes rather than individual functions or organisational structures. This is because it is the business processes which actually deliver services to customers. Furthermore, as processes are rarely confined to a single department, looking only at the operation of an aspect of a process will lose sight of the greater whole.

The greatest benefit is also achieved by focusing efforts on those processes which are most valued by the organisation's customers e.g. the processing of housing benefit claims, the collection of council tax, the provision of advice and services direct to members of the public. The use of BPR for internal functions may achieve cost savings but it is unlikely to have a direct influence on how an organisation is perceived by its external customers and clients.

In order to develop a set of re-engineering priorities, work is required to identify the key concerns, priorities and expectations of the local authority's customers and clients. This can be achieved using focus groups, surveys and structured workshops. It is also important to identify potential 'breakpoints', those areas where change could lead to significant improvement in customer-client perceptions of the organisation.

A key element of BPR is benchmarking performance against other organisations providing the same or a similar service (*see* Chapter 9). This can assist in identifying areas where significant improvements could be made and in setting standards and targets.

159

At several stages throughout a re-engineering programme a detailed and rigorous analysis of the business's processes is necessary. At these points, process mapping and simulation is commonly used to describe what is happening at present and to explore alternative ways of achieving the organisation's objective. There is a danger here that the indiscriminate use of techniques will lead to a state of 'analysis paralysis'. This may occur through a lack of understanding of the process or if the corporate culture is more comfortable spending money on analysis than the creation of new and better processes.

Mapping existing processes should, therefore, be allowed to proceed no further than is immediately necessary. Businesses need to remind themselves of the reasons for mapping a process which may be:

- to set down on paper the current way of doing things in order to help the formation of a vision for a new process

- to provide a detailed performance baseline against which improvements can be measured

- to assist in identifying opportunities for short-term improvements

- to demonstrate (if the mapping process produces a 'spaghetti-like' diagram) the urgent need for improvement

The tools and techniques used to analyse a business process depend upon the characteristics of the process. For example the tools used to analyse a repetitive process involving physical inventory include approaches such as 'routing by walking about' and statistical quality control. In situations where process characteristics include either high speed, high levels of complexity, high transaction volumes, or high cost, dynamic simulation may be appropriate.

The achievement of breakpoints is an essential element of BPR. However, many managers are concerned that there will be no breakpoints to be found, or that if a 'breakpoint' is too readily identified, it may not really be one. Such concern is understandable; however, experience suggests that breakpoints will not be discovered unless an organisation deliberately sets out to find them through the identification and evaluation of new and innovative ways of doing things. In practice breakpoints may emerge in a number of ways: as the result of a rigorous analysis of current processes, from a benchmarking exercise or from listening closely to the views of customers and clients.

So, will BPR be of value to the new unitary authorities? If a local authority seeks solely to merge the arrangements operating in predecessor authorities with minimal change to culture or working practices the answer will be no. If a local authority is committed to the implementation of a new vision the answer may well be yes. A question which senior managers and councillors should ask themselves is: How well does the authority meet the expectations of customers/council tax payers for efficiency, effectiveness and customer care? If there is room for substantial improvement, BPR may provide the means of delivering the change required.

Tool/technique 3: **Priority based budgeting**

Priority based budgeting (PBB) is a method for performance improvement which is well proven in the public and private sector. Designed to overcome the weaknesses of traditional incremental budgeting it is an effective method for undertaking a radical review of resource allocation. Although less intensive than BPR, it can deliver wide-ranging improvements including:

- the re-allocation of resources in line with service objectives and priorities

- achievable cost reductions

- improvements to efficiency and cost effectiveness

- ownership of, and commitment to, budget changes by service managers

PBB is structured planning process carried out by service managers, with support and direction from senior managers and councillors typically through a steering group. The process involves managers in:

- identifying service objectives

- analysing their activities, outputs and resources

- identifying improvements in working methods

- identifying and assessing the impact and benefits of different service levels starting from a 'zero' base

PBB may be applied to both direct and support services. A typical exercise would involve the review of 10 - 15 related budget subjects. If the review area was defined as leisure services, for example, the individual budget subjects could include leisure centre provision, the letting of public halls and the provision of play schemes. A number of PBB exercises can be carried out at the same time and the results can be brought together to facilitate the reallocation of resources between service areas.

The process of PBB is similar to zero base budgeting in that for each budget subject a number of service levels are identified which may be categorised as:

- **minimum service** - service level considered essential to meet statutory requirements

- **intermediate service** - an improvement on the minimum but less than that currently provided

- **current service** - a service level which is equivalent to the current level of service

- **enhanced service** - an improvement on the current service

Each service level should take into account improvements in working methods identified as part of the process. In practice more than one intermediate level or more than one enhanced level may be identified.

The steering group plays a key role in the process by:

- setting planning guidelines and performance targets

- reviewing and challenging managers' proposals

- determining priorities for, and the funding of, discretionary services

PBB could play an important role in assisting new authorities to allocate resources according to new objectives and priorities. It would also improve communication and understanding between councillors, senior managers and service managers by providing a rational framework for discussion and decision making. In particular, councillors would gain a better understanding of the range of the services provided by the authority and their resource implications, senior managers would gain a better understanding of political priorities and service managers would have the opportunity to present service options directly to members and senior officers.

Priority based budgeting is resource intensive, particularly when first introduced. Many local authorities have, therefore, phased its introduction over a period of time so that learning from an initial exercise can be passed on within the organisation. A phased approach can also assist a local authority in managing the implementation of change. The case study overleaf (Figure 10.3) provides an example of how PBB has been used in practice by a regional council.

Three major spending departments were taken through the PBB process as part of the authority's response to the threat of capping. As a result:

- numerous possible method improvements were identified giving options for cost reduction without impact on service levels

- a wide range of possible service levels were established for all main service areas enabling priorities to be reassessed

- members were given the opportunity to make service priority and resource allocation decisions together in a way they found both challenging and rewarding

- officers were provided with an additional mechanism for quantifying the costs of policy initiatives

- the process was extended to all other departments and is now being built into the regular budgeting cycle.

The officer responsible for managing the process said at the end 'The authority will never be the same again.'

Figure 10.3 A regional council: case study

Tool/technique 4: **Activity based costing/management**

The key to success for all organisations whether they are in the private or public sector is to continue to do the 'right things' better. This means managing carefully the things that the organisation does, the activities and processes, and improving them continuously. There are many different approaches to improvement, but many of them involve some degree of activity based costing.

Activity Based Costing (ABC) is a technique through which resources (costs) are related to outputs and hence, through processes, to the products and services provided to customers/clients. ABC enables a better understanding of costs, the generation of costs and how costs might be reduced.

If ABC is done well, it can underpin a whole series of initiatives. For example, it can assist in:

- the identification of non value-added activities and under-utilised resources

- benchmarking and cost reduction exercises
- BPR and PBB
- the introduction of continuous Activity Based Management (ABM) systems

ABM is the continuous management of an organisation through systems which focus on activity costs, setting improvement targets, work planning and the avoidance of costly performance variations. It ensures that organisations do the right things better, and so complements other improvement approaches and shares with them the same vision of excellence.

The principles of excellence upon which ABM is based are:

- to manage activities not resources
- to streamline activities within processes
- to eliminate wasteful activities
- to improve activities continuously
- to do activities right consistently
- to adjust capacity to activity workload

The introduction of service level agreements, internal trading accounts and CCT have over the last few years greatly improved activity and cost management within local authorities. Many elements of activity based costing have already been introduced although not usually as part of a comprehensive technique or approach such as ABM. As a result, the quality and completeness of data can be variable, and managers and staff may lack a full understanding of how activity analysis or ABM can assist in improving performance or reducing costs.

Local authorities in the 1990s and beyond will increasingly require information systems which will enable them to manage activities, outputs and costs on a continuous basis. Local authority client functions will need to know the impact on costs of changes to service levels. They will also want to ensure that they are getting value for money. Local authority provider functions will need a thorough understanding of their cost structures and the action required to achieve financial targets.

ABM is not a standardised approach but needs to be tailored to specific organisational requirements. Depending on where an organisation is now, it can assist in calculating and understanding cost structures, reducing costs and improving performance. It is a particularly relevant concept when designing new management information systems. New local authorities may, therefore, benefit from considering whether and how ABM could assist them to manage their costs and services more effectively.

Conclusion

This chapter provides a brief introduction to some of the most well-known methodologies for performance management and performance improvement. All of these methodologies could make a major contribution towards the transformation of how local authorities operate and the services they provide. BPR, PBB and ABM all relate directly to resource allocation and can lead to cost reduction if required. A comparison of the main features of these methodologies is given in Figure 10.4.

All these methodologies will only deliver a lasting change in an organisation if they also change the behaviour and attitudes of staff. This requires the careful integration of both the technological and behavioural aspects of the changes that are made. For senior managers it is the process of managing these changes which will reduce the risk of failure and provide the opportunity to make substantial improvements.

The corporate culture of an organisation may act as both a barrier to change and a lever for positive improvement. Senior managers should therefore seek to make the culture and the process mutually reinforcing. For some local authorities this will mean moving people away from a technical to a customer focus. For others it may mean replacing a command and control culture with one of empowerment and trust in which the sharing of knowledge is the norm.

One way of building commitment to any programme of change is to show early success. This is achieved through the use of pilot programmes or the identification of 'quick-wins'. Both of these enable performance improvements to be demonstrated in a relatively short space of time and so build up credibility and commitment.

Finally, the success of any tool of performance improvement will depend on having the commitment of senior managers and councillors who will champion the change process, act as sustaining sponsors to staff, ensure that the necessary resources are assigned to the programme, remove any barriers to progress that arise, ensure that the programme is fully integrated with other initiatives and play a key role in monitoring progress and results. This will be a key role for senior managers and councillors in the late 1990s and beyond.

Comparison of methodologies for performance improvement

	BPR	PBB	ABM
Vision	Deliver key objectives and priorities efficiently and effectively		
Coverage	One or more core business processes	Overhead and service functions	Total, comprehensive coverage of business
Differentiating objectives	Radical step change in performance	Resources allocated according to priorities Performance improvement	Management of continuous improvement
Differentiating features	One-off review	One-off or phased review	On-going system
	Driven by project team under senior sponsor	Undertaken by management with direction and support from project team	Undertaken by management with direction and support from project team
	Customer focus and external benchmarking	Planning guidelines based on strategic objectives	Activity and process analysis and costing
	Innovative thinking driven by Break Point targets	Activity, methods and service level analysis	Improvement driven by externally based targets
	Systematic management of change	Challenge, review and prioritisation process	Planning, budgeting and reporting system
Tool box	Common resource management techniques, for example activity analysis, process mapping, cost driver analysis, benchmarking, target costing		

Figure 10.4

11

INFORMATION STRATEGY AND MANAGEMENT

Introduction

This section outlines the main stages in formulating strategies for information. It also considers the implications of compulsory competitive tendering (CCT) for the future provision of Information Technology (IT) services.

The table below shows the stages in developing and managing information strategies across the three main stages of the change programme.

Table 11.1 Information strategy and management

Tools/techniques	Taking stock	Merging and building confidence	Transformation/ achieving change
Information strategy and management	Review of provision	Specifying requirements/ agreement of strategies	
		Procuring of <--------	Systems -------->
			Managing and review of supply via contracts and agreements

Information strategy and management

Information is a key resource for both new and existing local authorities because it supports the achievement of goals and objectives. It is a vital factor in the provision of services and provides the basis on which performance can be monitored. The management of information is, therefore, critical to success.

Successful information management requires the establishment and operation of strategies for information, information systems and information technology (IT). These three strategies are part of a hierarchy which ensures that information is managed in a way which contributes to the achievement of the authority's goals and objectives. The hierarchy comprises:

- corporate and departmental (or functional) objectives which set out where the authority is going, its priorities and what it plans to achieve over the strategic period

- corporate and departmental (or functional) plans setting out how it proposes to achieve those objectives and how it will monitor performance against those targets

- the information strategy which defines the information needed to support the corporate and departmental plans and objectives

- the information systems strategy setting out the systems needed to provide the defined information

- the information technology strategy defining the technologies which will be adopted to support the information systems

Information strategies depend crucially on the clear definition of where the authority/department is going, how it proposes to get there and how it will measure progress along the way. In preparing an information strategy, an authority needs to decide:

- what information is needed

- who uses it

- where it will come from

- how its integrity will be maintained

Information is used for operational and management processes. Experience of reviewing numerous local authorities has shown that operational data from which information can be derived are, for the most part, comprehensive and up to date. The operational needs enforce disciplines which ensure that this is the case. However, the vital management information needed to monitor performance and allow the authority to manage strategically is, in the great majority of authorities, weak and inadequate. Authorities can be said to have a lot of data but not much information.

The key to providing quality management information (MI) is first to determine what MI is needed and by whom. Unless this is done, MI will always be produced on an ad hoc basis using databases and systems which do not acknowledge the MI needs.

Preparation of performance indicators will require the combination of data from more than one operational database, eg activity and financial data to provide a cost per activity. This demands the ability to match across systems and introduces a requirement for standard references.

It is critical to define how information flows around the authority and between the authority and other bodies. Data integrity demands that, although data may be held more than once, it should not be entered more than once. If it is, then it is not possible to know which of the two or more databases for, say, students or properties, is the accurate one. Without a strategy, this situation can easily arise particularly where the emphasis will be on pragmatic business solutions to enable service providers to compete.

Knowing where the data needed to provide management information, are held, is critical to good information management. An information audit should indicate who maintains what data, in what form, and how they are transferred. In most authorities, this is likely to indicate an array of systems, data references, technologies, levels of accuracy and duplication. In a new local authority made up, say, of part of a former county and two or more former districts, the problems will be increased.

The integrity of management information depends on the integrity of the data which are used to provide it. A basic principle of MI is that it should be derived from operational data wherever possible. Where this is not possible, one has to question the value of the resultant MI. Experience of data which are held purely for management purposes is that there is insufficient incentive, on a day-to-day basis, to keep it up to date and ensure its accuracy.

New local authorities will inherit systems from their predecessors. Decisions will be required on the systems to be adopted for each service, but, in many cases, the system chosen will be one being used by one of the former authorities. There is enormous potential for the current situation on management information, which is less than satisfactory, to become considerably worse. However, the wholesale replacement of systems is not practical. The development of a pragmatic but effective strategy to integrate information systems using a variety of technologies and incompatible definitions of data will be high on the list of priorities for new authorities.

This strategy should be driven by agreed and clearly defined information needs and will often be based on providing the means to combine and manipulate data through 'add on' management information systems. Priorities will need to be determined which take on board the implications of white-collar and housing management compulsory competitive tendering within two years of the creation of the authority. This is difficult in the metropolitan authorities which exist already. The difficulties facing authorities which are yet to be created are considerably increased.

Compulsory Competitive Tendering

As outlined in Chapter 9, the fact that new authorities face compulsory competitive tendering (CCT) (including tendering of computer services) within two years of their inauguration means that it is imperative to plan for CCT at the earliest possible stage. This means determining suitable structures and management processes for the competitive environment.

In terms of structure, it is now accepted that it is necessary to separate client functions from those of the contractor. Client responsibilities exist in the centre in respect of corporate needs and in service departments for their needs. In overall terms, the client is responsible for:

- deciding on what to buy to support the achievement of business objectives (i.e. strategy)
- staying abreast of technology so that opportunities offered by IT can be taken where appropriate
- specifying requirements for systems
- procuring those systems
- managing supply via contracts and agreements

There is a relationship between central and departmental clients where the central client provides support and expertise to the department or provides the complete client function where the department wishes it. The central client function will often also provide business analysis services to departments to assist them in identifying how IT can be optimised in support of their business.

Where the central client is providing services to a department, i.e. acting as an agent, it is important that these services are provided on a charge-out basis rather than being treated as an overhead. This will be in the spirit of the CCT environment and will help to discourage the growth of large client functions unconstrained by the need to demonstrate cost effectiveness.

The success of the central IT client function is critical to new local authorities' ability to secure the infrastructure support they need. However, the track record to date of existing authorities is poor. This can be attributed to a lack of interest from suitably qualified people and the head of IT client functions typically not being appointed at a sufficiently senior level. In many cases, this has resulted in poor appointments and an inability to gain the respect of senior management. Without this, the central client function cannot be effective.

We turn below to the preparation for the CCT of IT services. It should be borne in mind however that new authorities arising from reorganisation may choose not to inherit or replace systems but instead decide to manage IT services facilities from the start. It will still be necessary for the client-side to specify services and set up contract arrangements although in this case the specification would require issue and agreement before vesting day.

Turning to the IT contractor functions, which will virtually all be subject to CCT, there are two key issues:

- viability to survive in a CCT environment
- quality of services provided to the authority

Viability is determined by the current level of cost effectiveness and particularly the ability to adjust resources to match demand. In new authorities, cost effectiveness will be significantly affected by the need to bring together the systems from the constituent authorities.

IT contractors need to operate commercially to have a chance of survival. Briefly, this means:

- providing services under agreements which define the service, performance, responsibilities and cost
- being allowed to set prices to achieve the required return on investment
- using sound techniques for estimating costs and managing operational services and projects
- being capable of adjusting costs and resources to match business won
- deciding when to bid for services and when not to

Resource management will be especially difficult for new authorities because of:

- the danger of inheriting equipment on which there are large leases outstanding
- the need to provide initial machine capacity which will exceed that needed in the future
- the significant initial development workload which will decline dramatically after the transitional period. There will be a temptation to write off the initial investment over too long a period, employ staff on permanent contracts and not to recognise what will happen to demand over the first five years

This underlines the need for a clear strategy which is matched to business needs and based on sound projections of the possible effects of white-collar CCT. This is critical to the IT contractor, who needs to know what is likely to happen to the customer base. It is also critical when preparing specifications for CCT purposes in the case of IT and when negotiating contracts for supply of IT services.

All of this is set against a background of complexity during the early months of the new authority. Experience from the abolition of the metropolitan counties in 1986 was that it took 18 months to 2 years to disaggregate the county systems and close down the installations. In many new unitary authorities, there will be a need to do this as well as to aggregate and standardise district systems. New authorities thus face an enormous task with a pre-set timescale for CCT.

One of the difficulties to be overcome will be maintenance of former authority IT services during the transition. Faced with working in an installation which is closing, staff may well vote with their feet. This problem was dealt with in a variety of ways in 1986, some of which choices are not available today. For example, Birmingham City took over the large West Midlands installation and offered all staff a permanent job thereby ensuring a smooth transition and an early close down within 18 months. Only facilities management (FM) companies are likely to be in a position of offer such a facility today and this is a strong pointer to what is likely to happen.

IT has been acknowledged as a key issue for new authorities. Service provision is becoming increasingly dependent on IT which underlines the need for a smooth transition and appropriate strategies for the future. Add to this the demands of CCT and the importance of starting the planning process as soon as possible is clear.

12

CHANGE MANAGEMENT

Introduction

This chapter outlines techniques that will assist in the identification of specific problems that may limit the effectiveness of the implementation of the change programme. In particular, it focuses on some of the human factors which must be considered if change is to be achieved.

Table 12.1 below shows the techniques covered and provides an indication of the stage in the change process where they might be appropriate.

Table 12.1 Change management

Tools/techniques	Taking stock	Merging and building confidence	Transformation/ achieving change
1 Sponsor evaluation	Determine level of sponsor commitment to change/early warning of risks	Strengthen sponsorship if commitment reducing	Evaluate sponsor commitment to further change
2 Culture assessment	Identify required changes in culture	Review that cultural changes are taking place	Compression of culture at beginning and end of the process
3 Change Project description		Defining the scope of change	Assessing change objectives have been achieved
4 Implementation problems assessment	Identification of factors which have assisted/thwarted past change initiatives	Identify and respond to 'barriers' developing during implementation	Identify negative 'after effects' of change

Tool/technique 1: **Sponsor evaluation**

Definition

For major change to be successfully implemented, the change sponsors - the senior members of management who must authorise the change - must demonstrate strong, decisive commitment to the change programme. They may be heads of departments, elected members or more junior officials in specialist functions. Strong commitment is vital to ensure that the change agents are effective and supported in their work.

The sponsor evaluation tool is designed to assess sponsor commitment to the change proposed. If high levels of sponsor commitment are not shown, this will increase the risk of implementation failure.

This tool is applied by change managers using a series of analytical tests to assess the degree of sponsor commitment against a set of critical success criteria - for example assessing whether sponsors are willing to make sacrifices to ensure the success of the change programme. The overall analysis, the sponsor factor, can then be benchmarked against comparable scores for other organisations, particularly those which have implemented major change successfully.

When to apply it

This tool should ideally be applied at an early stage, the seeds of failure may be sown almost before the change programme has really begun because insufficient attention has been paid to bringing the change programme sponsors in line fully behind the programme. But it can also have other uses. It should be used:

- while change is being considered or during initial planning

- before the change programme is formally announced to staff in the authority

- at any time after the announcement has been made, where it is felt necessary to review the level of commitment, there may be some loss of enthusiasm and further effort is needed

- after the change programme is completed - has it really lived up to sponsor expectations and is there still support for further change in the future?

How it will help

This is likely to be most helpful in:

- providing early warning for potential commitment problems and possible implementation failure - there may be unexpected sources of resistance where early warning can help to influence the focus of resources at the planning stage

174

- determining the level of sponsor commitment towards the change - is everyone in the senior team fully signed up or is there the risk that some staff will be more lukewarm when the going gets tough?

- analysing possible fluctuations in commitment during the implementation process - assessing whether wavering is taking place, and the degree of action required to pull the programme back on course

- identifying sponsor commitment generated after implementation - nothing breeds success like success, but will this make it easier or harder for the next change programme?

How it can be used successfully

Where the analysis shows a low risk, then there is a major opportunity to undertake and successfully implement a major change programme, although sponsor commitment should never be taken for granted and there may still be problem areas that will need continued vigilance.

Where there is a moderate risk level shown, this may not imply failure, but implementation is likely to be more complicated. This may highlight the need to spend more time convincing sponsors that change involves them and to commit more resources to sponsor education and support.

High risk levels rarely succeed in achieving full implementation. With this result, change agents must undertake one of three main options:

- strengthen sponsorship - use the application of the tool to demonstrate the importance of commitment

- identify alternative sponsorship - are there any other powerful supporters who can legitimise the change?

- prepare to fail - ideally by not proceeding at all, but with political pressures for 'change without making changes', contingency plans should be made to deal with the problems that will arise when the change programme fails to meet expectations

Tool/technique 2: **Culture assessment**

Definition

Culture assessment is designed to assess the consistency between the existing culture and the culture required to drive the change. It also assesses the overall strength of the existing culture.

The strength of a culture reflects the degree of day-to-day influence it exerts over its staff and its operations. Assessment of it is an important part of analysing the basis for the change programme.

When to apply

It can be applied at any time in the change programme - ahead of the programme to help in planning, during the programme to assist with review and afterwards to make comparisons with the culture at the outset.

How it will help

This tool is a valuable means of:

- providing early warning of possible inconsistencies between the existing culture and the change proposed

- determining specific inconsistencies between the existing culture and the change

- analysing any inconsistencies that may develop during the implementation process

- identifying the nature of cultural inconsistencies after implementation

How it can be used successfully

The tool measures two main factors. Firstly, it measures the consistency of the culture, where comparisons between the current culture and the requirements to undertake the proposed change are assessed. High consistency indicates favourable conditions for successful implementation are likely to exist, low consistency suggests serious risks exist and must be addressed. Secondly, it assesses the strength of the culture, where a strong culture that is inconsistent with a change programme presents a serious implementation barrier.

A large operational support unit within the Ministry of Defence wanted to effect extensive changes to its organisation and management, reducing unnecessary tiers of management and improving corporate communications and devolving more decision-making from headquarters to frontline managers, with the added benefit of improving efficiency and reducing overheads. The culture assessment tool enabled senior managers to form a better understanding of current problems, to anticipate the level of resistance to organisational change and plan an effective response to it, and to assess the willingness of operational staff to implement a range of structure options. The culture assessment identified a strong culture, inconsistent with a wider programme of change and gave a strong indication of the further work required to develop the beliefs, behaviours and assumptions present in the existing culture if the full benefits of the change were to be gained.

Figure 12.1 Cultural assessment: case study

Tool/technique 3: Change project description

Definition

In preparing for major change it is important for sponsors and change agents to define clearly the nature of the change as well as the scope of the impact it will have on the intended targets - the individuals or groups of staff who must actually change the way they work. In this, the process suggested parallels the description of a project plan outline, contained in Chapter 8.

If the definition of the change programme is not jointly understood by both sponsors and agents before planning the implementation, then confusion, misdirected energy and wasted time and effort can result which could lead to failed implementation.

This tool uses a series of tests to clarify the parameters of the change proposed with the focus on:

- identifying the key components of the change programme
- setting the technical and human objectives
- defining the key constraints

- outlining the sponsor and agent roles and responsibilities to legitimise the change
- helping the targets of change to understand and sign up to the change proposed

When to apply it

This tool forms an important component of the planning process bringing the change programme sponsors and agents together in defining the bounds and scope of the change programme:

- while change is being considered or during initial planning
- before the change programme is formally announced to staff in the authority

It can also be used again and updated if more data come to light during the course of a change programme:

- at any time after the announcement has been made, where it is felt necessary to reinforce the level of joint commitment and agreement as circumstances develop

How it will help

For successful change to occur, sponsors and agents must discuss and agree on the following:

- where the starting point is
- where the change programme is intended to head
- how they are to get where they are going
- how to know when they have got there - how to assess whether the change objectives have been achieved

When these questions go unanswered many organisations engage in inappropriate activities and invariably achieve poor results.

The change project description tool can assist in posing these questions and obtaining appropriate answers. Where the questions are unanswered, then the areas where remedial action is required can be identified.

A large unit within a government department required a programme of change to unravel a confused management structure characterised by a lack of role clarity, overloading of key senior positions leading to slow response times and difficulties in decision making, together with management information systems, financial reporting and administrative arrangements that fell short of requirements.

The change project descriptions laid out the desired and achievable objectives for the changes involved, combined with the phasing of the programme with a timetable and project milestones for implementation. It identified the expectations placed on the senior management team to work together and devise a new organisational strategy, showing areas of concern where managers were insufficiently committed to the change and unclear about their role in managing and communicating the need for change to their staff within a conventional civil service pay and grading structure.

Senior management strategy workshops were identified as a key mechanism for analysing the essential building blocks of the organisation and using these to design and develop the change programme; also helping to achieve full senior level agreement, involvement and commitment to the change proposed.

The project description identified the need for greater teamwork, new ways of working and improved management skills to gain the support and cooperation of all staff in undertaking the change proposed.

Finally, the test of success of the change programme was defined in terms of improved decision making processes, faster response times, higher quality services to customers, changes in workloads and progress towards further devolution of financial and management controls and accountabilities for the unit within the department.

Figure 12.2 Change project description: case study

Tool/technique 4: **Implementation problems assessment**

Definition

The inability to implement change fully is a critical risk area for authorities - a major change programme will fail if the organisation lacks the capacity to translate senior management directives into tangible results.

One of the key factors affecting an authority's ability to implement change is past track record. Implementation problems in the past are likely to be repeated in new change projects though the circumstances of a new authority may help. An assessment of previous implementation experience can help in planning future change programmes, identifying problem areas and providing the basis for ways of dealing with them successfully in the future.

This tool is applied by change managers using a series of analytical tests to analyse implementation problems against a set of critical success criteria, for example assessing the extent to which low expectations of staff have hampered the success of change programmes in the past. The overall analysis, the implementation problems factor, can then be benchmarked against comparable scores for other organisations, particularly those which have implemented major change successfully.

When to apply

This tool should mainly be applied at an early stage - learning from past experience before planning the change programme in detail. It should be used:

- while change is being considered or during initial planning
- before the change programme is formally announced to staff in the authority

But, it can also be used:

- after the announcement has been made - where it is felt necessary to analyse problems that have emerged in the course of the programme
- after the change programme is completed - are there any new problems because of the experience?

How it will help

The tool can help in several different ways:

- providing early warning for potential problems and possible implementation failure areas

- determining the authority's predisposition towards change, assessing the extent to which staff are committed

- analysing any barriers that may arise during the implementation process - will looking back into past problems shed any light on a solution?

- identifying new barriers that may have developed after implementation - if this means going through a pain barrier, will there be any negative after effects?

How it can be used successfully

The tool can help to assess the impact of the legacy of the past: where there are high risk factors, the amount of effort and resource required and the targeting of that effort to deal with the negative effects of that legacy can be determined in advance. Using the data collected can help to build a more precise plan for different projects within the overall twin-track, change programme. The case study below (Figure 12.3) provides an example of how the tool has been used to identify specific implementation problems.

Prioritisation of past problems can direct management attention to the key areas. For example, a large unit within a government department was seeking to change the organisational structure to prepare for possible agency status. The implementation problems assessment tool revealed the priority problems from previous efforts at restructuring, identifying those problems which would require priority attention in changing the organisation:

- Lack of co-operation between departmental heads

- Absence of an effective senior level committee structure

- Inward looking departmental focus with insufficient attention to the overall goals and objectives

- A lack of understanding of change proposals inadequately explained by top management

- Low expectations of success amongst staff

This analysis encouraged senior staff to re-examine their approach and work more closely together in developing a new structure. Using external facilitation they used a high-level strategy workshop to resolve differences and develop agreed recommendations for change to the organisation structure rather than have it imposed by the head of the unit.

Figure 12.3 Implementation problems assessment: case study

13

ORGANISATION DEVELOPMENT

Introduction

This section outlines the tools and techniques that will facilitate the development of a preferred organisational design together with corresponding roles of staff and working methods. It also highlights methods for encouraging staff to work together in implementing change and encouraging feedback on the success of the implementation process and it emphasises the need for review during each stage in the development of new arrangements.

Table 13.1 Organisation development

Tools/techniques	Taking stock	Merging and building confidence	Transformation/ achieving change
1 Organisation design	• Define objectives • Establish cultural style • Agree principles for design • Identify options/ evaluation criteria • Evaluate options • Agree design		
2 Business planning	• Status review	• Strategic analysis and preparation of detailed plans	• Implementation of plans and performance review. Roll forward plan

Table 13.1 Organisation development (contd)

Tools/techniques	Taking stock	Merging and building confidence	Transformation/ achieving change
3 Team building	• Define roles • Agree working methods • Build consensus	• Developing cohesion during implementation stage <--------	------->
4 Focus groups	• Identify key issues	• Provide "feedback" on the implementation of the change process <--------	------->
5 Workshops	• Determine printing of key issues	• Formulate and agree recommendations for action	• Problem-solving identifying future goals

Tool/technique 1: Organisation design

The design of a new local authority is an experience which does not come about often and therefore it provides both opportunities and risks. The organisational design selected and implemented at the outset is likely to form the basis of the local authority for many years. From that point onwards change is more likely to be incremental as it is rare for any organisation to have the time or resources to tear up voluntarily its entire organisational structure and to start again. Later organisational changes are likely to relate to the redesign of individual departments within the predetermined overall structure for service reasons (e.g. the purchaser/provider divide in social work). The need for future (incremental) change is likely to be identified through the annual business planning process (*see* Tool/technique 2 of this chapter).

Those given the responsibility for the design of the new authority, must therefore be aware of the legacy which their efforts will leave, and the need to ensure that the best possible organisation form is selected. This applies to both stages of organisational design which will have to be gone through, i.e.:

- outline of organisational structures
- detailed systems and structures of the whole of the organisation and its parts.

As a general principal, authorities will be seeking an organisation which is robust, yet flexible, with systems which both support the implementation of its objectives at the strategic and operational level, and ensures clear performance measurement.

The design of new organisational structures is never a totally risk free process, and should not be undertaken in isolation from the environment within which the future organisation will be operating. Authorities which come together as a result of the implementation of the proposals which are accepted for the restructuring of local government within any area will necessarily have associated historical structures and infrastructures. New authorities will therefore need carefully to consider how to minimise the risks that may arise from changing these, without unduly constraining and inhibiting the design process.

There are a number of tools and techniques of organisational design which can be used to assist the design process. Properly used, these tools and techniques should ensure that the optimum design is selected for the new organisation and that it is successfully implemented, managed and monitored.

Set out below are the six steps of organisational design:

Step 1	Define objectives of the organisation
Step 2	Establish cultural style
Step 3	Agree principles for design
Step 4	Identify options and evaluation criteria
Step 5	Evaluate options and implementation issues
Step 6	Agree design process

Figure 13.1 Six steps of organisation design

A stepped approach such as this provides a clear framework for the process of building up the organisational design, ensuring clarity at each stage and consistency of approach. It also enables a clear communication strategy to be developed, to ensure that consultation and discussions are pre-programmed and that an effective means of disseminating and receiving information is established. Finally, it should provide a timetable and project plan, openly available and used as a working project management tool.

Step 1: Define objectives

One of the first issues to be addressed will be to determine the objectives of the authority, and therefore the type of design which will most effectively meet these objectives. For example, the Government has emphasised its preference for new authorities to be 'enabling', rather than supply focused. The process of objective setting will need to consider whether this is in fact a key objective for the authority, or whether a more provider driven organisation is appropriate. Similarly, each authority will need to determine whether they want to place emphasis on a decentralised or centrally based organisation. It will need to agree its approach to internal management and political management issues. Organisation structure will depend on all these points, and authorities will need to be clear about their objectives to design an organisation structure.

Step 2: Establish cultural style

Just as defining the objectives of the organisation will begin to shape the new structure, establishing the cultural style will start to identify the structural components which will be required to achieve these objectives. Key questions will need to be set out and addressed: for example, what will the authority's management philosophy be?; is the authority going to follow traditional approaches, or take a more radical view? Some of these issues are discussed in Part I, Chapter 4 and they are also thoroughly debated in the recent Local Government Management Board Paper (1993).

Step 3: Principles for organisational design

The authority will need to identify the principles by which the design of the new organisation is going to be guided and supported. Such principles will need to be formulated in consultation with the identified change sponsors and managers and representatives of all groups whose commitment to the change process will be key to its successful implementation. The design principle will need to focus on the following areas (Figure 13.2):

Service delivery
- minimisation of risk to service delivery during transition to and implementation of the new organisation
- capacity to ensure full range of consistent services at local level

Strategy
- strategic capability
- capacity to handle managerial change
- capacity to engage with wider and localised agencies

External interface
- capacity to manage demand of local and national requirements
- ability to influence policy on major issues affecting the locality and to act as advocate on behalf of all groups represented by the authority

Internal structure
- facilitate the development and motivation of human resources
- ensure accountability
- support policy and operational needs

Figure 13.2 Step 3: Key areas of organisational design

The principles which are developed to guide the design process must be both realistic and practical, and capable of clear articulation within the change process.

Step 4: Identify options and evaluation criteria

There will be a range of options which will need to be considered within the context of the organisational objectives, culture and design principles. There will also be a need to identify a clear basis for financial evaluation. However, at this stage in the development of the organisation, there is likely to be a spectrum of options which will be considered worthy of a first level evaluation. The options will be of a high level, setting out broad structures and frameworks. This will be an opportunity, therefore, to examine the principles and objectives in more detail and to discuss how the general organisational shape may develop.

Step 5: Evaluate options and implementation issues

The first high level review will have identified those options within the spectrum which are not able to meet the objectives set for the new organisation, or which would not be able to comply with the agreed design principles. A small number of options will then need to be considered in more depth against more detailed evaluation criteria derived from consideration at the outset of the process of the authority's objectives and cultural style. The feasibility of each option also needs to be evaluated, using the techniques described in the previous section. An organisational design which is impractical to implement or which lacks flexibility in its early days, will be discarded at this point. It will be important also to examine implementation issues at this stage including resource requirements, timing, legal issues, and project management.

Step 6: *Agree detailed design process*

Once the preferred outline structure is agreed, the processes set out above will need to be repeated to facilitate the detailed design of the elements of the organisation. This may be undertaken on a service by service basis, departmentally or geographically, depending on the organisation design. Whichever is the most appropriate, it is important to adopt the same disciplined approach based on the guiding principles identified at the outset.

Tool/technique 2: **Business planning**

A common theme of this book is that each authority needs to plan and implement change at a pace which suits its own needs. The key message is that whether a radical or incremental change programme is favoured, it will be implemented more effectively if a co-ordinated and strategic approach is taken. This section demonstrates how the preparation, implementation and updating of a business plan can provide a clear sense of direction and a framework within which to manage the process of change and organisation development.

Advantages of business planning

In the local government context, business planning is an important way of demonstrating the commitment of the management team to the future plans and targets of the authority. The production of the plan can in itself be useful in generating a common sense of purpose for the new team. Additional benefits of business planning are that it:

- gives real meaning to strategic objectives

- stimulates decisive action

- focuses attention on difficult choices including competitive threats and opportunities and balance between the investment of resources

- encourages risk assessment and management

- develops the people who must deliver the outcome.

This helps to encourage a common sense of purpose amongst committee members and staff at all levels.

Key elements of business planning

There is no set formula for a business plan. Figure 13.3 sets out the business planning framework and the key elements of the process are considered in more detail below.

Stage 1: where are we now?

The first stage (*see* Table 13.2) of business planning involves a critical examination of the internal and external environment of the authority which will reveal the scope for change and the ability of the authority to deliver it. Tools such as benchmarking and the use of 'best of breed' groups (*see* Chapters 9) will assist authorities in identifying the competitive gap between itself and other service providers and the use of risk assessment (*see* Chapter 7) will highlight the effect of failing to implement change where it is required. The use of a SWOT analysis at this stage is a simple method for considering the strengths and weaknesses of the authority highlighting good practice where it exists, and opportunities for improved performance. It also assists the authority to look beyond its internal organisation to opportunities to extend its involvement in the wider community such as developing its role as advocate at the regional, national and European level.

It is helpful at this stage to draw together a broadly based team comprising members and officers from across the authority and representatives of service users to provide a range of views and perspectives and ensure that the picture created is as accurate as possible.

Stage 2: where do we want to go?

The second stage (*see* Table 13.3) of the process focuses on the authority developing a set of 'core values' or principles shared by all those who participate in the management and delivery of services by the authority. The core values will reflect the desired culture of the organisation and form the basis of the key aims and objectives, that will drive future service delivery and shape the structure and systems of the authority. Strategy workshops (see Chapter 7, Tool/technique 1) will be a useful tool at this stage to agree core values and formulate and rank strategic objectives. Clearly, it will be necessary to link key objectives to a financial analysis of what is feasible for the authority to commit itself to. The use of cost benefit analysis (*see* Chapter 7) will also assist in the preparation of options and the ranking of priorities. Similarly, the use of budgeting techniques such as priority based budgeting to review resource allocation in accordance with priorities; and activity based costing to identify non 'value added' activities and under utilised resources, will be helpful at this stage (*see* Chapter 10).

Finally, the key elements of the management and information strategy needed to support the implementation of the chosen key aims and objectives should be 'mapped' at this stage.

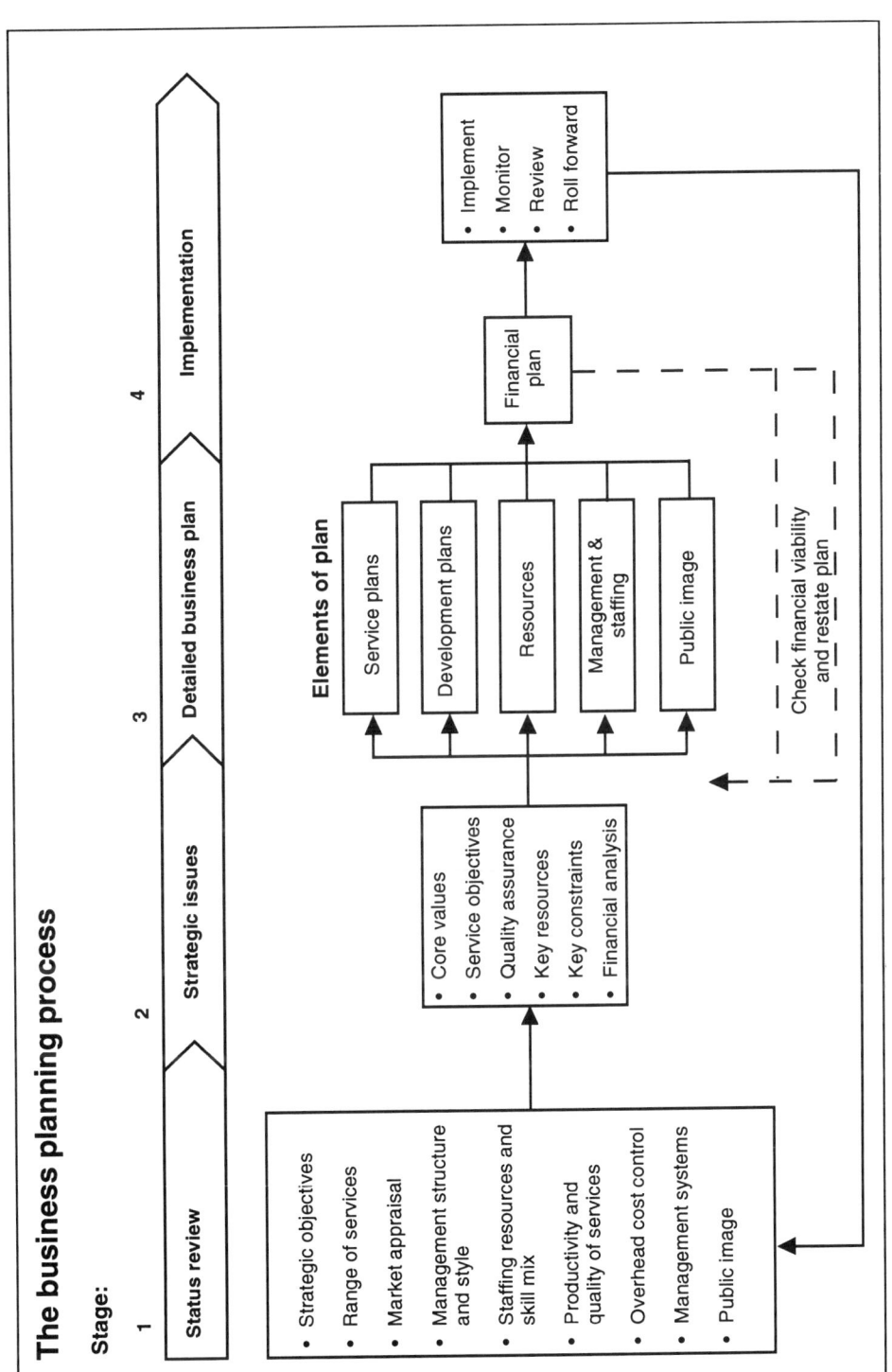

The business planning process

Stage:

1	2	3	4
Status review	Strategic issues	Detailed business plan	Implementation

Elements of plan

- Strategic objectives
- Range of services
- Market appraisal
- Management structure and style
- Staffing resources and skill mix
- Productivity and quality of services
- Overhead cost control
- Management systems
- Public image

- Core values
- Service objectives
- Quality assurance
- Key resources
- Key constraints
- Financial analysis

- Service plans
- Development plans
- Resources
- Management & staffing
- Public image

Financial plan

- Implement
- Monitor
- Review
- Roll forward

Check financial viability and restate plan

Figure 13.3

Table 13.2 Stage 1 of business plan

Stage 1	2	3	4
Status Review Internal assessment: - organisation/culture - systems - people External assessment: - legislation - markets - competition SWOT analysis: - strengths - weaknesses - opportunities - threats			

Table 13.3 Stage 2 of business plan

Stage 1	2	3	4
Strategic Issues Core values: Key aims and objectives Services: - needs to be met - area of operations - customer satisfaction Resources: - financial analysis - information strategy - management strategy			

Stage 3: how do we get there?

During the third stage (*see* Table 13.4), detailed plans are drawn up covering all aspects of the authority's work. The plans must then be assessed against the financial plans and resources of the authority (including staff, land and buildings) to ensure their viability and to be re-worked if necessary.

A key aspect to this stage is developing a marketing strategy that will communicate key objectives and service standards to the authority's customers and which will incorporate an effective mechanism for assessing customer satisfaction and identifying new needs.

It is worth noting at this point that authorities may find it helpful to establish a hierarchy of plans at the corporate, functional and service level, so that each plan contains an appropriate level of detail to be useful to its main audience.

Table 13.4 Stage 3 of business plan

Stage 1	2	3	4
Detailed Plan Service objectives: - quality of provision - customer satisfaction Marketing: - to customers and the public - to external agencies - to Central and European government Resources: - money - people - land Management and staffing: - developing committee skills - developing managerial skills - training and staff development - recruitment and retention Development plans: - area of operation (geographical) - area of operation (needs met) - scale of operation			

Stage 4: what must we do?

The fourth and final stage of the process (*see* Table 13.5) requires key actions to be set that will translate plans into clearly defined activities to be allocated to specific staff. A process of monitoring and review should also be specified which sets fixed dates/periods for the monitoring process and defines the methods with which progress will be reviewed and assessed. A common trap that many authorities fall into is to measure that specific tasks have been undertaken but not the quality of achievement. It is helpful therefore to develop relevant performance indicators that can provide a benchmark for assessing the quality of achievement and ensure that strategic objectives are being met (Chapter 10 outlines the process of performance management and the key factors influencing successful performance).

In summary, business planning is a dynamic process that encourages authorities to constantly review and update their plans to reflect changing circumstances, new opportunities, unforeseen threats and customer feedback.

Table 13.5 Stage 4 of business plan

Stage 1	2	3	4
Implementation			

- Implementation - turning plans into action

- Performance measurement

- Review

- Roll forward - to take account of real performance and external/ internal changes.

Tool/technique 3: **Team building**

Context

Implementating a new organisational structure and managing the transition process (in the case of setting up new authorities) will require new groups of people to work together. People will need to work together who:

- have not worked together before

- may hold different attitudes and beliefs about work
- will be likely to have experienced different management styles and approaches
- may be resistant or hostile to the changes
- may have different professional and social backgrounds

The culmination of these factors could have a damaging effect on service delivery if they are not appropriately managed.

There will be both temporary teams, for example developing plans and implementing change and permanent groups, working in new or existing service areas. They will need to develop quickly into functioning bodies, particularly where a service is being provided directly to the public.

New teams will require:

- definition of roles
- agreement of working methods
- rapid assimilation of new ideas, and
- delivery of effective services within a short timescale

There is strong need to forge these teams into effective functioning units ready to provide services to their customers and to operate 'normally' in as short a time as possible. Ideally, a group should have a carefully selected membership, with a mix of skills, roles and personalities appropriate to the task. In reality, permanent teams formed through a merger of existing groups of staff are unlikely to be so well matched.

The theory of group behaviour tells us that groups need to go through four stages in their development prior to achieving full functionality. In general these stages are called testing, conflict, development of cohesion and functionality. They are more easily remembered as:

- forming
- storming
- norming, and
- performing

Table 13.6 describes the key features of each stage.

The stages of group development outlined in the table can be 'forced' so that the group reaches the performing stage more quickly and valuable time is preserved. This is particularly important where a service is being continually provided to customers during the process of change. The most effective and commonly used method of speeding up the process is team building.

Table 13.6 Stages of group development

Stage of group development	Key features of the stage
Testing/Forming	• Individuals 'size each other up' • Group members assess each other's capabilities • Getting to know each other takes precedence over completing the task at hand
Conflict/Storming	• Individuals struggle for dominance within the group - jockeying for position • Sub-groups may form within the team • The task is often not achieved as effort is expended on conflict
Development of Cohesion/Norming	• The group develops ways of working to achieve the desired end result • Groups may start to socialise and develop unique signs or phrases which signal group membership
Functionality/Performing	• The team members know their roles and work accordingly • Work is completed with few problems • Members recognise the skills of other members • Decisions are reached quickly and with minimal conflict

Team building is the process whereby a team completes a series of exercises, whether real or imaginary, to speed up the process of achieving group functionality. The process is usually undertaken away from the normal working environment to avoid team members falling into their traditional roles, behaviours and attitudes.

A team building event normally lasts from half a day to two days although some events can be longer and more demanding. They are ideally held away from the normal day-to-day place of work and should be facilitated by an experienced external moderator. It is essential that the facilitator has considerable knowledge and expertise in the analysis of group dynamics, to ensure that the greatest benefit can be gained from the team building event.

The facilitator designs a series of events which aim to replicate many of the issues which teams may encounter in their normal work. On occasion this can be a real work project or problem which the team has to resolve. In addressing the issues which form the basis of the sessions, the group is compelled to work together to achieve the end results.

The focused nature of these sessions can sometimes result in high levels of emotion as the beliefs and attitudes of individuals are challenged. For this reason the environment for the team building must be a supportive one and the need for a neutral facilitator is strong. Sometimes the facilitator can provide counselling to individuals to support the team building process.

Several tools and techniques can be used to enhance the team building process. These are shown in Figure 13.4 .

Tools and techniques used in team building

- self-assessment questionnaires which examine the perceptions of members as to the functioning of the team;

- group and individual counselling undertaken by the facilitator to encourage group analysis of performance or reasons for lack of performance;

- competition between groups can enhance intra-group cohesion, but can also encourage non-productive rivalry if taken too seriously;

- a timed exercise which focuses team members on results;

- a combination of physical and mental activities which stimulate group members to explore and understand each other's strengths and weaknesses;

- activities which cannot be completed without every group member having an input to the process.

Figure 13.4 Tools and techniques used in team building

Using team building

Team building is a technique which is particularly helpful where teams have a strategic, managerial or decision making function. They can, however, be relatively expensive to put together and require a trained facilitator. Situations where the technique can be particularly useful are:

- building consensus - especially within management teams

- maintaining essential services to the customer during the change period

- where the group needs to establish a new identity

- where there is adversity in the environment external to the group

- where the group needs to function quickly to achieve credibility

A cascading programme of team building events can be useful as a tool for aiding the process of change within the organisation. The management team should be the first team to undergo the team building process followed by a rolling out of the process through the organisation. If the focus for the event is the building of new skills or attitudes, such as customer care or total quality, then the process has a dual purpose. It builds functioning teams and carries the new messages of the 'new' authority.

Tool/technique 4: Focus groups

Before any changes take place the organisation will 'take stock' of its current position. This examination will certainly include: the internal aspects of the way in which services are managed; human and financial resources deployed; and the current structure and systems in place. Account will also be taken of customer perceptions of service delivery and the standing of the authority within the local community.

There are likely to be a whole range of areas which need to be addressed before any changes occur and some issues of particular concern will be evident. Questions which may arise are:

- Does our organisational structure meet our current and future needs?

- How effective is management at the strategic and operational level?

- What systems will we need to provide effective management information for the future?

- Is there a mis-match between skills that are available and those which are required?

- Will we need to develop our human resources to meet the needs which result from the changes?

- Does our culture provide the right environment for successful change?

- What changes could we make to enhance the services we provide?

- What services are we providing?

- Are they the services the customers want or need?

- Do we provide them well?

- How could these services be improved?

- Should we be providing other services?

- What services are of most value to the customers?

- What services do we want to provide in the future?

An effective technique which can be employed to research these issues is the focus-group approach. This is a marketing technique often used in the private sector by a wide range of companies in all areas of business and is increasingly relevant in the public sector.

Setting up focus groups

Focus groups consist of a small number of people, usually numbering 6 - 10, who come together to discuss a specific project, service or other aspect of a business. The group is led by a trained and skilled facilitator who needs to be knowledgeable and experienced in the subject matter and in this technique. It is particularly important that the facilitator should be skilled in the analysis of group dynamics and the perceptions of participants, otherwise the results of the focus group could be misleading.

The aim of the focus group is to encourage participants to contribute to a discussion on the subject at hand which generates information on their perceptions, beliefs and attitudes, and which reveals important details about service provision. For this reason it is usually advisable to make the groups as informal as possible to encourage a free and open discussion.

Employee focus groups should comprise staff drawn from a broad perspective in the following ways:

- at random

- self selected volunteers

- a vertical cross-section - different levels in one function

- a diagonal cross-section - different levels and functions

External focus groups usually comprise volunteer customers who are involved in an aspect of the service either as a user or as a community representative. The sample of customers selected to take part in the groups needs to reflect the breadth of the service itself and, for this reason, it may be necessary to hold more than one focus group to ensure full representation.

The facilitator will usually open the discussion with a broad open question: 'how do you feel when you come into one of the council offices?' or 'how does it feel to work in this organisation?'. This will be followed up by other questions addressing various issues which the facilitator wishes to discuss. The facilitator focuses the discussion, hence the name of the technique, but they also ensure that every group member has the opportunity to speak and express their opinions.

A key advantage of the focus group approach to information gathering is the freedom with which participants can express their opinions without being identified individually. The report of the session is a consensual view of the group or a mix of views expressed on the day.

The discussion between participants can reveal a great deal of information about the services the authority provides, how they are managed and what the key issues are. Customer focus groups can provide an insight into customer perceptions of the quality of your service, satisfaction levels with the current service and can point the way forward to areas for further investigation. Results from a focus group session should be treated with caution and generalisations from the data should be avoided where possible.

Advantages of focus groups:

- they are a useful way of taking stock

- opinions can be expressed freely as they are non-attributable

- the trained facilitator ensures the discussion concentrates on key issues

- the groups can act as motivational tools as they encourage participation and stimulate commitment

- high quality feedback is provided at relatively low cost compared to other survey methods

- beliefs and opinions can be exposed without the need for a questionnaire

- important issues can be easily clarified and followed up immediately

Tool/technique 5: **Workshops**

Information and data gained through the use of focus groups are likely to identify the key issues which the change management programme should address. It may be useful to examine these issues in the context of a workshop consisting of appointed change managers in order to:

- determine the priority of the issues which have been highlighted

- formulate and agree recommendations for action

Table 13.7 summarises and contrasts the functions of focus groups and strategy workshops and highlight the many differences in purpose, operation and participation. The key difference, in summary, is that focus groups produce information for others to use in making decisions, whereas strategy workshops are a forum for taking decisions.

Table 13.7 Contrast of focus groups with strategy workshops

	Focus goups	*Workshops*
Purposes	• to stimulate honest views about the service • to provide data for others to use in taking decisions • to obtain a cross-section of views • to act as a motivational tool for staff - people like to be asked • to provide high quality feed- back at relatively low cost	• to make recommendations for action • to resolve problems • to build commitment to solutions • to act as a team building focus • to promote a greater understanding of issues
Participants	• facilitator/consultant • 10-12 people invited from a cross-section of staff or customers	• facilitator/consultant • ideally six-eight senior managers directly involved in the areas concerned

Table 13.7 (contd)

	Focus goups	*Workshops*
Operation	• usually two hours long • tightly controlled by the facilitator who asks a series of open questions about key areas • confidentiality is essential • facilitator ensure all participants have an opportunity to speak • the output is reported	• can last up to two days • vigorous and focused debate to form decisions and make plans • previously circulated information is often used as the basis for discussion • consultants and staff often make presentations • clear actions usually identified and individuals given responsibility for their achievement

14

INDIVIDUAL DEVELOPMENT

Introduction

This chapter concentrates on tools and techniques which will be useful in preparing staff for implementing the change programme and accepting the direct effect of change on them as individuals. In particular, the techniques described help the identification of the required change management skills and suggests relevant training techniques to assist in the personal development of staff. Table 14.1 shows the five techniques which are recommended and the stages in the change process where they can be used.

Table 14.1 Individual development

Tools/techniques	Taking stock	Merging and building confidence	Transformation/ achieving change
1 Leadership coaching	Analysis of skills	Strengthening of skills	Continuous skills assessment to meet changing needs
2 Counselling	Stress counselling/ preparing for change	'out' counselling of staff facing redundancy	Group counselling of teams
3 Assessing change management styles	Reviewing management styles	Improving the effectiveness of change management styles	Continuous assessment that chosen style encourages achievement of objectives

Table 14.1 (contd)

Tools/techniques	Taking stock	Merging and building confidence	Transformation/ achieving change
4 Change management skills training	Establish training needs Identify change agents/advocates to receive training and establish "training pyramid"	Implement training programmes	Respond to evolving training needs
5 Developing resilience	Devise training plan to assist staff in responding positively to change Focus plan on staff in greatest need	---------------------------- This tool should be used through each stage of the change process ----------------------------	----> ---->

Tool/technique 1: **Leadership coaching**

The study of leadership in the management of change has received widespread attention over the last decade since the publication in 1982 of the Peters and Waterman book *In search of excellence*. The authors studied excellent companies to assess the key factors which made them so successful. One of the critical factors for success was the presence of a strong and charismatic leader to guide the organisation through the doubts and uncertainties of the change process.

In a study by Larry D Alexander (Mayon-White 1986) inadequate leadership and direction by departmental and corporate managers was described as being the cause of poorly implemented change on 59% of occasions. The consequences of poor implementation can, in the most extreme form, determine the ultimate success or failure of the organisation in its new operating environment.

Leadership of change requires:

- hard work
- thinking through the change to its conclusion so that a vision of the new organisation is constantly in mind
- the building of consensus with managers via informal discussion, feedback and influence

- fostering of objectives which directly achieve the desired changes

- monitoring and enforcement of change

- acceptance of the need to change oneself

The need for strong and effective leadership during a period of change is perhaps self-evident. And yet, how many organisations assume leaders are born and not made, or that the leadership skills required during periods of long term stability are those best suited to the demands of rapid change programmes? And, can all the required skills be found in one person?

The study of leaders and leadership has shown that the skills required for effective leadership for change can be learned by managers. Leadership coaching is a technique used to achieve this purpose.

The process of leadership coaching

The technique of leadership coaching is used by senior and middle managers to enhance their performance during periods of rapid change within their organisations. The technique involves the following stages.

Table 14.2 Four stages in the process of leadership coaching

Stage 1 A self-assessment of the strengths and weaknesses of the manager. There are many proprietary questionnaires which have been designed for the self-evaluation of managerial skills. It is important when completing them that honest judgements are made by the participant.

Stage 2 An outside assessment of strengths and weaknesses.
This should be undertaken by a facilitator trained and experienced in leadership coaching. The facilitator interviews the manager and makes an assessment of their current skills compared to the ideal skills profile for an effective leader of change.

Stage 3 Building on the strengths of the manager.
This is a key area where the manager practices new behaviours and skills which enhance the areas of strength identified in the stages 1 and 2. The facilitator can use role playing techniques and examples of good practice to encourage enhanced performance. It is important that the manager is encouraged to be open and responsive to constructive criticism provided by the coach.

Stage 4 Addressing weaknesses.
As in Stage 3, the facilitator examines with the manager the areas of leadership skills and behaviour which are counterproductive to the change process or which require substantial enhancement in order to perform as a more effective leader in the change process. This stage of the coaching is critical to the overall success of the coaching technique.

The facilitator's role is a major element of successful leadership coaching. Ideally the coach should be:

- highly accomplished in leadership coaching

- experienced and knowledgeable in the area of business concerned

- external to the organisation so that he or she is independent from the internal political processes of the authority

There are many factors which are likely to contribute to an effective leadership coaching process. These can include:

- The sessions should be conducted on a one-to-one basis - facilitator and manager

- The high level skill and experience of the facilitator in drawing out more effective leadership skills from the manager

- The coaching sessions should be focused on everyday problems encountered by the manager

- The facilitator should be knowledgeable and experienced in the business area of the manager so that practical problems can be addressed in the coaching sessions

- The environment should be supportive and confidentiality maintained

- The most effective coaching is undertaken over the long-term, building up skills over time. But short-term sessions can provide the impetus for skills enhancement

- Receptiveness and openness to change

The coaching process is one of a portfolio of techniques which can be used to enhance the performance of managers during the period of transformation and beyond. Training in skills which complement and enhance the leadership coaching process can provide essential confidence and support to the managers involved. Useful skills include:

- presentation skills

- influencing skills

- communications skills

- interpersonal skills

- negotiating skills

Using leadership coaching

Coaching can be useful to any managers involved in change. However, the cost of a trained facilitator on a one-to-one basis can be considerable if all managers in the authority use the process. It is often considered to be more effective if the coaching is confined to key senior managers in the change process: the chief executive, the management team and perhaps also the political leaders of the authority. This ensures that the process of transformation is carried through effectively using a top-down approach.

A key disadvantage of leadership coaching is the time which needs to be set aside by the manager for the coaching sessions. Many managers are under considerable pressure during the change process and it may appear that the coaching sessions are not as important as other, more pressing, operational problems. However, setting aside time for coaching can provide substantial benefits to the manager and to the change process as a whole.

Tool/technique 2: Counselling

There will be many people within old and new authorities who have difficulty coming to terms with the process of transition and long-term change, because of:

- changes in staffing needs requiring retraining, redeployment, or redundancy
- changes in ways of working which confront strongly held beliefs about the validity of current working practices
- alterations to the management structure, style and processes which require staff to work differently in familiar jobs

These changes, and many others, will have considerable repercussions on staff working in the organisation at various times during the change process. Indeed, situations are also likely to occur along the way which challenge even the staunchest supporter of the new vision for the authority. These challenges may include:

- 'moving the goalposts', particularly in a political context
- new factors being introduced which complicate the process, for example new legislation
- difficult tasks to be completed, particularly redundancies, which require reserves of tact and diplomacy and which can be stressful for the bearer of bad news as well as for the staff member concerned
- tasks which require protracted negotiations with staff, outside contractors, politicians or other authorities

While some staff will respond positively to the demands the changes place upon them, others are likely to question in forceful terms the reasons for the changes and the capabilities of the managers involved! The various responses to change over time have been documented in many studies and were discussed in Part I, Chapter 3. These are summarised for convenience in Table 14.3.

Table 14.3 Responses to change

Positive responses to change	Time	Negative responses to change
• Uninformed Optimism	Start of changes	• Immobilisation
		• Denial
• Informed Pessimism		
		• Anger
• Hopeful Realism		• Bargaining
• Informed Optimism		• Depression
		• Testing
• Completion/Satisfaction	End of changes	• Acceptance

The positive responses can be dealt with in team situations and harnessed for productive use by the new organisation. Negative responses, however, can prove very damaging to the health and future well-being of the authority and, in some cases, damaging to the individual as well. Staff responses which have been encountered by other public sector bodies which undergo radical change have included:

- industrial action by staff
- sabotage of plans or facilities
- withdrawal of goodwill
- increased stress levels
- depression

The external manifestations of change resistance (the first three listed above) can usually be confronted relatively effectively by the managers of change. The last two responses, increased stress levels and depression, can be far harder to diagnose and deal with. It is in this area that the technique of counselling is often used.

The counselling process

Counselling works by challenging the beliefs and attitudes of the individual in a non-threatening environment, allowing the individual to address issues without fear of failure. The technique encourages people to confront their own barriers to achievement in the new working environment which the change process has brought about.

Trained counsellors are commonly used by organisations to provide a counselling service which meets the needs of staff members affected by the transformation process. A counselling service usually has the following features:

- counsellors are trained and experienced in organisational work
- the service is paid for by the authority
- confidentiality is preserved
- any staff member can use the service

Many managers are sceptical about the value of such a service especially during periods of change when budgets are tight and management achievement is measured by financial criteria. However, the benefits of the process tend to far outweigh the disadvantages particularly in the long-term. Key advantages of using counselling in the change process are outlined below.

- Staff are provided with a safety valve for their frustration and anger which results from changes over which they feel they have little power or influence.

- Negative and unconstructive dysfunctional change responses can be re-directed into positive action benefiting both the individual, who gains greater satisfaction from his or her work, and the organisation, which gains a staff member working towards the authority's objectives.

- Staff feel their difficulties concerning the change are respected, understood and, to a certain extent, provided for.

The main issue in providing a counselling service is the overall cost of the service and whether it can be justified in the circumstances. It is never easy to decide the value of counselling to an authority, but if the number of days absence lost due to stress and related problems is taken into account, the decision to initiate counselling for employees can become clearer.

Uses for counselling

Counselling can be effectively used in many areas of the change process and, indeed, in organisations not undergoing periods of dramatic transformation. Specific uses can be identified as:

- Stress counselling - to reduce the stress of staff working through the changes. This is especially true of situations where staff are working in new

project groups where tight deadlines have to be met, or where staff are
required to work in new teams under new managers with different styles of
management.

- Counselling out - whereby individuals are helped to confront the new
  environment prior to the redundancy occurring. It is well recognised that
  people actively helped to leave organisations are more likely to be re-
  employed quickly.

- Group counselling - a process whereby teams which are not functioning
  effectively are counselled both individually and as a group to identify and
  address the reasons for the lack of functionality. This area of counselling is
  often used in conjunction with teambuilding.

Tool/technique 3: **Assessing change management styles**

Definition

A range of personal style assessment tools is available, such as the Myers Briggs
Type Indicator Test.

Their use in the change management context is a way of helping change agents
and change advocates to become more aware of their style of communications,
helping them to apply their change management skills more effectively to change
programmes.

When to apply it

This tool can be applied at any time during the training and development of
change managers required to support the change programme. Since the aim is to
encourage greater self-awareness and enhance communication skills as part of the
change process, the earlier in the programme it can be used the better.

How it will help

Change managers will become more aware of the way they can use their
communication skills through the change targets to influence staff, to understand
the change process and embrace the change proposed. The change agent will
build a better understanding of:

- the way they function, for example as a deep thinker, a dynamic problem
  solver or a tenacious pursuer of a problem who never gives up, so that they

can visualise better how they will behave in undertaking a change programme

- their strengths - the way they behave at their best, for example as leaders and visionaries motivating staff by example, or as patient and empathetic listeners who win staff over by their belief in teamwork and cooperation, so that they can build on these strengths and use them effectively in the change programme

- their weaknesses - the way they behave at their worst, perhaps as 'long on vision but short on action', or having a tendency to short-term thinking and 'knee-jerk' reaction without thought for the longer-term implications of an action, helping the change agent to avoid the worst aspects of behaviour in developing the change programme

- the way they behave under stress - perhaps the most important and relevant aspect in dealing with change programmes, where change agents learn how to deal with the behavioural type that most often emerges when under pressure to achieve major change; to the all-important change targets this may take the form of appearing aloof instead of wise, of appearing subjective instead of dynamic, or overly narrow-minded instead of focused

How it can be used successfully?

This tool can help in a variety of ways to improve the skills of change agents in their role as managers and implementers of change and to assist them in communicating messages about change to help the change targets develop a better understanding of change and change management techniques, to reduce resistance to change and build resilience, and to avoid the occurrence of black holes in the communication of change.

Tool/technique 4: **Change management skills training**

Definition

A training course to provide change managers with a portfolio of essential change management concepts, tools and techniques.

'Training the trainers' is a proven, cost-effective means of ensuring that the many change management concepts, tools and techniques which will generally be new to staff within the authority are transferred from the core of expert advisers and specialists to the wider body of staff chosen to be change agents or change advocates within the authority.

They in turn can train new change agents and change advocates and the base of the training pyramid can thereby be expanded so that the required number of staff with a basic understanding of change concepts is created who can pass on this knowledge to the 'change targets' within the authority. They can also be trained to use many of the tools and techniques shown throughout Part II of the book. Many of the methods used employ classic consulting and training techniques, including:

- facilitation skills - working alongside staff to help them analyse problems, design and develop solutions and apply implementation programmes effectively. The facilitator is a catalyst, helping to set the scene, intervening only where there is an obvious block to inhibit progress. This often involves learning how to act as facilitator in a workshop, a focus group or to organise and run a 'best of' group

- coaching and skills transfer - transferring specific skills by practical example in undertaking project work or by explaining particular tools and techniques by means of worked case studies or presentations; the emphasis is on applied work and goes beyond conventional lecturing or teaching in a fully interactive process

- training courses - learning how to run a formal training course with a pre-prepared agenda and course materials, either to develop understanding of a specific change management tool or the more generic skills that are need to for change management

- leadership coaching - demonstrating the skills needed to manage change projects as sponsors or agents of change

- teamworking skills - developing the approach towards cross-functional knowledge sharing and information exchange needed to institute best practice in the change process

- data collection and surveying techniques - many of the change management tools and techniques involve using interviewing and formal surveying techniques to gather data on staff attitudes and it is important for change agents and change advocates to know how to introduce them, who to involve, what questions to ask and how to analyse the results

- handbooks and manuals - staff engaged in change management programmes will need to have accessible sources of reference to help them undertake their work and to continue learning or refreshing their skills. This form of training or distance learning will be an important part of the change programme and can include:
  - recommended reading lists and formal published literature
  - tailored briefing materials, possibly linked to the overall communication of change

- handbooks and manuals, (a loose-leaf format may be helpful), allowing change agents to build up their sources of reference as they learn more about change tools and techniques, receive more training and develop their skills on, for example, project management, communications, benchmarking and risk management.

When to apply

Change management skills training can be introduced at almost any stage in the change management programme - identifying key change agents for training at an early stage, then extending the programme on a phased and selective basis to focus on training managers who need to deal with areas where higher risks or problems have been identified, for example in the change project description.

How it will help

The training programme will extend the numbers of change managers and extend the pool of staff who have an understanding of the key change issues, the problems that must be addressed and the range of tools and techniques that can be called on to help. This will help to lower the risks of failure in implementing change and achieving the transformation of the authority. Change agents, advocates and 'targets' can benefit from carefully managed training courses, tailored to suit the needs of the authority.

How it can be used successfully

See Figure 14.1 below.

An operational unit within a large department was seeking to implement a major change programme immediately prior to being market tested in an effort to improve efficiency and effectiveness and assist the in-house team to submit a credible bid for the contract and win the market test.

The unit operated out of several geographically distributed bases and a project manager was appointed in each location to manage a small team of staff to undertake a wide range of efficiency and effectiveness projects. To raise change management skill levels and encourage effective teamworking and cooperation between project managers at different sites, a training course was organised to provide the project managers with an understanding of key change management skills. They could then pass this knowledge on to the members of their project teams and assist them in managing the change implications of their projects more effectively.

The course focused on a range of change management tools and techniques including basic project management and leadership skills. One project manager was given responsibility for continuing the training of other managers in change management skills as a project in its own right, providing effective support in change management skills to assist in the successful implementation of the other efficiency and effectiveness projects. Updates and refresher training in change management tools and techniques have been continued in a training module attached to the regular project progress meetings.

Figure 14.1 Change management skills training: case study

Tool/technique 5: **Developing resilience**

Definition

Resilience is the ability to cope with change; resilient people are positive, focused, flexible, organised and proactive. Training can help to build this resilience so that staff in the authority are able to:

- regain their sense of equilibrium more quickly when change disrupts their expectations - 'the shock of the new'

- maintain their productivity during a period of uncertainty and ambiguity as the change programme progresses

- remain physically and emotionally healthy in the face of uncertainty

- avoid symptoms of overload - 'future shock'

- rebound from the demands of the change programme stronger and better prepared for change than before

Resilience training is focused on developing understanding of the core characteristics of a resilient individual. Staff are trained to identify their personal strengths and weaknesses and practice the skills necessary to enhance their ability to assimilate change programmes. Change agents can learn what they have to do to support themselves and their staff in the development of greater personal resilience. Staff will learn how to acquire new resilience and to conserve their existing ability to assimilate change.

When to apply

Training in resilience can be given at almost any time during the change programme but higher priority should be given to key staff who are showing signs of resistance to change or emotional upset.

How it will help

People involved in major organisation change enhance their resilience when they:

- realise that people want to be in control of their lives and that what everyone fears is the ambiguity caused by the disruption of expectations that change brings

- are able to exercise some degree of control over what happens to them during a change programme

- can assimilate change at a speed commensurate with the pace of the events taking place around them

- understand the implications of organisational change

- assimilate all of the change they face within their ability to absorb change

During the training course, therefore, it is intended that staff will learn how to:

- understand the importance of individual resilience in their work and lives in general

- build on their existing resilience and develop new resilience skills

- clarify the consequences of their action during the change process and its impact on their personal and on the organisation's resilience

- contribute to raising their own productivity during change

- manage their response to change more effectively

- spread the word about change to their colleagues

How it can be used successfully

By developing personal resilience staff will be better prepared to respond to change by gaining a sense of control in the midst of ambiguity, anticipating their personal responses to change and by focusing on the opportunities rather than the dangers that major change appears to present.

They will not get overloaded with change and will be more likely to respond positively to the change proposals.

15

COMMUNICATIONS, PR AND MEDIA MANAGEMENT

Introduction

This final chapter outlines approaches to internal and external communication during the change management process and to public relations and press management.

The table below shows the key aspects covered and an indication of when they might be used.

Table 15.1 Communications, PR and media management

Tools/techniques	Taking stock	Merging and building confidence	Transformation/ achieving change
1 Communications	• Determine methods of communication • Communicate background to change	• Communicate new values/vision • Stress continuity • Ensure 'two way' channel of communication	• Reinforce values vision • Address concerns
2 PR & press management	• Agreeing key messages • Familiarisation with local media • Commission research on local perceptions	• Networking with media/develop target relationships • Train 'spokesmen'	• Allocate responsibilities in accordance with press strategy

Tool/technique 1: **Communications**

It is inevitable that much uncertainty will surround the process of merging local authorities, particularly for the staff involved. The majority of staff from the predecessor authorities are likely to transfer to the new authority. The success of the merger will largely depend on encouraging these staff to support the merger process and identify with the new management. Therefore, while it will not be possible to remove all of the uncertainties immediately, the importance of early communications, internally and externally, cannot be overemphasised.

Both the message and the method of communication will require careful consideration. The detailed contents of early communications will depend on the circumstances. However, they will need to be delivered in a way that helps maintain morale and reinforces the core beliefs and values of the new organisation. These beliefs and values will not be shared by staff unless they are first understood, and they will not be understood unless they are effectively communicated.

Communication must also be sensitive to people's concerns, if it is to allay fear of change and assist in building resilience. 'Signing up' to the shared vision will be influenced by the need for job reductions and rationalisation, and the communications structure must anticipate any new or recurring fears. External support similarly will be more likely to be forthcoming if public concerns are recognised.

This section covers the following:

- internal issues
- external issues
- stages in the process
- methods of communication

The issues surrounding general public awareness of the changes are discussed in the section entitled *PR and press management.*

Internal issues

A number of issues need to be covered in communications to management, staff and unions. These include:

- reasons for the reorganisation and an indication of future priorities and plans
- any immediate changes in the management or organisation of their department
- details of reporting relationships indicating clearly what is expected, right down the hierarchy

- reassurances, where possible, of business as usual
- reassurances regarding remuneration and benefits (including pensions and redundancy policy) and an indication of planned enhancements where possible
- an indication of actions or reviews planned in the short-term and who will be involved
- key aspects of vision and strategy - for example service policies and priorities, performance standards and policies on whether particular services will be delivered in-house or through a third party
- what is being communicated to clients and suppliers and what they should themselves convey in their day-to-day contact

External issues

A range of external parties will also have concerns about the reorganisation, and will want to know how it will affect their relationship with the authority. These will include:

- clients/customers
- suppliers
- other statutory bodies or agencies with whom the authority works
- voluntary organisations working in the area

The key message of reassurance for these parties should again be: business as usual. In other words, in the short-term the authority should aim, wherever possible, to ensure:

- continuity of service delivery
- continuity of purchasing arrangements
- continuity in relationships with other statutory or voluntary organisations

Where changes are unavoidable, the reasons should be carefully explained to all parties affected and put in the context of the key aspects of the vision and strategy of the new authority.

Stages in the process

Communication will be important throughout the process of planning and implementing the merger. Some of the key considerations at the various stages are described below.

Pre-merger

The consideration before merger should be to:

- determine methods of communication to staff and external parties

- communicate background of reorganisation, stages involved and approach to implementation, giving assurance as far as possible of 'business as usual'

- communicate makeup of planning team(s), their roles and responsibilities

- indicate how further information can be obtained by those with questions

At or around date of merger

Near the date of merger it will be necessary to:

- acknowledge that this is an intensive period of communication to launch new organisation both internally and externally

- stress continuity and the positive opportunities to build on the foundations already laid

- use all avenues of communication necessary to reach the whole community

Post merger

At this stage ongoing communication at regular intervals will be necessary in order to reinforce earlier messages, demonstrate progress and address any further concerns raised by staff or external parties.

Methods of communications

A variety of means of communication are possible. Innovative methods can help. Although conventional newsletters, notices and circulars and consultations with staff representatives will continue to have an important place in the communications system, these can be supplemented with considerable advantage by low cost initiatives that refresh and revitalise links with the whole workforce, and also with the authority's consumers and electorate. The communication approaches are detailed in Chapter 5 and include:

- roadshows

- group discussions

- team briefings and 'cascades'

- videos

In practice, a range of communication methods will need to be exploited depending on the nature of the target group, the sensitivity of the issues involved, the time and resources available. Table 15.2 summarises some of the advantages and disadvantages of different communication methods.

When planning the communication process, it will be necessary to consider the overall pattern as well as the methods to be used. The normal order of communication for most issues would be:

- management affected
- staff affected
- external parties affected

Table 15.2 Methods of communication

	Written	Verbal
Examples	Personal letters Memos/notices Glossy newsheets	Face to face Group meetings
Benefits	• can include detailed explanations for future reference • new logo emphasises new corporate identity • ensures consistent message is clearly communicated • enables wide distribution simultaneously	• more personal - can adopt presentation to needs of audience • provides opportunity for questions, discussion and feedback • giving time emphasises importance of message • visual presentation may be more effective
Disadvantages	• may not be read and understood • may not address concerns of the reader • if not carefully worded, may provoke further questions • glossy productions take time and money to produce	• need to ensure consistent message is communicated in each interview/meeting • need to be able to deal with awkward questions • potentially time consuming • may need to phase meetings

The appropriate level of detail to be communicated will vary between staff, management, clients, suppliers and other external bodies. Consideration should be given to the level of knowledge of the target audience as well as to the sensitivity of the information being communicated.

It is important to ensure that there is high quality two-way internal communication. Structures and processes within the authority should include arrangements for messages and feedback to travel upwards from junior staff to senior management, and inwards from the periphery to the centre. This will enable the two-way exchange of ideas and concerns, and help management to assess whether the communications process is operating effectively. Upward communication can be facilitated in several ways, e.g.:

- allowing questions or discussion in group meetings

- nominating certain officers as reference points for staff with questions on particular issues

- establishing a contact point or telephone hotline to deal with (or refer elsewhere if appropriate) queries from members of the public or other external parties

If the feedback received indicates that the message is not getting across, or that misinformation is causing confusion, this should be addressed as soon as possible by reinforcing the communications process. Restoring clarity will help avoid the potentially negative impact that confusion or uncertainty would have on staff morale or public perception.

Tool/technique 2: **PR and media management**

Establishing the identity of the new authority will be an important part of a successful merger. It will be important for the authority to increase the public's general awareness and understanding of the changes, and manage media coverage. The process of communicating with staff and external parties with whom the authority deals with directly has been discussed in the previous section though there is inevitably a degree of overlap between these various activities.

Public relations and media management are not activities that can be reduced to a set of standard procedures. Establishing a good reputation takes time and commitment. Successful management of public relations during a period of major reorganisation will require a co-ordinated publicity strategy, which stretches over a realistic timeframe. Unfortunately, a good reputation can be lost very quickly. Hence it is important to ensure that the reality of service delivery matches the expectations generated by the publicity machine, and that officers dealing with enquiries from the public or the press are adequately trained and briefed.

The following issues are considered below:

- establishing objectives

- getting the message across

- press management

- evaluation

Establishing objectives

In order to achieve the most effective publicity from a limited budget and resources, it is necessary to be clear from the outset about the objectives. The first step to setting these objectives is to establish the starting position, that is, to understand clearly current public and customer perceptions. This can be achieved through a combination of approaches including:

- discussion with staff regarding their views on public perception
- the results of recent, relevant market research (see section on customer satisfaction)
- a review of recent media coverage

This research is an important first step. Without a reasonable assessment of current public views, it will be impossible to measure the benefit derived from subsequent investment in publicity. Once a picture of current perceptions has been established, the key objectives of the publicity strategy can be defined. Some possible objectives are listed in Table 15.3 below, together with examples of issues likely to be of concern to members of the public during the process of merging authorities.

When setting objectives, it is important to be clear about who the target audience is. From a local authority's perspective, the general public can be viewed as two overlapping groups of people. These are:

- the citizens living within the authority's boundaries (to whom the authority is democratically accountable)
- the customers of particular services provided by the authority

Table 15.3 Objectives of publicity

Objectives	Examples of issues and concerns
To inform	Will I still get the same service? Will it cost more?
To reassure	Why is there a reorganisation? What does it mean for me and for my community?
To influence	Do the new boundaries make sense? Are the changes a threat or an opportunity?

Local people will have different priorities depending on their stage in life and the particular package of services they currently benefit from. For example, parents with school age children will have a particular concern as customers for education services. Others will be more concerned with other services for which they are customers, such as refuse collection, leisure services or homecare. However, as citizens (and as council tax payers), local people will also have a valid general interest in the provision of services regardless of which package of services they are currently benefiting from directly.

People's opinion of a local authority will be based on a combination of factors, including the extent to which they agree with the political decisions made and their level of satisfaction with the services they receive directly. Hence, any successful publicity campaign will need to take account of the diverse range of interests and priorities of local people, and effectively reach people as both citizens and customers.

Getting the message across

Given the diverse range of priorities of local people and the scale of change involved, it will be necessary to develop a co-ordinated strategy to get the message across effectively. An authority will need to select an appropriate range of approaches that will reach the whole community while remaining within budgetary constraints. A number of possible methods of reaching local people are listed in Table 15.4 together with an indication of some of the issues to be considered in relation to each method.

Table 15.4 Publicity tools

Publicity tool	Issues to consider
Publicity events	Takes time to plan and arrange. May achieve good short-term impact, but difficult to ensure target audience is reached. Costs will vary significantly depending on type of event.
Appearance at existing events	Similar issues to publicity events. This approach may save time and money, though it may mean that the effect of the message is diluted.
Publicity materials (eg service guides)	If in a user friendly format, can be informative and provide a useful reference. Preparation time and printing costs need to be allowed for. Can be effectively targeted. Distribution can be achieved on back of other activities eg distribution of council tax bills.
Posters and advertisements	Helpful to increase general awareness as part of a wider campaign. May achieve good short term impact.

Table 15.4 (contd)

Publicity tool	Issues to consider
Displays at service outlets	Combination of publicity materials and visual display. Maybe an effective way of reaching the users of a particular service.
Information points or helplines	Allows scope for personal interaction and responsiveness to individual concerns and queries. Maybe expensive as it requires appropriate human resourcing, though this may be part time (linked to other activities).

A number of criteria should be considered when deciding which combination of methods to use as part of a co-ordinated and balanced publicity strategy. These include:

- achieving a balance between increasing general awareness and reaching particular target groups

- using the available budgetary resources most effectively

- achieving a balance between short-term impact and long-term gain

- the level of time input, skills and experience required from staff

- the period of time required to prepare and implement different options

Press management

The media have a significant influence on public perceptions. It is inevitable that local authorities will receive coverage during a process of major reorganisation. While in many cases this may present an opportunity to increase public awareness of the changes, the media are also likely to focus on any problems, anomalies or controversies they identify. It is not possible to control what newspapers print or television and media journalists report. However, it is possible over time to develop a constructive relationship with appropriate representatives of the press, which should provide a bridge to influence their reporting. Given the sensitivity of members to local opinion, and the desire to provide services which are responsive to public expectations (which may be reflected in the press) developing this relationship is very important.

Before deciding the level of resources to invest in media management and setting out an appropriate action plan, a key strategic question needs to be addressed. This is, whether to pursue a reactive or a proactive strategy or a combination of the two. A reactive strategy aims to provide a rapid and effective response to media enquiries or coverage, which enables the authority's views to be represented and accurate information to be distributed. A proactive strategy requires greater investment than this. The aim is to actively generate media interest and achieve positive press coverage.

The stages involved in developing relationships with the media are similar, regardless of which strategy is chosen. The stages are as follows:

Stage 1: Familiarisation - this involves establishing which parts of the local media might cover local authority issues, how influential they are and who the journalists are; e.g.:

- which programmes on local radio

- which sections in local newspapers

- what about regional television?

Stage 2: Develop targets - develop relationships with priority journalists who are most likely to influence the target audience and establish their approach to their work (e.g. reporting deadlines, topics of interest, format of articles).

Stage 3: Allocate responsibilities - depending on the publicity strategy and objectives which have been set. Appoint spokes people on key issues or to represent service areas. If they do not have PR experience, ensure they receive training on dealing with the media and a full briefing on the authority's publicity objectives.

Where a proactive strategy is being pursued, there are a variety of methods of facilitating coverage. These include:

- producing press releases

- photocall opportunities (an alternative to this is to supply pictures directly, ensuring that they are of an appropriate size and quality)

- media briefings

- contributing feature articles

- letters or items for opinion columns

Evaluation

In order to ensure that the chosen publicity objectives are being achieved and that resources are being used effectively, it is essential that progress is monitored and evaluated. While it may not be possible to measure progress exactly, a reasonable indication will be given by:

- repeating research on local perceptions a year later to see whether this has moved in the desired direction

- monitoring those outputs which are measurable (e.g. the level of positive media coverage).

References

Audit Commission (1990) *We can't go on meeting like this: the changing role of local authority members* (HMSO, London)

Bloch, Alice and Peter John (1991) *Attitudes to local government: a survey of electors* (Joseph Rowntree Foundation, York)

Briggs Myers, Isobel *Type Indicator Test* (Consulting Psychologists Press Ltd, licensed to Oxford Psychologists Press Ltd 1976)

Cmnd. 9797: report of the Committee of Inquiry into the Conduct of Local Authority Business (Chairman: David Widdicombe) (HMSO, London, 1986)

Community leadership and representation: unlocking the potential: the report of the Working Party on the Internal Management of Local Authorities in England (HMSO, London, 1993)

Conner, Daryl (1993) *Managing at the speed of change: how resilient managers succeed and prosper where others fail* (Villard Books, New York)

Game, Chris and Steve Leach with Geoff Williams (1993) *Councillor recruitment and turnover: an approaching precipice?* (Local Government Management Board, Luton)

Leach, Steve et al. (1991) *After abolition: the operation of the post-1986 metropolitan government system in England* (Institute of Local Government Studies, University of Birmingham, Birmingham)

Local Government Management Board (1993) *Fitness for purpose: shaping new patterns of organisation and management* (LGMB, Luton)

Loughlin, Martin (1992) *Administrative accountability in local government* (Joseph Rowntree Foundation, York)

Management Consultancies Association (1993) *Chief executives views on project management performance* (MCA, London)

Mayon-White, Bill (1986) *Planning and Managing* Change Open University

Peters, Thomas J and Robert H Waterman, Jr (1980) *In search of excellence: lessons from America's best-run companies* (Harper and Row, London)

Rao, Nirmala (1993) *Managing change: councillors and the new local government* (Joseph Rowntree Foundation, York)

Report of the Committee on the Financial Aspects of Corporate Governance (Chairman: Adrian Cadbury) (Gee & Co, London, 1992)

Terez, Tom (1990) *Managing change in the 1990s: strategies for the operations manager* (Arrow Associates, Charlotte, NC)

Transfer of Undertakings (Protection of Employment) Regulations 1981

Young, Ken and Mary Davies (1990) *The politics of local government since Widdicombe* (Joseph Rowntree Foundation, York)